THE ANARCHY TOUR

MICK O'SHEA

OMNIBUS PRESS

London / New York / Paris / Sydney / Copenhagen / Berlin / Madrid / Tokyo

Exclusive Distributors
Music Sales Limited, 14/15 Berners Street, London, W1T 3LJ.

Music Sales Corporation,
180 Madison Avenue, 24th Floor, New York, NY 10016, USA.

Macmillan Distribution Services,
56 Parkwest Drive, Derrimut, Vic 3030, Australia.

Images courtesy of Bob Gruen, Getty Images, Rex Features and Corbis Images.

Every effort has been made to trace the copyright holders of the
photographs in this book but one or two were unreachable.
We would be grateful if the photographers concerned would contact us.

Printed in Croatia

A catalogue record for this book is available from the British Library.

Visit Omnibus Press on the web at www.omnibuspress.com

Contents

In Memoriam

Malcolm McLaren
1946 – 2009

Joe Strummer
1952 – 2002

Johnny Thunders
1952 – 1991

Jerry "Niggs" Nolan
1946 – 1992

Rolf "Nils" Stevenson
1953 – 2002

Dave Goodman
1951 – 2005

Tracie O'Keefe
1960 – 1978

Bill Grundy
1923 – 1993

Sid Vicious
1957 – 1979

Introduction

While renovating the exterior to his World's End retro clothing emporium at 430 King's Road which during the latter part of 1973 he ran with his business partner and on/off girlfriend Vivienne Westwood, future Sex Pistols manager Malcolm McLaren daubed Jean Jacques Rousseau's telling aphorism: 'Craft Must Have Clothes, But The Truth Loves To Go Naked' on the shop's lintel. What had seemed an immovable maxim back in Rousseau's day wasn't quite so rigid by the mid-seventies, and on Monday, November 1, 1976 – whilst delivering a face-saving counter salvo against those newspapers that were openly mocking both himself, and his ailing Labour government in equal measure – beleaguered Prime Minister James Callaghan attempted to deflect some of the blame by paraphrasing Mark Twain's humorous adage: "A lie can be half-way around the world before the truth has got its boots on."

Then as now, Fleet Street's editors-in-chief were collectively diligent in keeping the truth from ruining a good story – and a classic example of the press' Machiavellian mindset at work came a calendar month after Callaghan's emboldened speech in the House of Commons with the vitriolic vilification of the Sex Pistols following their now-legendary appearance on the *Today* show on Wednesday, December 1, 1976.

What should have been an inconsequential three-minute interview intended to give the Sex Pistols the opportunity to plug their debut single, 'Anarchy In The UK', and a promotional 19-date UK tour set to commence in two day's time, descended into farce when the show's boorish host Bill Grundy wilfully goaded Sex Pistols' guitarist Steve Jones into calling him, "You dirty bastard, you dirty fucker, what a fucking rotter".

Of course, Steve wasn't the first person to say "fuck" on live television as that dubious honour had already gone to the colourful and controversial film and theatre critic Kenneth Tynan* back in 1965. But whereas Tynan's four-letter faux pas came during a late-evening BBC debate on censorship, the *Today* show was a half-hour regional magazine news programme aired from Monday to Friday between 6.30 and 7p.m. Though the blame should have been placed firmly and squarely at Grundy's door over the "air turning blue" that chilly December evening, Fleet Street was gearing up to charge, try, and convict the Sex Pistols before the show's credits had even finished rolling. The reason for this was because much like today mid-seventies Britain was in the icy grip of financial recession, and Jim Callaghan's government had been forced to go cap-in-hand to the International Monetary Fund (IMF) to save sterling from the humiliation of devaluation. Indeed, since Labour had come to power some two years earlier, the country had been subjected to power cuts, a three-day working week, and inflation hitting a staggering 29.6 per cent. And with no royal wedding in the offing, Fleet Street was desperate to find a way of distracting the disaffected public. And the Sex Pistols' teatime tête-à-tête with Grundy gave them the perfect pantomime villains in the run up to Christmas. It was nigh on perfect…

I was a 14-year-old lad growing up in the Lancashire mill town of Accrington when Fleet Street first declared war on the Sex Pistols. Their overkill coverage of the *Today* show debacle not only wrenched the group from relative obscurity and propelled them onto the front pages of every broadsheet and tabloid newspaper in the land, but also left the forthcoming Anarchy Tour itinerary in tatters. Because the *Today* show was broadcast only within the London area, I was blithely unaware of the "Filth", or the ensuing "Fury" that swept the nation the following day, and wouldn't have known a Sex Pistol from one of Disco-Tex's Sex-O-Lettes!

Indeed, such was my general ambivalence towards pop music at the time that I didn't become aware of the Sex Pistols – or punk rock – until the subsequent front-page furore surrounding the release of 'God Save The Queen' the following spring. Even then, I assumed that while the group had a singer calling himself Johnny Rotten and a bass player called Sid Vicious, the Sex Pistols were just another of the Status Quo style long-haired, denim-clad outfits that were clogging up the pop charts. Since both 'Anarchy In The UK' and 'God Save The Queen' were banned from daytime radio play-lists, I didn't actually become attuned to what the Pistols were doing until inadvertently catching 'Pretty Vacant' on the Sunday evening Radio One Top 40 rundown. Then of course, seeing the promo video of the band performing the song on *Top Of The Pops* the following week changed my life forever.

December 2011 saw the 35th anniversary of the ill-fated Anarchy Tour – wonderfully recreated by the Sex Pistols Experience – which means that only those of a certain age will remember the month when the musical landscape was irrevocably changed by them. This book is the first to investigate thoroughly all aspects of the Anarchy Tour, and how it cast the Sex Pistols as social pariahs, The Damned as punk pariahs, saw heroin introduced to the London Punk scene courtesy of The Heartbreakers, and placed The Clash on the first rung of the ladder to national – and international – stardom. It also exposes a once proud nation's vulnerability to loud-mouthed anarchists, its hostility to change and the eternal truism that establishment attempts to ban anything always make it more popular.

Mick O'Shea
Still Living The Dream. . .
April 2012

The Dates

Friday, 3 December	**Norwich East Anglia University**	**Cancelled**
Saturday, 4 December	**Derby Kings Hall**	**Cancelled**
Sunday, 5 December	**Newcastle City Hall**	**Cancelled**
Monday, 6 December	**Leeds Polytechnic**	**Played**
Tuesday, 7 December	**Bournemouth Village Bowl**	**Cancelled**
Tuesday, 7 December	Sheffield University	*Fell Through*
Thursday, 9 December	**Manchester Electric Circus**	**Played**
Friday, 10 December	**Lancaster University**	**Cancelled**
Friday, 10 December	Preston Charter	*Fell Through*
Saturday, 11 December	**Liverpool Stadium**	**Cancelled**
Saturday, 11 December	The Cavern	*Fell Through*
Monday, 13 December	**Bristol Colston Hall**	**Cancelled**
Monday, 13 December	Bristol University	*Fell Through*
Tuesday, 14 December	**Cardiff Top Rank**	**Cancelled**
Tuesday, 14 December	Caerphilly Castle Cinema	*Played*
Wednesday, 15 December	**Glasgow Apollo**	**Cancelled**
Wednesday, 15 December	Wolverhampton Lafayette	*Fell Through*
Thursday, 16 December	**Dundee Caird Hall**	**Cancelled**
Friday, 17 December	**Sheffield City Hall**	**Cancelled**
Friday, 17 December	Carlisle Market Hall	*Fell Through*
Saturday, 18 December	**Southend Kursaal**	**Cancelled**
Saturday, 18 December	Maidenhead Skindles	*Fell Through*
Sunday, 19 December	**Guildford Civic Hall**	**Cancelled**
Sunday, 19 December	Manchester Electric Circus	*Played*
Monday, 20 December	**Birmingham Town Hall**	**Cancelled**
Monday, 20 December	Bingley Hall	*Fell Through*
Monday, 20 December	Cleethorpes Winter Gardens	*Played*
Tuesday, 21 December	**Plymouth Woods Centre**	**Played**
Wednesday, 22 December	**Torquay 400 Ballroom**	**Cancelled**
Wednesday, 22 December	Paignton Penelope's Ballroom	*Fell Through*
Wednesday, 22 December	Plymouth Woods Centre	*Played*
Sunday, 26 December	**London Roxy Theatre**	**Cancelled**

The original 19 venues in red, with alternate venues in italics

CHAPTER ONE

Vive le Rock... 'n' Roll

"I was this strange guy with this mad dream. I was trying to do with the Sex Pistols what I had failed to do with the New York Dolls. I was taking the nuances of Richard Hell, the faggy, pop side of the New York Dolls, the politics of boredom, and mashing it all together to make a statement, maybe the final statement, and piss off the rock 'n' roll scene. That's what I was doing. I wasn't doing anything new. I was waiting my turn to make the statement I'd been trying to make since I was 14."

Malcolm McLaren

Contrary to Sex Pistols legend, the destination board on the coach that pulled away from the kerb outside the Pistols' W1 HQ on Denmark Street on Friday, December 3, 1976, didn't read "Nowhere" or "Boredom" like the twin coaches adorning the back of the 'Pretty Vacant' picture sleeve the following July, but was – with no irony intended – left blank. But while such portentous overtones make for interesting reading, it is worth remembering that any chartered coach would leave its destination board blank if it wouldn't be stopping off en route to pick up paying passengers. That said, however, following the Sex Pistols' now-legendary appearance on the *Today* show two days earlier, it's a wonder Sir Reg Goodwin, the residing leader of the Greater London Council, didn't order Sex Pistols' manager Malcolm McLaren to daub red crosses on the coach's side panels to warn the soon-to-be outraged citizens of the towns and cities on the tour's original 19-date itinerary of the foul-mouthed Sex Pistols' impending approach.

Edgar Allan Poe's Prince Prospero staged elegant masquerade balls to keep the "Red Death" away from his castle walls, but Goodwin and the rest of Britain's outraged councillors resorted to less fanciful means in their determination to do everything within their collective powers to keep the Sex Pistols and their pogoing, ill-mannered ilk away from their cosy realms. Indeed, Glasgow's reigning Lord Provost, Peter McCann, drolly declared that "Scotland had enough hooligans of its own without importing them from across the border", and was so resolute in his determination to keep the Sex Pistols away from his fair city that he revoked the Glasgow Apollo's entertainment licence for the night in question.

Had it not been for the Sex Pistols' now legendary appearance on *Today* that wintry Wednesday evening in early December 1976, it's likely no one would even remember Thames TV's early evening regional news magazine programme which followed directly after the national ITV news at 6p.m. As with every other weekday, the line-up for that evening's show would have been mapped out in advance at a production meeting earlier in the day. As ever, it focused on the national news topics of concern to Londoners, specifically the passing of the Criminal Law Bill aimed at doing away with jury trials for minor offences such as disturbance of the peace or petty theft, and covered prominent local issues from the pages of London's flagship newspaper, the *Evening Standard*. Given that *Today* immediately preceded Thames' early-evening light entertainment schedule, the show would usually end with a warm-hearted tale or a music clip to put the viewing public in a more relaxed mood.

That particular evening's show was set to end with an extended clip of the promo video for Queen's latest single, 'Somebody To Love', which was already riding high in the pop chart. However, *Today*'s producer, Mike Housego, was looking for somebody to blame on being made aware that owing to an oversight the video hadn't actually been given clearance for broadcast by the all-important Musicians' Union. Other reports on an evening eternally steeped in controversy suggest that Queen had been forced to pull out because their flamboyant frontman, Freddie Mercury, was still recovering from major dental treatment. But this doesn't really stand up under scrutiny because it implies that Queen were to perform their latest single live in the studio, and a group busy rehearsing for their first world tour – set to commence in the US the following month – was surely beyond miming on tea-time television.

Regardless of the reason for Queen's eleventh-hour withdrawal, the clock was ticking and Housego suddenly found himself with a three-minute hole to fill. As Queen were signed to EMI, which had a 50 per cent stake in Thames TV, he put a call in to EMI's offices in Manchester Square to speak with the label's head of promotions, Eric "Monster" Hall. While Hall was anxious to help – if only to make amends for the glaring omission in forgetting to get the video cleared for broadcasting – there was little he could realistically do at such short notice.

"Queen and Freddie Mercury cancelled their appearance on *Today,* so the programme came to me looking for someone else," confirmed Hall later. "I suggested trying the Sex Pistols who'd just signed to EMI. I never liked the Sex Pistols' music, but I always knew they were going to be 'monster'"

Another enduring urban myth surrounding the Pistols is that it was the desperation of the hour which led Eric Hall to propose the Sex Pistols as a possible replacement but according to Brian Southall's highly informative book *Sex Pistols: 90 Days At EMI*, it was in fact Housego who enquired about the group's availability. EMI held significant shareholding in Thames and he would have been privy to the insider gossip at Manchester Square where everyone at the label who was involved in promoting the Sex Pistols believed the group was capable of becoming the next Beatles.

At first glance – and given what we all now know about the Sex Pistols' short-lived turbulent career – this may seem like an idle boast. Nevertheless, it's worth remembering that prior to taking the world by storm The Beatles were just another rough and ready beat combo cutting their musical teeth on Hamburg's notorious Reeperbahn – and enjoying everything that the city's red-light area had to offer. Back in Liverpool, too, they wore leather jackets, cursed on stage and adopted an all-for-one gang mentality that in hindsight seems not unlike the punk credentials of the Pistols.

Malcolm, however, hadn't the slightest inclination of grooming the Sex Pistols to become the new "Fab Four" or England's answer to The Monkees (who were of course America's manufactured answer to The Beatles). While there is a strong argument that he wanted to create the Bay City Rollers of outrage – "Shang-a-lanarchy in the UK" – the only real design he had for the Pistols was one which would enable him to promote SEX (as his shop was now called), and sell lots of T-shirts and bondage trousers into the bargain. But of course, how Malcolm found himself managing the group in the first place is a necessary diversion to understanding the origins of the Anarchy Tour.

"It was fate that I stumbled upon a hole in the wall at the darkest end of the King's Road that they called the World's End," McLaren would state in *Q* magazine's *Never Mind The Jubilee Punk Special*. "There I ran a shop which sold vestiges from the past, ruins from the fifties, records and clothes that were truly authentic, that were indebted to pop culture but also soon became pop culture themselves.

"To begin with that shop was just a haven for myself and a few friends. But soon under a variety of names and guises it attracted a whole group of people, who were disenchanted with the world around them. They would come and sit in the shop. They wanted to be a part of this thing we were creating."

At the time of the Anarchy Tour, Malcolm Robert Andrew McLaren was 30 years old, and an experienced trouble-maker. He was born and raised in Stoke Newington, north London, which at the time was a respectable, solid Jewish neighbourhood. His parents had separated when he was just 18 months old, his mother Emily preferring to spend illicit weekends in Monte Carlo with the new man in her life – Selfridge's supremo, Sir Charles Clore – while Malcolm and four-year-old brother Stuart were being raised by their maternal grandmother, Rose Corre.

Other than seeing him develop an effete 'Little Lord Fauntleroy' persona, the absence of a father figure appears to have had no adverse effect on Malcolm. Although both boys were largely ignored by their mother, Malcolm enjoyed the greater share of Grandma Rose's affections, and rather than follow Stuart into primary education he persuaded Rose to teach him from her cosy front parlour.

The old adage about leading a horse to water perfectly sums up Malcolm's early schooling, for although his mother managed to wrestle him from her mother's clutches and deliver him to a "proper" place of learning, she was left powerless when he failed to take any interest in the school's curriculum. In a last desperate attempt to get him through his 11+ exam, which in those days was the only means for those from a less-than-privileged background to advance to grammar school, she hired a private tutor. But the plan backfired as taking on double helpings of something he already despised with a passion was anathema to a firebrand like Malcolm, who deliberately frustrated all attempts to further his learning and duly failed the exam.

Malcolm McLaren outside Let It Rock

When Malcolm left school in the summer of 1961 he had just two O levels to show for his efforts. There followed shorts stints having to work for a living – first at Sandeman's Port & Sherry wine merchants in Orange Street, Piccadilly, and then as a retail clerk at a West End haberdashery in the Burlington Arcade – before he swallowed his resentment at the education system and returned to schooling in the spring of 1963, enrolling as a part-time student at St. Martins School of Art where the Sex Pistols would make their live debut some 12 years later. In order to return to full-time education he would require another two O level passes, and so having gained the necessary qualifications by taking a summer "booster" course at a school in Edgware, he enrolled at Harrow Art School where he befriended Gordon Swire, whose striking elder sister, Vivienne, was of course to play such a significant role in his life.

Following on from Harrow – by which time he'd become a father – Malcolm enrolled at the Croydon College of Art and Design to study painting. Whilst there, he participated in the so-called "Croydon Student Sit-In" of June 1968, in which he and 300 or so of his fellow students barricaded themselves within the college's South Norwood annexe in imitation of their Parisian counterparts who'd brought France to a virtual standstill, and forced De Gaulle into dissolving the National Assembly.

His next school was Goldsmiths, where aside from studying film and photography, he embarked on an affair with Helen Mininberg[1*] – later Helen Wellington-Lloyd – and married a Turkish-French student called Jocelyn Hakim so she could remain in Britain and continue with her studies. Malcolm supposedly used the £50 Hakim had paid him to ensure that he arrived at Lewisham Registrar Office at the appointed hour to fund his Goldsmiths student project, while the £2,000 it would subsequently take to secure a divorce inevitably fell to Grandma Rose.

During the summer of 1969, Malcolm attempted to ingratiate himself with his fellow Goldsmiths students by unveiling plans to stage a free music festival – to be staged in the amphitheatre situated to the rear of the college's art annex – with an impressive line-up boasting both The Pretty Things and King Crimson. Not surprisingly, news of the festival spread across London's college circuit and come the day of the festival some 20,000 students descended on Goldsmiths. As the disgruntled masses grew more restless when each and every one of the named acts failed to show, those in authority tried to maintain order as best they could, but with thousands of lager-fuelled freeloaders helping themselves to whatever they could stash and carry, the day quickly descended into chaos.

Having miraculously escaped expulsion over the festival debacle, Malcolm decided to keep a low profile and concentrate on his student project – a conceptual film based on London's Oxford Street, and the dehumanising effect of the consumer market – for which he borrowed Goldsmiths' one and only functioning camera. Although a film of sorts was slowly taking shape, Malcolm inevitably lost interest in Oxford Street's anarchic history, and instead focused his attention on his all-time rock 'n' roll hero Billy Fury, who'd been managed by Larry Parnes, and had enjoyed run of UK Top 10 hits between 1960 and 1965.

The ideas may have flowed freely, but Jocelyn Hakim's £50 had long since been spent. After one last desperate – and fruitless – attempt to raise finance from Larry Parnes, Malcolm shelved the film and drew a finite line under his art school wanderings by walking away from Goldsmiths. Though a lack of funding had forced Malcolm to put his film project on ice, those closest to him fully expected him to reactivate his filmic passions at some point in the future. He just needed another vehicle to finance his ambitions.

---

1   "Helen of Troy" in *The Great Rock 'N' Roll Swindle.*

The Sex Pistols and others have gone on record saying how the not-so-Svengali-like Malcolm panicked in the immediate wake of the *Today* show. His immediate thought, however, would have been, "How does this affect me?" for despite the group having secured a recording contract and released a single, the shop was still his main priority. While Vivienne was a dab hand with a needle and thread, they still needed the raw materials with which to make their clothes, and there was a possibility that their suppliers might cease deliveries – in a fit of moral indignation on learning he was the Pistols' manager.

In the *Never Mind The Sex Pistols* DVD, Malcolm claims to have been unmoved when EMI terminated the Sex Pistols' contract in January 1977 as there was "always another whore further down the street". This, of course, was his view three decades after the event, and if the music industry had deigned to close its collective legs on the Pistols then he'd have been forced to go cap-in-hand to an independent label such as Stiff or Chiswick – which would have been anathema to Malcolm. Even if – though neither Malcolm nor EMI Records MD Leslie Hill made any mention of it at the time – Richard Branson is to be believed and he did make an offer to take the Sex Pistols off of EMI's hands the day after the Pistols' appearance on *Today*, having to do business with "Mr Pickle" – as Malcolm referred to Branson – at such an early stage in the Sex Pistols' career without the sizeable A&M advance shoring up his defences, would have been equally unbearable for Malcolm.

Though McLaren was undoubtedly guilty of gilding the lily in his self-aggrandisement of his role in the *Today* saga, not even he could have predicted the societal backlash against the Pistols. It wasn't so much a knee-jerk reaction as a tectonic shift. His fascination with the Paris riots of May 1968 – which he subsequently claimed to have witnessed first-hand – is of course well documented. While he was under no illusion that the British government would follow France's lead by bringing in the Army to quell a major riot, his active participation in the Croydon sit-in, coupled with the Goldsmiths festival fiasco, would had given him an insight into how those in authority reacted in the face of youthful belligerence.

It was Malcolm, after all, who christened the group in the knowledge that the name alone would inspire – at the very least – a degree of disdain or – even better – outrage. "Taking their name partly from the shop, SEX, I then added the word Pistols," he told *Q* magazine. "I was looking for something with sexual implications, a name that could act as a metaphor. Here was a group, the Sex Pistols, that would and did shoot down anything we didn't like, which in our case was absolutely everything."

SEX wasn't your average high street fashion boutique, at least not in mid-seventies Britain. It tended to attract an unusual clientele, one of whom was a 19-year-old Shepherd's Bush reprobate called Steve Jones. When Steve – a self-confessed kleptomaniac – wasn't on the lookout for a "five-fingered discount", he could more often than not be found badgering Malcolm to manage Swanker (or The Strand, depending on whose account you believe), the group he and his mates Paul Cook and Warwick "Wally" Nightingale formed shortly after leaving school. Aside from a manager the trio were also in need of a bass player as Paul's brother-in-law Del couldn't be relied on in this capacity.

Though Malcolm hooked the trio up with his Saturday lad Glen Matlock, who just happened to be teaching himself bass, and was happy to occasionally put his hand in his pocket to pay for them to rent a rehearsal room at the Covent Garden Community Centre, it wasn't until the summer of 1975 that he began to pay attention to what they were doing. The reason for this sudden surge in interest was due to his having witnessed the musical revolution that was rapidly taking shape on the other side of the Atlantic.

Having been seduced by the New York Dolls' "awkward, trashy vibe" when the brash five-piece group – whom he subsequently described as being "the worst striptease rock act you could imagine" – visited 430 King's Road while in London during a European jaunt the previous November, he'd left Vivienne to mind the store – and his old friend and business associate, Bernard Rhodes, to keep an eye on Steve's group, while he jetted over to New York to try and reinvigorate the Dolls' ailing career.

Despite being hailed the "Queens" of New York, the Dolls' collective appetite for drink and drugs had exacted a heavy toll, and their once-promising career appeared to be in freefall. Indeed, the Dolls were little more than dead men walking on Malcolm's arrival, and his decision to have them trade in their thrift store threads for the red patent leather ensembles Vivienne had crafted back in London, and play in front of a backdrop bearing the hammer and sickle at a time when American boys were coming home from Southeast Asia in body bags draped in the Stars and Stripes, would prove a red flag to an already bullish audience.

Unsurprisingly, Malcolm's initial foray into music management wasn't the success he might have hoped, but at least his American adventure had allowed him a glimpse into the future. Elton John, Fleetwood Mac, and The Eagles might still be packing them in at Madison Square Garden, but the next generation of rock fans was flocking to a seedy club called CBGBs situated on New York's Lower East Side, where exciting new bands such as Television, Talking Heads and The Ramones – who cared little for musical proficiency – were taking rock 'n' roll back to its roots. Naturally enough, Malcolm's haberdasher's eye wasn't slow in taking note of the scene's equally stripped-back fashions – particularly Television's Rimbaud-esque bassist Richard Hell, whose hacked hair and ripped-up clothing would soon inspire a cultural revolution. After all, this was music by the kids, for the kids, and of the kids – and watching it all unfold in front of his eyes reminded him of what Steve Jones and his friends were doing back in London.

Steve Jones, Alan Jones, Chrissie Hynde, Sue Catwoman and Vivienne Westwood at the SEX shop

Malcolm knew he would have a limited time-frame – six months at the most – before news of what was happening across the pond filtered through to London. Having convinced the Dolls' corkscrew-haired guitarist Sylvain Sylvain that his future lay in London fronting Steve's group, he returned to London armed with Sylvain's much-cherished cream-finish Gibson Les Paul guitar. Unbeknownst to Sylvain, however, when Malcolm boarded his plane at JFK Airport, he did so with a slip of paper bearing Richard Hell's contact number nestled in his wallet. Indeed, by the time he'd gone through passport control at Heathrow he'd already decided that Sylvain was surplus to his requirements.

Malcolm's first executive decision on taking the soon-to-be-rechristened Sex Pistols under his wing was to hand Sylvain's Les Paul to a bemused Steve, thus indicating that Wally Nightingale's days in the group were numbered. What Malcolm didn't know, however, was that Richard Hell was using heroin as a stimulant for his poetry and songwriting, and that regardless of whatever promises Malcolm had made before leaving for the airport Hell soon opted to remain in New York where heroin was easily obtainable. Malcolm couldn't even revert back to his original

New York Dolls

intention of bringing Sylvain over in Hell's stead, as the guitarist had reunited with the Dolls' singer, David Johansen, for a revamped New York Dolls' tour of Japan.

However, Malcolm wasn't too disheartened. With Steve furtively learning guitar, he let it be known that his errant charges were on the lookout for a charismatic frontman.

Not long after he and Malcolm visited Glasgow to meet with leather and rubber suppliers, Bernie Rhodes made Malcolm aware of a bunch of tearaways who were making a nuisance of themselves by terrorising the tourists on the King's Road, and whose leader was a kid with hacked-off green hair and a manic-eyed, 1,000-yard stare. Vivienne had also seen the kid in question in the shop. Though Malcolm had yet to see this "Spiky John" character for himself, he instinctively knew Steve's group had found their ideal frontman.

As it turned out Malcolm didn't have to wait long before coming face to face with John Lydon, the acerbic 19-year-old north Londoner who would ultimately become his *bête noire*. Glen, who'd encountered John and his Clockwork Orange-esque coterie of friends in the shop one August Saturday afternoon, cajoled John into meeting up with Steve, Paul and Malcolm at the Roebuck Pub[2]* – situated a couple of blocks further down the King's Road – later that same evening.

Years later, when interviewed for *The Filth & The Fury* movie, Steve Jones – who inadvertently gave John his "Rotten" moniker owing to the state of his "dog-end teeth" – would opine that Malcolm and John's constant butting of heads throughout the former's tenure as Sex Pistols manager was due to their both being Capricorns. Of course, Steve's astrology was obviously a little hazy as John and Malcolm were in fact born under Aquarius – which may account for the hot air both were known to spout on occasion.

That night at the Roebuck John drove Malcolm to distraction with his feigned disinterest. Steve was equally riled at John's obtuse manner and came within an E-string of kissing his subsequent career goodbye, but Malcolm persevered and pressed John, whose singing he likened to an out-of-tune violin, into agreeing to an ad hoc audition at the shop. As there were no instruments to hand, Steve, Paul and Glen sat watching as John warbled along to Alice Cooper's 'I'm Eighteen' from the SEX jukebox, with a plastic showerhead serving as a surrogate microphone. "Rotten looked the part with his green hair, but he couldn't sing," Steve later told *Punk*. "Then again, we couldn't play, so it was OK."

Bernie Rhodes was an interested observer. "Steve, Paul and Glen weren't sure about John at first, but I said to them, 'Well, can any of you write lyrics? You need him,'" he recalls. "Steve and Paul were already thick with each other, and Glen – being middle-class – thought that he and John could form a similar alliance... if John liked The Beatles."

Accompanying John that night was his sidekick, the mild-mannered John Gray. "We'd only gone to the Roebuck to meet with Steve and Paul," he told the author. "And as Glen had told us the group was rehearsing somewhere over Bermondsey Wharf, it never crossed my mind that John would be expected to audition."

Malcolm returned to the flat on Nightingale Lane where he, Vivienne and their two boys were living at the time and no doubt regaled Vivienne with a rundown of the evening's events. But when Vivienne subsequently met John, she told Malcolm he'd got the wrong guy. She had another "Spiky John" in mind who would enter the picture soon enough.

Gray was also on hand to accompany John to the Crunchy Frog pub in Rotherhithe in south-east London for a live rehearsal. Glen and Paul were happy enough to give John his chance, but Steve was still unmoved and he'd convinced the others that John was a timewaster who probably wouldn't even show up. But show up John did, and his doing so is testament to how much he wanted the gig. Walking around Bermondsey – Millwall territory – dressed as he was, and his and Gray's being "Gooners" (Arsenal fans) to boot, was literally risking life and limb. Malcolm had been beside himself on hearing the planned rehearsal hadn't gone ahead, but designated peacemaker Glen made the requisite call to John, and having withstood a tirade of abuse, he convinced John that his, Steve's and Paul's failure to show up on the night had just been a simple misunderstanding.

With the clock ticking Malcolm was anxious to get the group to the next stage, and so rather than have them wasting time schlepping across London to short-term rehearsal rooms, he handed over the £1,000 deposit for a two-storey rehearsal space at the rear of Denmark Street in the West End. Back in the fifties and sixties, Denmark Street – colloquially known as "Tin Pan Alley" – had been the hub of England's vibrant pop scene, and it was from here that pop impresario Larry Parnes – who'd managed Malcolm's ultimate musical hero, Billy Fury – had run his musical empire.

---

2   In 2012 it was trading as the Beaufort House restaurant.

CHAPTER TWO

Anarchy In The UK

"It's true that Malcolm wanted the Sex Pistols to be the new Bay City Rollers. He also wanted to be the singer/frontman because he craved attention...but he didn't have the balls to do it."

Bernard Rhodes

On Thursday, November 6, 1975, after three months of solid rehearsing, the Sex Pistols were unleashed onto an unsuspecting audience when they played support to a rock'n'roll revivalist combo called Bazooka Joe – featuring a future Adam Ant on bass – at St. Martins School of Art on Charing Cross Road where Glen was enrolled as a student. To commemorate the 30th anniversary of this particular slice of musical history, Glen would one day return to his alma mater to unveil a blue plaque, but on the night itself, the Pistols' "don't-give-a-fuck" attitude ruffled a few feathers and someone from either the college – or more likely Bazooka Joe's entourage – pulled the plug midway through their 30-minute set.

"We was going really mad cos this was our first gig, and we was all really nervous," Paul Cook said in *Sex Pistols: The Inside Story*. "And suddenly you had this great big hand pop out, and someone pulled the plug out like. Someone switched the power off."

The Sex Pistols, however, remained unbowed, and at their second outing at the Central School of Art & Design in Holborn the following evening they were allowed to complete their set without interruption. Yet while Glen was responsible for booking these debut shows, once the group was active it was Malcolm who busied himself with either booking or blagging them support slots at various colleges on the London circuit, both in the run-up to Christmas and into the New Year.

Andy Czezowski, who would go on to open London's seminal punk haunt, the Roxy, some 12 months later, was already aware of the Sex Pistols owing to his being Malcolm and Vivienne's accountant. He subsequently said in Jon Savage's punk opus *England's Dreaming* that at the early Sex Pistols shows the audience reaction was "50 per cent indifference, 25 per cent hostility, 20 per cent hilarity, and five per cent immediate empathy".

Amongst that insightful five per cent were some who were instantly attuned to what the Sex Pistols were doing and – though not having yet bought the T-shirt – were astute enough to know it was time to roll over to the other side of the bed.

Of course, the Sex Pistols playing in and around London didn't impinge too much on Malcolm's time but when the group began making noises about playing further afield – or "Bumblebeeland" as

The Pistols in the studio, left to right: Johnny, Paul, Steve and Glen

he referred to the provinces – to further enhance their reputation, he co-opted an acquaintance, Nils Stevenson, into serving as road manager.

"Malcolm managed to push himself between Vivienne and me and I found myself much more interested in him," Nils said in *Punk*. "We talked and talked drunkenly about doing this club together. Then, one night, he mentioned that he managed this group who he said were going to be the next Bay City Rollers. I thought 'That sounds like shit. What are you talking about?'"

Dalston-born Nils, who at the time was running a second-hand clothes stall on Beaufort Street market further along the King's Road, first came onto Malcolm's radar owing to his infatuation with Vivienne. Nils says that he and Vivienne went out on a couple of dates, but even had Malcolm been the jealous type then Vivienne's being some 13 years older than Nils meant the would-be lothario's ardour would go unrequited.

Like Malcolm, Nils was an art school dropout. Neither was he averse to living on his wits whenever the situation arose, which of course made him the perfect candidate for what Malcolm had in mind when offering him the job. An added bonus of Nils' acceptance came with his bringing along his older brother Ray, a professional rock photographer of some renown having served an apprenticeship of sorts on the mid-sixties scene, who came out of self-imposed exile working as a cab driver to serve as the Sex Pistols' in-house photographer.

Nils' first exposure to the Sex Pistols live experience came when they got an unexpected break supporting current media darlings Eddie & the Hot Rods at the Marquee Club on Wardour Street on Thursday, February 12, 1976. For everyone in the Pistols' camp, the support slot was seen as a means of paving the way to their getting a shot at headlining the prestigious Soho venue. But an altercation with the Hot Rods' management over John's wilful mistreatment of the headliners' PA led to their being banned from the club – the first of several expulsions the group would accrue in the months ahead.

Having only previously met with Steve and Paul – whom he subsequently described as being "just a couple of football hooligans" – Nils wasn't entirely sure why Malcolm was so excited about the group, but from the moment John walked on stage at the Marquee he was utterly transfixed – and by the end of the first song, he knew he just had to be involved.

In one of those rare quirks of fate that can never be properly explained away, the Sex Pistols' "break" came about not because of their performance – as electrifying as it undoubtedly was – but rather due to Steve inadvertently grabbing the attention of *NME* staff writer Neil Spencer (who was there primarily

to review the Hot Rods), with his now-legendary "We're not into music, we're into chaos" comment. The banner headline to Spencer's subsequent review in the February 21, 1976 edition of *NME*, which tellingly made no mention whatsoever of the Hot Rods, was the first to gave notice that things were perhaps never going to be the same again: 'Don't Look Over Your Shoulder But The Sex Pistols Are Coming'.

The Sex Pistols were indeed coming – and were doing so with all guns blazing. Aside from playing London's familiar rock'n'roll haunts such as the Marquee and the Nashville Rooms – where they first encountered their soon-to-be-in-house sound engineer Dave Goodman – they were also content to play strip clubs, ballrooms and the occasional disco. The most significant breakthrough, however, came with their being offered a Tuesday night residency at the 100 Club on Oxford Street.

Away from the capital, they put in plenty of legwork traversing the highways and byways of the land, taking their "Do-It-Yourself" message to the provincial masses. Of course, the majority of said masses remained largely unmoved – in some venues the group was asked to stop playing because it was interfering with either billiards or bingo – but there was always a smattering of kids in the audience who were fed up of hearing about how great rock'n'roll had been back in the day, and who were waiting for something new that they could latch onto and call their own. Amongst these cliques there would be one or two aspiring musicians who – like their clued-up counterparts in London – latched on to the Pistols' message and changed their own game plan accordingly. Though no one would have guessed it from listening to Radio One, or watching *Top Of The Pops*, ever so slowly a scene began to develop.

Somewhat apocryphally, the first indication that a counter-cultural revolution was underway came on Sunday, July 4, 1976, when the then five-piece Clash made their live debut supporting the Sex Pistols at the Black Swan in Sheffield. On discovering that Malcolm had no intention of offering him a co-management deal with the Pistols – a deal he believed was his rightful reward for having looked after the band in Malcolm's absence – Bernard Rhodes had put The Clash together to rival the Pistols.

"I loved Malcolm, but he fucked me over on the T-shirts, and then he fucked me over on the Pistols," Bernard Rhodes says today. "I was the one looking after them whilst he was in New York with the New York Dolls. When he came back to London he was like, 'It's my group'.

"I thought, 'Right, if that's the way you want to play it,' I'm gonna fuck you over. And I did it by planting a bomb with a slow-burning fuse under his chair. A green-haired bomb called John. Because I knew immediately that John would fuck Malcolm over. He was obnoxious and southern Irish, so he had a chip on his shoulder."

Like Malcolm, Bernard – or Bernie as he was known during his tenure as The Clash's manager – was of Jewish descent. He'd been raised in London's East End by his Russian émigré mother who, unlike his father had managed to escape the Jewish pogroms in the mother country. Within weeks of arriving in London, she'd purchased a forged birth certificate on the black market to establish citizenship in the UK, as well as escape possible deportation back to Russia. During the late fifties and early sixties, she worked as a seamstress for several tailors on Savile Row, including Huntsman & Co and Hawes & Curtis. It was while she was working at Hawes & Curtis that John Pearse – who a decade or so later would found the renowned King's Road psychedelic fashion emporium Granny Takes A Trip – was apprenticed to her.

"I grew up on the streets with prostitutes and black blues musicians keeping an eye out for me whilst my mother made suits for people like Cary Grant," says Bernard. "Being from the streets as they were is why I got on so well with John and Steve."

By the summer of 1963, having emulated Malcolm by enrolling at art school, Bernard moved into a flat with Pearse in St. John's Wood, which – thanks to Mick Jagger having one of his mistresses ensconced in the flat above – became a hangout for a colourful coterie of flower-powering misfits such as Donovan, The Who's Pete Townshend and Roger Daltrey, and the soon-to-be-famous Marc Bolan.

Malcolm and Bernard first encountered and befriended each other on London's so-called sixties Soho coffee bar scene – particularly the 2I's Coffee Bar on Old Compton Street where Britain's rock'n'roll pioneers Cliff Richard and Tommy Steele had first started out. When Malcolm and Vivienne first set up stall at 430 King's Road, Bernard, who among his many ventures was running a stall in the nearby Antiquarius Antiques Market selling second-hand leather jackets, would put forward ideas for T-shirts, the most notable being one with the slogan 'You're Gonna Wake Up One Morning And Know Which Side Of The Bed You've Been Lying On', which became the UK punk scene's early manifesto.

"Malcolm and Vivienne were jealous of me because my second-hand clothing was shifting as fast as I put it out on the stall, faster than theirs," he says. "They didn't like that, and that's why they brought me in."

Needless to say, while Malcolm was happy to assimilate Bernard's ideas into his own agenda, he'd flatly refused to make Bernard a partner in either SEX, or the Sex Pistols.

Two days after The Clash made their debut, The Damned supported the Sex Pistols at the 100 Club, which owing to the Pistols' residency was by now regarded as the as yet unnamed scene's spiritual home. "The gigs at the 100 Club were good because they were regular gigs," Paul Cook reflected in *Rotten: No Irish, No Blacks, No Dogs*. "We relied on it each week as a regular place. I suppose that's what actually started the punk movement going."

In the *Never Mind The Sex Pistols* DVD Malcolm states that he hadn't wanted to sign the group to a record label – or indeed, even to release any records. However, once *Melody Maker* and *Sounds* began devoting significant column inches to the nascent UK punk scene – in which both were lauding the Pistols as the scene's kingpins – Malcolm couldn't allow one of the bandwagon jumpers to take over the reins. The first step in exposing "London's best-kept secret" to a wider audience came in arranging for Dave Goodman to record some demos with the group so that he might then go out and solicit interst in their wares.

The Sex Pistols' debut demo session – staged at renowned pop mogul Mickie Most's Majestic Studios back in May – hadn't produced the required results, so it was decided to record the group at Denmark Street, this being their natural habitat, so to speak. At the end of August, having despatched a tape of Goodman's efforts to the leading lights in the music industry, Malcolm arranged a show at the Screen On The Green Cinema in Islington, north London, to showcase the Pistols' live talents. "All the dates until then had been building up to the Screen On The Green," Nils Stevenson told *Punk*. "That was when it all came together – the group, the audience, the event."

Aside from screening a couple of Kenneth Anger movies, Malcolm invited The Clash, and Manchester's proto-punksters, Buzzcocks, to augment the billing. However, what was initially viewed as a show of altruism on Malcolm's part was soon seen for what it really was – a means of showing the assembled A&R teams that the Sex Pistols were the only real game in town. For while both The Clash and Buzzcocks' sets suffered from poor sound, the problems with the PA were magically rectified for when the Pistols took to the stage. While sabotaging the PA to undermine the opposition is something of a time-honoured trick in the industry, Malcolm humiliated The Clash further still by having them provide the materials for – and erect – the makeshift stage, as well as go out and fly-post the posters.

"We'd played with the Pistols before, but as there'd been some friction in the past between Malcolm and Bernie, they made us build the stage," Paul Simonon recalled. "I don't mind a bit of manual work, but to do that all day with the scaffolding and stuff and then go and play was a bit much, I thought."

When the "Midnite Special", as it was billed, failed to garner any concrete interest from the assembled A&R teams, Malcolm hit on the notion of staging a festival to rival the recently staged inaugural European Punk Rock Festival at Mont de Marsan in southern France. The Sex Pistols had been scheduled to perform at this event before having their invitation revoked owing to the UK press' exaggerated reports of violence at their shows. The Clash pulled out in a show of solidarity with the Pistols, but The Damned saw no reason to follow suit and boarded the coach to Dover along with festival headliners Eddie & the Hot Rods. This was seen as the first crack in the veneer of the UK punk scene's so-called "unholy triumvirate".

Of course, once having announced a Punk Festival – to be staged over consecutive evenings on September 20 and 21 – Malcolm had to then find enough punk bands to fill the bill. Having pencilled in The Clash, The Damned, and The Vibrators (featuring a guest spot from Chris Spedding who'd overseen the Pistols' demo session at Majestic Studios), Malcolm again invited Buzzcocks down from Manchester, as well as French punk outfit Stinky Toys. Even then, there were still sizeable holes in the billing, and to remedy the problem he invited Siouxsie & the Banshees (billed as Suzie & the Banshees), and Subway Sect to make their respective debuts.

The festival was an unqualified success in terms of promoting the bands and alerting a wider audience to the emerging scene, but in a moment of madness Sid Vicious threw a beer glass at the stage during The Damned's performance, which prompted the 100 Club to affect an immediate ban on all punk rock acts. The "did he, or didn't he" argument over Sid's supposed glass-throwing antics has raged ever since, but Siouxsie and her bassist Steve Severin – who were both standing next to Sid at the time – are adamant that he was guilty as subsequently charged.

It was initially believed that Sid was merely expressing his displeasure at The Damned's performance on the night, but the reality was that the Croydon-based quartet had been bragging to all and sundry – most notably the *Melody Maker* – that they were "miles better than the Sex Pistols", and had more recently pipped his beloved Pistols to the post by securing a record contract with Stiff Records. They would, of course, go on to steal more of the Pistols' thunder by becoming the first UK punk act to release a single – 'New Rose' – the following month.

"[We] were always shunned from the punk in-group because [we] didn't give a shit," Captain Sensible said in *England's Dreaming*. "There was very little camaraderie among the punk groups. In London there was a certain snobbery, but out of town it was fine: we were very approachable. We'd always be drinking with the people who came to see us."

Watching *The Great Rock 'N' Roll Swindle*, and the cartoon cash register ringing up six and seven-figure sums from the likes of EMI, A&M, Virgin and Warner Bros, one could be forgiven for thinking the Sex Pistols were able to take their pick of major record companies. Yet, the musical merry-go-round didn't actually get into gear until after the group's appearance on the *Today* show. For while all the major labels were aware of the Pistols, and had sent along representatives to the 100 Club, each and every one of them – with the possible exception of Polydor's Chris Parry – went away again still believing punk was another flash-in-the-pan fad. Indeed, EMI's A&R head, Nick Mobbs, who would pip Chris Parry to the post in securing the Pistols' signatures a fortnight or so later, admits that he couldn't be bothered to make the short walk over to the 100 Club from nearby Wardour Street where Giggles (one of EMI's latest acquisitions) were showcasing at the Marquee.

Fortunately, however, the label's in-house engineer, Mike Thorne, and EMI International's Graham Fletcher did make the journey, and it was largely due to their persistence that Mobbs cut short a trip to Venice to see Wings in order to catch the group performing in Doncaster. Although Mobbs could see why Thorne and Fletcher were so excited about the Pistols, he remained unconvinced as to whether EMI was the right label for the group. So the dilemma facing Malcolm when he visited EMI's plush offices at Manchester Square to present his case to Mobbs one overcast October morning wasn't what he was going tell Polydor's Chris Parry (who was so convinced he'd got the group that he'd booked them studio time), or about the £40,000 he was asking for the group's signatures, but rather that he had to overcome the A&R chief's own personal doubts as to whether the Sex Pistols' rough and ready live sound would translate onto vinyl.

Malcolm had prepared his brief well in advance, and he refused to allow Mobbs' personal musical tastes to enter the equation. He sealed the deal by convincing Mobbs if he wasn't willing to sign a hot new act that was right here in front of his eyes then EMI was living in the past, and the label might as well shut up shop. Having convinced Mobbs, he then refused to leave the latter's office until the contract had been drawn up, and only then did he hail a cab to Denmark Street to collect the group.

The Sex Pistols' contract was signed, sealed and delivered in a single day, making it the fastest-ever signing in EMI's illustrious history. Also covering EMI's overseas territories, it was a two-album deal over an initial two-year period with two further one-year options (exercisable only by the label). The group, or rather Malcolm's newly incorporated management company, Glitterbest – as per Clause 17 of the managerial contract – received a £40,000 non-returnable advance, £20,000 of which was paid on signing with the remaining £20,000 to be paid on the corresponding date 12 months later. EMI would also shoulder reasonable recording costs which

Dave Vanian and Brian James of The Damned

could be recouped from future royalties. The group would have record sleeve approval, as well as a say in the choice of producer – which EMI would pay for.

Now that EMI had the Sex Pistols' signatures on the dotted line, its Group Repertoire Division had to decide which of its labels – EMI, Parlophone, or Harvest – would be best suited to take the group forward. Having had the likes of Pink Floyd, Be Bop Deluxe, Kevin Ayres and Soft Machine on its roster, the general consensus within Manchester Square was that it should be Harvest, but on hearing of this the group made it abundantly clear to all concerned that they weren't going to be associated with what they dismissed as a "hippie label". If it said EMI on the contract, then it was going to say EMI on the record.

With EMI gearing up for the impending Christmas rush, the Pistols had just 24 hours to celebrate following in the hallowed footsteps of John, Paul, George and Ringo, before they – accompanied by Dave Goodman – headed into Lansdowne Studios in upmarket Holland Park to record 'Anarchy In The UK'. EMI had initially wanted 'Pretty Vacant' for the debut single, feeling the song was more radio-friendly and therefore more likely to generate sales.

The group spent seven weary days holed up inside Lansdowne playing 'Anarchy' over and over again without having anything to show for their labours – let alone a slice of EMI's £10,000 budget. With the original November 19 release date pushed back another week, the recording party relocated to the decidedly more compact Wessex Studios in Highbury where they again wasted countless reels of expensive two-inch tape while Goodman vainly attempted to record them in a fashion that captured their live energy.

"EMI didn't want 'Anarchy [In The UK]'. They wanted a pop song, 'I'm So Pretty' as they called it. Glen was going along with that but 'Anarchy' was the strongest and that was what it was going to be," Goodman bemoaned in *England's Dreaming*. "I was called into EMI, and Mike Thorne had gone in there with Glen and done their own mix of my production. They played me this acetate, and I just freaked."

According to those in the know, the normal recording process for a single took an average of around three weeks, and the powers-that-be over at EMI were beginning to express doubts in Goodman's capabilities. As the days continued to slip by with no sign of Goodman producing the goods, the engineer was duly summoned to Manchester Square to be told he was off the project.[1*]

---

1   Dave Goodman's version of 'Anarchy In The UK' wouldn't surface until its inclusion on *The Great Rock 'N' Roll Swindle* soundtrack in March 1979.

Goodman's replacement at the Wessex console was the studio's affiliate producer Chris Thomas, who'd cut his teeth working on The Beatles' *White Album,* before going on to work with Procal Harum and Roxy Music as well as oversee the mixing of Pink Floyd's *Dark Side Of The Moon*. Thomas was familiar with the Sex Pistols' style as he'd accompanied his friend Chris Spedding to Malcolm's 'Midnite Special' at the Screen On The Green at the end of August. Even though Thomas would subsequently confess on *Classic Albums* that the group had left him largely unmoved, he was, however, suitably impressed with the chord changes on the version of 'Anarchy In The UK' that Mike Thorne had sent him and he tentatively agreed to meet the group at his home in Ealing.

While Thomas' no-nonsense approach to recording – and his favouring of overdubbing the guitars – may have bruised a certain spiky ego, no one could argue that Thomas wasn't a master of his craft for within five takes the finished song was in the can. He'd won the battle to get John to enunciate his lyrics, and also eradicated a discrepancy on the timing on Paul's snare drum by splicing two backing tracks together. Most importantly, while Goodman's four-minute-and-counting version had subsided into wave upon wave of meandering feedback, Thomas opted for a sonic shutdown by cutting the song immediately after John's 'Get pissed… Destroy' coda in the hope that the needle would actually leap up out of the groove to escape the invective.

'Anarchy In The UK' (EMI 2566) was released in the UK on November 26, 1976, with the first 2,000 copies issued in a plain black bag accompanied by Malcolm's old Suburban Press pal Jamie Reid's now iconic fold-out poster of a torn Union Jack held together with assorted safety pins and paper clips. Having already capitulated on two fronts in the choice of song, and the Sex Pistols' refusal to be housed with the company's subsidiary label, Harvest[2*], EMI also had to comply with Malcolm's wishes in avoiding the usual clichéd promotional packaging.

When the bemused head of EMI's marketing department had questioned how anybody was supposed to find the single, Malcolm responded by saying he didn't want just "anybody" to find the record, he only wanted the "somebodies" to go into their local record store and ask for it by name. This, of course, was in accordance with the terms of the contract, and the label again had little option but to comply.

Though Malcolm undoubtedly took pride in the fact that in just 12 months the Sex Pistols – under his auspices – had gone from playing to a handful of people in a tiny upstairs room at St. Martins to being hailed as leaders of an exciting musical craze, as well as being signed to one of the most prestigious record labels in the world, SEX was still where his priorities lay. Indeed, he and Vivienne were in the midst of drawing up plans to renovate the shop, so having his time taken up with organising the itinerary for a 19-date nationwide tour to promote 'Anarchy In The UK', as well as accompany the group on the road in the weeks leading up to Christmas – every shopkeeper's busiest period – must have been anathema to someone used to calling rather than following the tune.

---

2   Harvest was established in 1969 to cater for bands in the emerging progressive rock genre such as Pink Floyd.

CHAPTER THREE

Nothing, A Rude Word...

"If there's one thing that everyone – even if they've never listened to a rock 'n' roll record in their life – knows about the Sex Pistols, it's that we appeared on the Bill Grundy show, we swore and some bloke got so annoyed by us he kicked in his TV set."

Glen Matlock

Malcolm McLaren first began planning the Anarchy In The UK Tour while the Sex Pistols were holed up inside Lansdowne Studios recording their debut single. Though he hadn't had much involvement with the group's touring itinerary since handing over the mundane day-to-day managerial tasks to Nils Stevenson back in February, he was astute enough to recognise that the group – having played only around 60 shows to date – was still relatively unknown outside London, Manchester, and Birmingham. Indeed, there'd been occasions when they'd outnumbered the audience, and while the single would soon be out in the shops, he didn't feel the group had sufficient pulling power to go it alone. This anxiety stemmed not so much from the possibility of the Sex Pistols being left with egg on their faces, but rather due to a sizeable slice of the tour's costs coming out of the EMI advance that was nicely accruing interest in the Glitterbest account.

Had the Sex Pistols been an ordinary pop group, Malcolm could have eased the financial strain by inviting another of EMI's up-and-coming bands – or even a group signed to another label – onto the tour and have their label pick up a portion of the tab. But the Pistols were far from being a run-of-the-mill pop group. Though they were the leaders of what the music press was hailing as the most exciting scene to come out of England in a decade or more, The Damned were as yet the only other group on the scene to have secured a recording contract, albeit with Stiff Records, a recently incorporated independent label operating on a shoestring budget.

His options therefore somewhat limited, Malcolm turned his attention to the groups that were making waves in New York. The obvious choice from the Bowery groups was The Ramones, whose eponymous album – released on Sire Records in April 1976 – had served as a blueprint for many of the London bands paddling in the Sex Pistols' wake. Indeed, when The Ramones came over to London to play a couple of shows over the bicentennial weekend of July 4, 1976, at the Roundhouse and Dingwalls respectively, Malcolm had approached the renowned London promoter John Curd at the latter's home to see about getting the Pistols onto the Roundhouse bill. Legend has it that Curd responded by forcibly ejecting Malcolm out into the street, so it must have come as something of a surprise – if only to the UK music press – when Malcolm subsequently announced that The Ramones would be coming on the tour as co-headliners.

Aside from The Ramones, Malcolm had also invited Talking Heads – whose punk style came with a more sophisticated, syncopated beat – over from New York to share support duties with The Vibrators, who'd supported the Pistols at the 100 Club back in August, as well as appearing on the second night's bill at the 100 Club Punk Festival the following month. However, his efforts – not to mention the cost of several lengthy transatlantic telephone calls – counted for nothing, and he was forced into a major rethink when all three bands subsequently announced they were withdrawing from the tour.

Under the headline 'Pistols To Open New Roxy Venue – Ramones Out – Damned, Clash In', *NME* of December 4, 1976 reported: "The Ramones have pulled out of the big punk-rock package tour, in which they were to have co-headlined with the Sex Pistols. As a result the whole tour has now been completely revamped. It will be going ahead from the beginning of next month with the Pistols as sole billtoppers – supported by two other fast-rising British punk bands, The Damned and The Clash, plus American outfit Heartbreakers, fronted by former New York Doll Johnny Thunders.

"The climax of the revised tour itinerary will be two gigs at London's new Roxy Theatre in Harlesden on December 26 and Boxing Day 27 [sic], with December 28 being held for a third night if there is sufficient ticket demand.

"The Ramones apparently dropped out because they felt the original tour schedule had been set up too hurriedly, and without allowing them sufficient time to arrange promotion. Their manager said they were now thinking in terms of a British tour in the New Year which would be better organised.

"The Talking Heads, another U.S. outfit who were in the original package, have dropped out for the same reason."

The Ramones, left to right: Joey, Dee Dee, Johnny and Tommy

In hindsight, one can understand The Ramones' reasons for pulling out of the tour: having already wowed London with two sell-out shows the leather-clad rockers would have felt they were more than capable of filling other venues elsewhere in the UK under their own volition. Talking Heads' withdrawal could also perhaps be explained away as they were as yet unsigned, and Malcolm was unwilling to meet their expenses. Yet even now, it's difficult to understand The Vibrators' motives, for although they had secured a record deal with Mickie Most's RAK label in recent weeks, they were hardly in a position to snub the opportunity to promote themselves to a wider audience. Indeed, prior to their witnessing the Sex Pistols in action at the 100 Club – which led to a collective shearing of hair and a shedding of patchwork denims – they were just another aspiring outfit plying their trade on London's pub-rock circuit.

Captain Sensible

It's safe to assume that the thumbs down from Talking Heads and the Vibrators wouldn't have been seen as much of a setback at the Sex Pistols' Glitterbest HQ in Dryden Chambers, there being a dozen or more exciting new groups that had supported the Pistols in recent months to choose from, but The Ramones giving back-word did present Malcolm with something of a headache. Though many emerging English bands would have happily crawled over broken glass for the chance to undertake a national tour, he still needed a "name" group with bona fide punk credentials capable of putting bums on seats at each venue to ensure the tour wouldn't only prove a success in terms of maximising exposure and limiting unnecessary expenditure, but would also provide a springboard for the Pistols for the coming year. And that, much to Malcolm's chagrin, left but one viable option – The Damned.

It wasn't so much the simmering friction between the two bands that was the problem, but rather Malcolm's ongoing spat with The Damned's new manager Andrew Jakeman – a.k.a Jake Riviera – who'd set up Stiff Records with his fellow pub rock enthusiast, Dave Robinson. Malcolm had heard on the grapevine about how Riviera was openly dismissing him as nothing more than a "second-rate haberdasher".

Putting personalities and playground insults aside, however, the truth was that Malcolm had now grown accustomed to being regarded as the London punk scene's kingmaker and was reluctant to share the kudos with anyone. "Jake came from a pub-rock background and had no time for Malcolm who he saw as little more than a jumped-up schmutter [sic] merchant, with no understanding of the music or the business," Glen recalled in his autobiography, *I Was A Teenage Sex Pistol*. "Malcolm thought of Jake as a real pleb. The Bill Brown of rock 'n' roll he called him, nothing but darts, public bars and pints of bitter."

Though Malcolm had suffered the indignation of having had his transatlantic advances spurned not once but twice, he was still keen to add a little Lower East Side allure to the forthcoming tour. Following several desperate late-night telephone conversations, ex-New York Dolls Johnny Thunders and Jerry Nolan's new outfit, The Heartbreakers – which until recently had featured Richard Hell in the line-up – were added to the bill. However, despite Johnny and Jerry being regarded as "cause célebres" on the New York scene, none of the American labels were willing to offer them a recording deal due to their offstage activities. "There were times when I had to push Johnny on stage, and I had to put a bucket out so he could throw up between songs," Leee Black Childers recalls. "But you just deal with that reality. I never went into it [managing The Heartbreakers] thinking I was going to change them."

Though there are some who still defend Johnny and Jerry against accusations that The Heartbreakers were responsible for introducing heroin to the London punk scene – claiming heroin was readily available in the British capital for those who knew where to look for it – it's worth remembering that up until their arrival speed and weed were the only recreational drugs around. Further proof of this is provided by Childers who says that while Johnny and Jerry were thrilled to be going to London, there was no way they could be expected to undertake a three-week tour without their preferred drug du jour, and before leaving for the airport they stashed an ample supply of heroin amid their luggage to see them through the ride.

Given that Malcolm and Bernard had renewed their working relationship, it's somewhat surprising that Malcolm didn't consider inviting The Clash onto the Anarchy Tour's initial billing. After all, they'd played together several times by this juncture, most recently at Lanchester Polytechnic in Coventry where the polytechnic's Student Union had tried to withhold payment to both bands due to their supposed fascist leanings.

"It's ironic really, but my first gig working for The Clash came at Lanchester Polytechnic in my hometown of Coventry when they supported the Sex Pistols," says Steve "Roadent" Connelly, who would have the unique honour of working for both The Clash and the Pistols. "After the show, the Student Union held an emergency meeting where they refused to pay either group because they said 'White Riot' and 'God Save The Queen' – or 'No Future' as it was called at the time – were fascist songs."

Though The Clash were as yet without a recording deal, they were rapidly accruing a partisan audience of their own in and around London, and while the Anarchy Tour's itinerary had but one date in the capital, their fans would have thought nothing of bunking the train to Birmingham where the group had played at the end of October. Yet though The Clash were billed as "Special Guests" on the tour's revised itinerary, it was something of a misnomer as they were still bottom of the bill.

"Malcolm couldn't stand the fact that I'd put another group together," says Bernard. "And forget what you've read elsewhere, because that's the real reason why he put The Clash at the bottom of the bill on the Anarchy Tour. We might have been 'Special Guests', but we were still bottom of the bill. And while everyone might have been talking about punk following the Bill Grundy thing, we still had to open the shows on that tour – and that's difficult enough without the world watching you."

Once the tour billing was finally completed, Malcolm – with the help of Jamie Reid's girlfriend Sophie Richmond, whom he'd recently taken on as his assistant – could finally concentrate on finalising the logistics.

As one might expect of a newly signed group undertaking their first headline national tour, the venues – with the exception of the 3,000-capacity Glasgow Apollo – were of moderate size, and made up of civic and town halls, places of higher education, and clubs with an established music pedigree. Though 'Anarchy In The UK' name-checked both the IRA and the UDA, Malcolm – possibly for that very same reason – chose to avoid Northern Ireland and instead chose 19 towns and cities on the British mainland. If everything went according to script, then the tour, which would get underway with a show at Norwich's East Anglia University on Friday, December 3, and take in venues as far afield as Dundee, Cardiff, Bournemouth, and Torquay, would culminate with a triumphant homecoming show at the Roxy Theatre in Harlesden on Boxing Day, Sunday, December 26.

Malcolm certainly had his hands full. He was concerned about EMI's commitment to the Sex Pistols' cause, worrying about the practical details of the impending tour and, lest we forget, finalising plans for his shop's latest makeover. It's therefore something of a wonder that he found time to answer the phone when Eric Hall, EMI's Head of Promotions, called SEX late Wednesday afternoon, December 1, to say he'd secured the Pistols a plug on that evening's edition of the *Today* show.

At the time of Hall's call, the Sex Pistols, who were holed up at the Roxy Theatre in Harlesden with The Damned and The Clash rehearsing sets and changeovers, already had several TV appearances under their belt. They'd performed 'Anarchy In The UK' live on Granada TV's late-night avant garde music show *So It Goes*, hosted by self-confessed punk aficionado Tony Wilson; appeared on LWT's *London Weekend*

Show, on which they'd been filmed performing live at the Notre Dame Hall on November 15, as well as being interviewed at Denmark Street by the show's loquacious host, Janet Street-Porter; and they'd also had the 'Anarchy In The UK' promo video screened on BBC 1's own magazine news programme, *Nationwide*.

Though something of a shameless voyeur, Malcolm was always happy to further the Pistols' advancement via the television camera. Nevertheless, he was unlikely to have been very excited by Hall's latest "monster plug", an appearance on a tea-time London local news programme. Even the offer of a courtesy limo to pick the group up in Harlesden and ferry them to the studio failed to ignite his interest.

Hall, however, was used to thinking on his feet. And knowing the Pistols were about to embark on a national tour that was primarily to promote their debut single, he talked up the advantages of having the group appear on *Today*. Aside from having a clip of the 'Anarchy' promo video aired, the group would be able to plug both the single and the forthcoming tour. Although *Today* was broadcast only within the London area, with Thames TV being a commercial station the interview could be syndicated to Granada TV, Yorkshire TV, Tyne Tees, Anglia, and every other region on the tour's itinerary. Malcolm was still sceptical, but on hearing mention that The Heartbreakers and their retinue were due to land at Heathrow within the hour, Hall threw in the use of the courtesy limo for them to seal the deal.

"Malcolm was always desperate to be part of the system, whereas I was always looking to create an alternative," says Bernard of Malcolm's desire to be in the spotlight. "I hate the BBC, and that's why I wouldn't let The Clash do *Top Of The Pops*. Keep refusing to do things and they have to give you our own show."

With Hall being EMI's head of promotions, his plush office had a state-of-the-art television set, and the comfiest of sofas. Though he couldn't stick around to see the fruits of his labours owing to a long-standing commitment to meet Marc Bolan over at the BBC, before leaving for Shepherd's Bush he passed word to those staffers involved with the Sex Pistols who were still in the building – primarily EMI Group Repertoire Division's General Manager Paul Watts, Harvest Records head Mark Rye, his second-in-command Frank Brunger, and Nick Mobbs' secretary, Diane Wagg (Brunger's fiancée) – that the Pistols would be appearing on that evening's *Today* show.

Malcolm wasn't the only one to express indifference at Hall's dilemma, for when Nils called the Roxy Theatre to make the group aware of the change in plan the four Sex Pistols were not best pleased at having to curtail their rehearsal schedule to appear on what they considered to be just another poxy teatime TV show. Indeed, the musical landscape might have remained unchanged for several months – and that's only if EMI had agreed to release 'No Future' in Queen Elizabeth II's Silver Jubilee year – had Malcolm not quelled the mutiny by threatening to withhold the group's £25-per-week wages.

One might wonder why Malcolm – having had his own reservations about the Pistols appearing on regional TV – didn't accept the group's stance and call Hall to tell the EMI plugger that he would have to look elsewhere on the label's roster for a replacement act. Of course, in hindsight, we now know that the overriding factor in Malcolm's acquiescence was that having the group on prime-time television provided an opportunity for him to promote SEX's latest clothing line.

If he'd have had sufficient time he'd have probably grabbed a few items from off the rails and ferried them over to Harlesden for the group to change into before the limo arrived, though there was no guarantee that John and the others would play ball – especially in light of his having held them to ransom by threatening to withhold their wages. Then, remembering that Hall hadn't said anything about Thames' invitation being limited to the Sex Pistols per se, he called on occasional SEX employee – and fully paid up member of the Bromley Contingent – Simon Barker, to round up a few of his like-minded chums and get themselves over to Thames TV's studio on Marylebone Road.

Imagine then Malcom's chagrin on entering the Green Room – as studio hospitality suites are usually known – to find Siouxsie Sioux and Steve Severin knocking back the courtesy plonk alongside Simon and Simone Thomas – another occasional SEX employee. Siouxsie and Steve were both long-standing SEX

The Pistols and friends with Bill Grundy on the *Today* show

habitués, but since forming their own group they'd purposely distanced themselves from the Sex Pistols. Then again, if you're going to promote a DIY ethic, you can hardly take umbrage when someone actually sits up and takes notice.

"I was 16 at the time. My life revolved around David Bowie and Roxy Music and dressing up and going to gigs," Simone Thomas said in *Punk: The Illustrated History Of A Music Revolution*. "I'd met Siouxsie at a Roxy [Music] concert. She was from the same part of London as me, and she started going out with Steve Severin who was part of the same scene. One afternoon, Siouxsie called and asked if I'd like to be on TV. "

While everyone assumes Siouxsie and Steve were there because of Simon's endeavours, again, with hindsight, it's obvious that their inclusion was actually down to Nils. Still peeved at being denied what he believed he was rightfully owed – a percentage of the spoils from the EMI contract – Nils was now acting as the Banshees' manager, and as he'd taken over from Glen in sharing the upstairs room at Denmark Street with Steve, he'd had a set of keys copied so the Banshees would have somewhere to surreptitiously rehearse while the Sex Pistols were out on tour.

"Simon [Barker] got a call from Malcolm who said he'd pay our train fares if we went along to hang out and stand in the background," Siouxsie said in *Siouxsie & The Banshees: The Authorised Biography*. "We were shown into the Green Room where everything was free so we started drinking immediately. Everyone, the group [Sex Pistols] and us, were all getting completely pissed. Bill Grundy came in to see us and even then I was winding him up. He kept on leering at me."

Though the footage has never surfaced, Paul Cook says he and the rest of the Sex Pistols were lined up in front of the camera while an unseen female voice – mimicking Rolling Stones' one-time manager Andrew Loog Oldham's memorable line aimed at his own wayward charges – jokingly asked the viewers at home if they would willingly allow their daughters to go out with a Sex Pistol. The group was then escorted through to the compact set where the show's Manchester-born anchorman, Bill Grundy – who'd spent the afternoon getting soused with several of his journalistic buddies at *Punch* magazine – was sat waiting. Though the one-time geologist subsequently claimed to have never heard of either the Sex Pistols or punk rock until that day, he'd already encountered the group and their followers in the Green Room earlier, so he should have had some inkling as to what might happen if he didn't keep a tight rein on things.

"If you [were to] ask me about Mozart or Beethoven or Haydn, I think you might get an intelligent answer," Grundy said in *The Wicked Ways Of Malcolm McLaren*. "I didn't know anything about pop music and [when] I saw 'Bill and the Sex Pistols' [listed on *Today*'s running order] that was the first: I didn't know what the Sex Pistols was, is, or were. I thought that all I was going to do was introduce yet another ghastly pop group and – end of programme..."

Eric Hall, to his credit, had forewarned Today's producer Mike Housego that EMI's latest acquisitions were "monster hungry" for any publicity that would help promote the single, and that Grundy should be extra careful with the group. Housego, however, believed that a no-nonsense old pro like Grundy would know how to handle a rock group. After all, he'd been the first television presenter to interview The Beatles back in October 1962, and the interview was an inconsequential three-minute affair slotted in at the end of the programme. What could possibly go wrong?

With Siouxsie, Steve Severin, Simon and Simone standing behind them, the Sex Pistols are seated – from left to right as the camera sees them – John, Steve, Glen and Paul, with Grundy sitting to their left. The full transcript of the interview is as follows:

Grundy: *Safety pins, Chains round the neck? And that's just the fellas, yeah, Innit?* [Appearing momentarily bewildered as he surveys the group and their bizarrely dressed retinue] *Eh...? I mean, it is just the fellas... yeah. They are punk rockers. The new craze, they tell me. They are heroes. Not the nice, clean Rolling Stones... you see they are as drunk as I am... they are clean by comparison. They're a group called the Sex Pistols, and I'm surrounded by all of them...*

Steve: [Reading from autocue] In action!

Grundy: *Just let us see the Sex Pistols in action...* [To Siouxsie and Simone] *Come on kids...*

Following a 30-second clip of Mike Mansfield's promo video for 'Anarchy In The UK', the camera cuts back to the studio:

Grundy: *I'm told that that group* [hitting his knee with the sheaf of papers he's holding] *have received £40,000 from a record company. Doesn't that seem to be ah... slightly anti-materialistic view of life?*

Glen: No, the more the merrier.

Grundy: *Really?*

Glen: Oh yeah.

Grundy: *Well, tell me more then.*

Steve [off camera]: We've fuckin' spent it, ain't we?

Grundy: *I don't know, have you?*

Glen: Yeah, it's all gone.

Grundy: *Really?*

Glen: Down the boozer.

Grundy: *Really? Good Lord! Now, I want to know one thing...*

Glen: What?

Grundy: *Are you serious, or are you just making me... trying to make me laugh?*

Glen: No, it's gone; gone.

Grundy: *Really?*

Glen: Yeah.

Grundy: *No, but I mean about what you're doing.*

Glen: Oh yeah.

Grundy: *You are serious?*

Glen: Mmm.

Grundy: *Beethoven, Mozart, Bach and Brahms have all died...*

John: They're all heroes of ours, ain't they?

Grundy: *Really? What... what are you saying, sir?*

John [his voice dripping with sarcasm]: They're wonderful people.

Grundy: *Are they?*

John: Oh yes! They really turn us on.

Grundy: *Well, suppose they turn other people on?*

John [mumbling]: That's just their tough shit.

Grundy: *It's what?*

John [snapping to attention]: Nothing! A rude word. Next question?

Grundy: *No, no, what was the rude word?*

John: Shit.

Grundy: *Was it really? Good heavens, you frighten me to death.*

John: Oh, all right, Siegfried…

Grundy [ignoring John and turning to Siouxsie and Simone]: *What about you girls behind?*

Glen [off camera]: He's like your dad, innee, this geezer?

Grundy [again to the girls]: *Are you, er…*

Glen [again off camera]: Or your granddad.

Grundy [to Siouxsie]: *Are you worried, or are you just enjoying yourself?*

Siouxsie: Enjoying myself.

Grundy: *Are you?*

Siouxsie: Yeah.

Grundy: *Ah, that's what I thought you were doing.*

Siouxsie: I always wanted to meet you.

Grundy: *Did you really?*

Siouxsie: Yeah.

Grundy: *We'll meet afterwards, shall we?* [Siouxsie does a camp pout]

Steve: You dirty sod. You dirty old man!

Grundy: *Well keep going, chief, keep going. Go on, you've got another five seconds. Say something outrageous.*

Steve: You dirty bastard!

Grundy: *Go on, again.*

Steve: You dirty fucker! [Nervous laughter from the others]

Grundy: *What a clever boy!*

Steve: What a fucking rotter.

Grundy: [Turning to camera] *Well, that's it for tonight. The other rocker, Eamonn* [Andrews], *I'm saying nothing else about him, will be back tomorrow. I'll be seeing you soon.* [Turning to the group] *I hope I'm not seeing you again. From me, though, goodnight.* [He then turns away from the camera but can be seen mouthing the words, "Oh shit"]

"The thing that really started the whole annoyance was the introduction to the show when Grundy was sitting in this chair and he was looking at a TV screen opposite him with an autocue," Malcolm said in *England's Dreaming*. "He was reading all his words and here were all the Sex Pistols sitting down reading it with him and that really set him off."

As the show's signature tune 'Windy' plays and the credits roll, Paul feigns a yawn, Glen glances around the studio, John absently glances at his watch, while Steve gets to his feet and playfully cavorts to the music. "The whole Bill Grundy incident was lovely. It was heaven," John Lydon said in *Rotten: No Irish, No Blacks, No Dogs*. "He ruined his own career. It wasn't me. At the time we were asked to appear, we were rehearsing on Craven Park Road in Harlesden for our forthcoming Anarchy Tour. EMI arranged an interview on the *Today* programme. *Today* was a show with idle banter and chat that was programmed to be on live TV that very day."

CHAPTER FOUR

Seen You in the Mirror...

> "The object of this particular item was to find out why people put safety pins through their noses; the same as if I'd been here 20 years ago I'd want to know why people wore drainpipe trousers and had Tony Curtis haircuts, or latterly why mods and rockers punched the shit out of one another on Brighton beach."
>
> Michael Housego

Having availed themselves of Thames TV's complimentary fare, it's hardly surprising that the Sex Pistols and their retinue were in jovial mood – early evidence of which came when Steve and John started reading out Grundy's lines from the autocue in an attempt to throw him off kilter. Glen says that he, John, and Paul were relatively sober in front of the cameras as all they'd managed to get their hands on in the Green Room were a couple of cans of lukewarm lager. Steve, however, as he subsequently recalled for the *Classic Albums* series, was "pretty fuckin' lit" by the time the cameras rolled owing to his having downed a copious amount of Blue Nun wine.

"[We got] slung in the Green Room with a fridge, and I remember downing about fucking four bottles of Blue Nun," Steve said in *The Filth & The Fury*. "We were in there forever. You know, it seems like we were in there for, like, over an hour – two hours, it seemed like – and I was just fucking having a good old time, pissed at this point by the time we went out there."

Having witnessed whatever shenanigans Steve and the rest of the group were getting up to prior to their coming onto the set, Grundy should have expected a little boisterous behaviour. All he'd needed to do to get them onside was tell them the first round at the pub round the corner was on him before the cameras rolled and then get on with what he'd been briefed to do – plug the new single, and ask a few innocuous questions about the group and their forthcoming tour. Instead, he wilfully chose to ignore the script – as well as the customary pleasantries – and launch into his tirade about punk rock being the latest craze.

"I thought, 'Well, I'm not going to be offended by that [the swearing], that's an absolute certainty,'" Grundy said in *The Wicked Ways Of Malcolm McLaren*. "And then there was a moment when I said, 'Look, if you're trying to offend me you're failing. I was in the Navy before you buggers were born and you don't

offend me.' I can't really remember what happened after that, except that their command of the English language appeared to consist only of four-letter words or six-letter words…

"I think I interviewed the prime minister that day. I mean it's that kind of a show, it varies a great deal. But there came a moment when I had to put us into VTR [Video Tape Recording], and while we were [in] VTR, in came a group of people whose hair appeared to have been spiked with machine oil. And with them were four girls who looked like – well, I am rather fond of women, but they were the sort of girls I wouldn't under any circumstances have, um, slept with."

Under the headline 'I DID IT TO SHOW THEY ARE JUST FOUL MOUTHED YOBS – GRUNDY SLAMS BACK AT CRITICS', the following day's *Sun* reported: "TV interviewer Bill Grundy yesterday defended his behaviour on the *Today* show, when a Punk Rock group used four-letter obscenities that shocked thousands of viewers.

"Grundy, facing a Thames TV enquiry over Wednesday's incident with the Sex Pistols, denied encouraging them to use bad language. 'The whole object of this exercise was to show that the group are foul-mouthed yobs. I think they proved this point and proved it quite well. I met them before the programme but they did not endear themselves to me. In fact, I detest them.'"

While no one was expecting an old curmudgeon like Bill Grundy – who would succumb to a heart attack in February 1993 aged 69 – to connect with what the Sex Pistols were doing. One might have at least expected him to try and establish some common ground. After all, he'd been the first man in television to interview The Beatles, who like the Pistols, had been signed to EMI. Instead, he chose to go straight for the jugular by suggesting the £40,000 advance from EMI was "contrary to their supposed anti-materialistic view of life". It's also strange that he chose not to mention EMI by name given that the conglomerate owned a 50 per cent share in Thames Television, the company that paid his wages.

"We were told that he [Grundy] was going to talk about the tour and the record and all that," Steve Jones grumbled in *The Filth & The Fury*. "The next thing I know he's, like... I got this – picked up this vibe – that he was trying to make us look stupid. And actually, there's a 'fuck' word even before they cottoned on to it, because he was drunk himself and he wasn't paying attention when he asked, like, 'Well, what do you do with the money?' And I said, 'We fucking spent it.' No one even heard that one until he focused on it later."

While the question of the £40,000 advance was no doubt aimed at all four group members, Glen was the only one showing much interest in the proceedings at this stage. His chirpy noncommittal responses, however, only seemed to further irritate Grundy, who instead of taking the hint and moving on, continued to press Glen about the sum. Needless to say, Grundy's frivolous questions about the advance soon began to grate – especially with Steve, who finally snapped and said – in a voice loud enough for everyone in the studio to hear – that they'd "fuckin' spent it".

Why Mike Housego – who must have heard Steve's outburst – didn't react is anyone's guess, but Grundy's response was utterly reprehensible. Instead of attempting to embarrass Steve by chastising him as one might an errant schoolboy, or at least by reminding the group that the programme was going out live, he not only continued with his inane line of questioning but went from the sublime to the ridiculous by throwing in a line about Beethoven, Mozart, Bach and Brahms having all died.

It's at this point that John, who'd been happy to take a back seat until now, picks up the gauntlet and offers a throwaway line about the composers all being heroes of theirs. It's easy to see from Grundy's reaction as he shifts in his chair to face John that this was what he'd

Bill Grundy

been waiting for, indeed hoping for, because aside from Steve wearing a risqué tits T-shirt, he, Paul, and Glen looked like three disaffected art school students, whereas John – with his ginger spikes framing his deathly white angular face – was looking every inch the anarchistic anti-Christ he was professing to be in song.

However, instead of seizing the initiative and perhaps challenging John's intellect by asking him to explain the opening salvo to 'Anarchy In The UK', he tried goading John by pressing him for a response to his quip about the composers being "wonderful people" who "really turn us on" and asking what if they [the composers] turned other people on? Realising that Grundy wasn't following a script but simply making it up as he went along, John loses interest and mumbles a line about it being "their tough shit".

Again, this should have been enough for Housego – or someone else charged with a clipboard – to get Malcolm, who was standing off camera watching history in the making, to signal for his boys to cease fire on the hapless Grundy. Failing that, then they should have at least got Grundy to change tack and do as he was supposed to by asking the group a pertinent question about either their new record or the impending tour.

Incredibly, no one does anything, and rather than acknowledge he was losing the plot by steering the rapidly sinking interview into calmer waters, Grundy pressed John into admitting to having said

"a rude word". Once again, Grundy failed to play his get-out-of-jail card by reminding everyone that this was a family show, and instead of asking the next question as John mockingly suggested, he compounds his folly by insisting that John repeat the expletive.

Had Grundy been sober enough to notice John's face visibly reddening in his monitor, he could still have salvaged the situation by offering the camera a knowing smile, and then making a joke about what Radio One DJs such as Tony Blackburn or Dave Lee Travis' reactions might be if they were asked to play a record called 'Anarchy In The UK' on their respective daytime shows. Instead, he chose to turn his attention to Siouxsie and Simone.

"Grundy was filthy dead, pissed drunk when we got there," John Lydon said in *Rotten: No Irish, No Blacks, No Dogs*. "We also had Siouxsie and the Bromley contingent with us. Grundy started coming on to the girlies, particularly Sioux. He behaved like a filthy, dirty old man, and that's what came out in the interview."

Somewhat surprisingly, Siouxsie went all coy at suddenly finding herself centre stage, and with the whole of London awaiting her response, punk's femme fatale could think of nothing else to say to Grundy other than how she'd always wanted to meet him. The comment was obviously meant tongue-in-cheek, given that Siouxsie was a svelte 21-year-old and Grundy was both overweight and the wrong side of 50. And while Siouxsie perhaps didn't realise it, she'd inadvertently handed Grundy a second opportunity to deliver a coup de grâce as all he needed to do was make a suggestive face to camera and he'd have been home and dry. Yet without giving any thought as to whether Siouxsie was anyone's girlfriend, he leeringly suggests that they should meet up after the show – and with the interview clearly going nowhere, Steve finally loses his rag with Grundy and calls him a "dirty sod".

It's worth pointing out here that whenever the camera was focused on Steve the viewers at home – many of whom would be impressionable school children – would see his T-shirt. When Jordan [long-standing SEX employee] had brazenly sported a swastika armband in the Granada TV studios during the recording of *So It Goes* – which went out at 10.30 p.m. on a Sunday evening – those in charge had insisted that the offending image be covered over with gaffer tape – yet a T-shirt bearing an image of a shapely pair of naked breasts was seemingly acceptable for prime-time family viewing. This, of course, was the publicity Malcolm had sought and he was probably making a mental note to himself to have a couple of hundred extra tits T-shirts printed up on the off-chance when Grundy ludicrously challenged Steve to "say something outrageous".

"Siouxsie told Grundy she had always wanted to meet him and I think she was being sincere," Steve said in *Rotten: No Irish, No Blacks, No Dogs*. He said to her, 'We'll meet after the show'. He was being an old sleazy bastard, so I started swearing at him. Actually John said 'shit', and nobody heard it. Then I started saying 'fuck this' and 'fuck that'. I thought they bleeped stuff on TV. It's common practice, and I can't work out why they didn't that day. Maybe somebody deliberately let it go out. It was amazing. But I had no qualms about telling this guy where to go."

"Steve on the Grundy show absolutely took over, because he was in his element," John said in *The Filth & The Fury*. "He completely understood that he was just talking, like, to a drunk, as you would a drunk in a pub, and he just topped him. And there was no reason or point for me to butt in or dominate or do anything."

Had Grundy made his career-ending offer to John then he still might have been spared, as John's riposte would have probably been something along the lines of, "Not until you say something intelligent, chief," and with honours even, everyone could have gone away happy. Steve, however – not being the sharpest note on the musical scale – simply responded as he would have done when dealing with an annoying drunk down the pub. "After Grundy it was a media circus," the guitarist said in *Punk*. "It was great in one sense that we were a household name, but it was kinda the start of the downfall of the group because it just pushed us way too fast."

While it was a measure of Grundy's conceited arrogance that he actually turned to the camera to tell

the viewers at home – who were all no doubt sitting in stunned silence – that he'd "be seeing them soon", inwardly he must have known that he'd seriously overstepped the mark. "Bill Grundy was a fat sexist beer monster who knew nothing about us and shouldn't have been interviewing us in the first place," John reflected in *Rotten: No Irish, No Blacks, No Dogs*. "All we did was point that out."

That Steve would choose to call Grundy a "rotter" – an antiquated term for a despicable or unpleasant character – would have been risible had it not been for its use in a Cadbury's Schweppes tonic water TV advertising campaign in the run-up to Christmas, which carried the tagline – spoken by caddish English actor William "Shhh... You Know Who" Franklyn – "You can always tell a rotter by his 'Schweppes'."

Interviewed on *Classic Albums*, John said that after the *Today* show he was unceremoniously dumped at the nearest Tube station and left to fend for himself, but the reality was that as the night was still young – and with a tour still to rehearse – the EMI limo ferried the group back to Harlesden where The Clash and The Damned were still feverishly running through their respective sets completely oblivious to the fact that the Sex Pistols' latest TV appearance had rendered their efforts redundant.

"We got into the car afterwards and shot off back to the rehearsal," Paul Cook said in *The Filth & the Fury*. "To be honest, I didn't think anything of it. We went out that night and got drunk like we usually did. We were going on our first tour the next day [sic] with this big American group, The Heartbreakers, plus The Clash and The Damned. We thought the Grundy thing wasn't that bad – a bit of swearing, but so what? Of course, we didn't know it was going out live."

The Heartbreakers were expected at the cinema at some point, and everyone – with the possible exception of John, who'd decried the New York Dolls in the lyrics to 'New York' – was desperate to meet Johnny and Jerry. "We had all been impressed by The Heartbreakers," Glen Matlock remembered. "They seemed confident and arrogant, but this was where we first discovered that their song 'Chinese Rocks' was about heroin – something I certainly wasn't keen on."

The Damned's bassist Captain Sensible also had cause to remember the Americans' arrival: "Our guitarist Brian James idolised Johnny Thunders of The Heartbreakers who he thought was a kindred spirit on the intoxicants front," he recalled for *Mojo*'s 20th anniversary Anarchy Tour retrospective in December 1996. "When The Heartbreakers rehearsed, Brian was up at the front the whole time. In between songs you could hear him yelling, 'Go, Johnny, go.' We were deeply embarrassed."

In his defence, James can't be held accountable for his actions owing to his idol having given him his first Quaalude tablet – after which everything "slowed down a bit". Things didn't merely slow down but went a little hazy, which explains why he believes the Roxy Theatre was "an old cinema in King's Cross" and that The Heartbreakers were on stage running through the set when the Sex Pistols burst in "laughing their heads off like a bunch of kids saying, 'You wouldn't fucking believe what just happened...'"

Walter Lure and Johnny Thunders

While the guys in The Clash and The Damned were made aware of what had occurred at the TV studios, according to The Heartbreakers' guitarist Walter Lure no one had thought the events of earlier worthy of mention. "We arrived at night and were picked up in a limo," Lure subsequently recalled. "We were taken to some hotel in Bayswater, and then went for burgers at the Great American Disaster or something. I thought that was funny. In the morning Jerry Nolan bought all the newspapers, and the Sex Pistols were on every god-damned front page. There was uproar. Jerry threw the papers on the bed screaming, 'Look at this shit, man. I knew it was a bad idea. I fucking knew it. It's all fucking Leee's fault.'"

Prominent among them was the *Daily Mirror* which pontificated: "Bleeps and the blame: The faceless bosses of Thames Television must share the shame of red-faced Bill Grundy. They deserve the rap because they knew well in advance that the Sex Pistols were likely to throw up a stream of verbal graffiti.

"That's punk rock style.

"London Weekend Television, who pre-recorded an interview with the group, had already bleeped out four-letter words.

"Yet Thames chose to let Bill Grundy do the chat with those four-letter words-men LIVE.

"Such programmes, as the Independent Broadcasting Authority should insist, belong, at best, to late-night viewing. With bleepers.

"Not tea-time with the children and Nan around."

Though Malcolm would subsequently adopt his "Svengali" mantle and claim to have orchestrated the *Today* situation in order to generate interest in the impending tour, there are ample first-hand accounts of his behaviour in the immediate aftermath to suggest otherwise.

"I didn't see Malcolm as a manipulating Svengali," John said of his erstwhile manager. "My favourite incident came after we'd all been on the Grundy show. In the heat of the moment, as the whole thing had begun to snowball, Malcolm was convinced the incident marked the end of the group. He thought we'd blown it. Instead the group landed on the front pages of the papers."

And Glen pretty much concurred with John's sentiments in *I Was A Teenage Sex Pistol*: "When we left the studio, Malcolm was shitting himself. Then the next day, once he'd seen the press coverage, it was all his big idea."

Having woken up to the possibilities the ensuing scandal made available to him, however, Malcolm was probably wishing Steve's tête-à-tête with Grundy had come before he'd invited The Damned onto the Anarchy Tour because thanks to Grundy's group-baiting, putting bums on seats was no longer going to be an issue. "I knew the Bill Grundy show [sic] was going to create a huge scandal. I genuinely believed it would be history in the making and in many ways it was," Malcolm reflected in *Please Kill Me*. "Because that night was the real beginning – from the media's and the general public's point of view – of what became known as 'punk rock'."

Perhaps not surprisingly, there were mixed reactions over the Sex Pistols' latest television appearance at Manchester Square. Those EMI staffers who were involved with marketing, and who lived by the time-honoured maxim that all publicity is good publicity, were rubbing their hands in festive glee over the number of records they were going to shift on the back of Grundy's ineptitude. One who saw things rather differently, however, was EMI Records Group Repertoire Division's General Manager, Paul Watts, whose lofty position in the chain of command gave him a greater insight into the big picture. EMI Records was merely a cog – albeit a very important and highly profitable cog – within a huge conglomerate machine – and a few thousand extra pre-Christmas record sales paled into insignificance against safeguarding the company's reputation.

EMI, or the Electric & Musical Industries to give the corporate giant its proper title, was formed in March 1931 following the merger of Britain's oldest record company, the Gramophone Company, made famous by its His Masters Voice label – founded in 1897 – and the Columbia Gramophone Company. It was also in 1931 that the newly incorporated company opened its legendary recording studios at Abbey Road in north-west London. Over the ensuing decade EMI built up a roster of artists including legendary composers Arturo Toscanini, Otto Klemperer, and Sir Edward Elgar. The label released its first LPs in 1952, while its first stereophonic recordings came three years later. In 1960 the company moved to 20 Manchester Square W1 (where it would remain for the next 35 years), and under the stewardship of its then chairman Sir Joseph Lockwood – and its acquisition of Cliff Richard and The Beatles – went on to become the best-known and most successful recording company in the world. In 1971 Electric & Musical Industries changed its name to EMI Ltd with the subsidiary Gramophone Company becoming EMI Records Ltd two years later.

Aside from its music interests, EMI was also involved in broadcasting equipment, notably providing the BBC with its first television transmitter, as well as investing in leisure industries such as restaurants, cinemas and hotels, not to

mention its heavy investment in the radical CAT[1*] brain scanner which would enable doctors to examine the inner workings of the human brain without resorting to surgery. The company could also count on 40 years of success with larger-scale electronics such as radar equipment and guided missiles, which were developed at EMI's laboratories in Hayes, Middlesex both during and after World War II.

"[Sir] John Read was concerned that the adverse publicity in America would impact on our ability to sell the EMI-Scan, this wonderful machine which let you x-ray inside peoples' heads instead of cutting them open," said Leslie Hill in *The Wicked Ways Of Malcolm McLaren*. "We had the American market sewn up and he was concerned because there were reports of the Sex Pistols on the front page of the *Los Angeles Times*. And that was scary."

By 1976, the sixth floor of EMI's Manchester Square citadel was the hallowed reserve of its chairman, Sir John Read, and board of directors – which at the time included Joseph Lockwood, as well as former Attorney General and Britain's chief prosecutor at Nuremberg, Lord Shawcross, and the Conservative Shadow Chancellor of the Exchequer, Geoffrey Howe. Further down in the company's chain of command were executives who were acutely aware that music and missiles didn't make for comfortable bedfellows and that EMI may end up with its fingers burned as a result. "Back at Manchester Square, Paul Watts, Diane Wagg, Frank Brunger and Mark Rye were among those who had gathered in [Eric] Hall's office to watch the show," Brian Southall recalled in *Sex Pistols: 90 Days At EMI*. "As [a] marketing man, Rye rubbed his hands and thought of all the records he was going to sell on the back of this, while his sidekick Brunger took the view that the [Sex] Pistols could not have done them any bigger favour from a publicity point of view. Wagg – 18 years old and unaware of the implications for the corporate side of things – just saw the funny side of it all."

Steve Jones, Johnny Rotten, Glen Matlock, Paul Cook, Malcolm McLaren and Nils Stevenson

EMI's Business Affairs Manager, Laurie Hall (no relation to Eric), was another who chose to view the positives: "We [EMI] must have been to a lesser or greater extent instrumental in getting them [Sex Pistols] on TV, as we are with any group," he subsequently told *Sex Pistols: The Inside Story*. "And any publicity of this sort is good."

This view was shared by many in the industry, regardless of whether they were sympathetic to the Sex Pistols' brand of rock'n'roll. Supersonic director Mike Mansfield, who made a promo film of the group, told *NME*: "The Sex Pistols are trying to do what the Stones did, but the Stones did it better. I'd never blow their cover. I know it's a calculated thing they're doing, and it's going to make them very successful. They've achieved a lot in one day."

While mobile phones were the realm of science-fiction fantasy in the mid-seventies, well-heeled suits within any blue-chip company always had their pagers to hand so as to be available during out-of-office hours, and those occupying senior positions at EMI were no different. So whilst Thames TV began issuing its regular on-air apology expressing regret over the foul language used during the interview – as it would do for the remainder of the evening – several black-tie dinner parties were interrupted when the four-letter fly landed in the corporate soup.

Eric Hall, still with Marc Bolan at the BBC and oblivious as to the chain reaction he'd inadvertently set in motion, was intrigued on being paged to take a call from Leslie Hill. He'd naturally assumed Hill's call was in relation to the "Bopping Elf", as the diminutive Bolan was known at EMI, and was initially taken aback when Hill – without bothering with the pleasantries – asked him if he'd had any calls regarding the Sex Pistols' appearance on *Today*. Hall instantly realised from Hill's tone that something had gone wrong, and he was savvy enough to know that whilst praise ascends, shit invariably descends.

"While an awful lot of people tuned in to the interview, several interested parties at EMI managed to miss it," Brian Southall recalled. "Whether we were on our way home, in the pub, or doing something really important I can't recall, but myself, (Leslie) Hill, (Bob) Mercer and (Nick) Mobbs were among those who missed the moment on TV. We very quickly found out about it."

Having been given "chapter and verse" on the evening's unsavoury events by his superior, Hall – realising he might be held accountable, if only for cajoling Malcolm into accepting the *Today* slot – called Dryden Chambers, hoping to speak to Malcolm. "I got a call in the office. [It was] Eric Hall, sounding seriously worried because he was obviously aware of the grossness of it in terms of TV convention," Sophie Richmond said in *England's Dreaming*. "That was immediately after the broadcast, and then I had to go to Heathrow to pick up The Heartbreakers. We saw it on ITN while we were waiting for them. Malcolm may have been going, 'Oh shit', but everybody else was exhilarated by getting all that attention. It was a kind of takeover."

Meanwhile the news was filtering out across England's green and pleasant land. "City Date For Rock Group In TV Row," reported the *Liverpool Echo* in its December 3 edition. "Sex Pistols, the Punk Rock group whose four-letter performance on television caused uproar with viewers and television authorities, will appear at the Liverpool Stadium a week tomorrow. The performance is part of their Anarchy In The UK tour.

"But group leader Johnny Rotten claimed: 'There will be no trouble.'

"Speaking from London, he said: 'This talk of violence is exaggerated. When we get on stage we just give it all we have got. Sometimes things happen which we are not really responsible for. But I can tell you there should be no trouble at the Stadium.'

"Thames Television has now suspended Bill Grundy, who presented the *Today* show which featured the group."

CHAPTER FIVE

The Filth & The Fury

"Oh, I think he [Grundy] was very clever. I don't think he was an old cunt really. It was kind of good. Who'd heard of Bill Grundy before that? He didn't mind. No matter what was said in the papers afterwards."

Glen Matlock

Burying bad news has become an accepted political strategy in recent times and in many ways the Sex Pistols became a victim of this. Britain in 1976 was in a state of financial crisis, successive governments having screwed up the economy while workers were put on a three-day week and the prime minister was obliged to go cap in hand to the International Monetary Fund to borrow a couple of billion to keep the country afloat. This didn't make for happy reading in the newspapers of the day so everyone, from the politicians to the editors to the reader themselves, needed some light relief. The word "fuck" came to the rescue.

While there's no doubting that the Britain of today (no pun intended) is a far more permissive society than it was when the Sex Pistols offended the Middle England masses, it's worth remembering that the verb "to fuck" had – at the time of the group's appearance on *Today* – been in existence for half a millennium or more. Even Shakespeare used the term on occasion, albeit in veiled euphemism, in *Henry V* scene four, when Pistol threatens to "firk" a soldier.

D.H. Lawrence's titillating novel, *Lady Chatterley's Lover* (first published in 1928), had scandalised Georgian society with its language, and couldn't be published openly in the UK until 1960, yet it succeeded in escaping punishment under the 1958 Obscene Publications Act. On November 13, 1965, the theatre critic Kenneth Tynan became the first person to say "fuck" on television during a debate about censorship, and since then scores of other books, plays, and films have featured similar dialogue. Indeed, Steve's outbursts were positively tame compared with comic duo Peter Cook and Dudley Moore's *Derek & Clive Live* album released on Island Records earlier in the year.

So while some will argue that going to see a risqué play or an X-rated film is a far cry from having foul language brought unsolicited into one's living room when children might be watching, it's worth remembering that – even in 1976 – the vast majority of children were familiar with every swear word in the lexicon by the time they went to secondary school. Indeed, if a similar occurrence were to happen today, it's fair to question whether the TV station responsible for airing the show would even bother with an on-air apology.

Yes, Bill Grundy was fully deserving of his two-week suspension – if only for his slipshod attitude towards the company which paid his not inconsiderable wages – while Steve perhaps – at the very worst – should have had his knuckles rapped for over-indulging in the Thames hospitality room. After all, there were plenty of studio personnel on hand to oversee what was occurring in there prior to the group going on air, and a simple reading of the transcript is enough for even the most jaundiced eye to see Grundy's culpability in trying to belittle the Sex Pistols when their friends, fans, and family would undoubtedly be watching. So for those in authority to instigate a witch-hunt against the group, which in effect denied them the basic democratic right to earn a living, was the true outrage in the whole sorry saga.

There's no way of guessing what the public's perception of the Sex Pistols' laddish behaviour on *Today*, or its view on the "punk rock cult" as a whole, would have been had the UK been enjoying a booming economy with jobs for all, but with the country in the grip one of its customary recessions, the powerbrokers on Fleet Street – who, having affiliations to either Labour or the Conservatives, and having therefore played an active part in running the country into the ground – were naturally on the lookout for anything which might deflect the public's gaze away from their respective failings. Similarly, the public, who were fed up with reading and hearing about the country's economic plight – especially in the run-up to Christmas – were happy to put Freud's theory of displacement into practice by projecting its collective frustrations onto a hitherto unknown scapegoat. This, of course, also raises the point as to whether punk rock could have flourished in Britain in a time of prosperity. After all, it had taken New York's near bankruptcy for The Ramones, Television and the other CBGBs bands to flourish, and while the Pistols never actually penned a song about being unemployed, the "unemployed youth" became – at least in the media's eye – the movement's stereotypical totem.

In *The Filth & The Fury*, John Lydon opines that the Sex Pistols happened when they did simply because the mid-seventies was the closest the UK had come in 200 years, since the Gordon Riots of 1780 – which are re-enacted in the opening scenes of *The Great Rock 'N' Roll Swindle* – to facing the very real prospect of anarchy on its streets. The decade, which had promised so much, had failed to deliver at almost every turn, and while morality-mongerers up and down the land clambered up onto their soapboxes to decry this latest example of a once-proud nation's sorry decline, as far as Fleet Street was concerned Christmas had come early that year.

Nils Stevenson

Instead of having to conjure up new angles with which to either defend or deride the government's on-going failings, the editors from both the tabloids and the supposedly more discerning broadsheets embarked on a feeding frenzy over the Sex Pistols and the shocking new music craze, punk rock. "Amazing response from the national press: the story's on every front page and news bulletin," Nils Stevenson later recalled. "We're no longer enigmatic freaks – we're suddenly despised 'punks'. People used to get out of my way, but they now barge me off the pavement."

Surprising though it might seem today, *The Sun* was perhaps the most charitable towards the Pistols in so much as its front page demanded to know 'Were The Pistols Loaded?', before going on to inform its readers of the two-week ban imposed by Thames TV's bosses on Grundy. Elsewhere the normally bellicose tabloid carried a brief interview with Vivienne Westwood, headlined: "These Hypocrites, By A Pop

Mum" which went on to report that "The hundreds of viewers who complained about the Sex Pistols' language were described yesterday as 'hypocrites' by Westwood, girlfriend of the group's manager. She said: 'I did not see the programme myself. But my children did, and they were not shocked by the swearing because I swear anyway.'

The Evening News also planted its flag in the group's corner with its equally challenging banner headline: "Grundy Goaded Punk Boys Says Record Chief". However, London's other premier evening newspaper, *The Evening Standard*, called it as it saw it and declared the group to be "Foul-Mouthed Yobs", while the *Daily Express* came in with "Punk? Call It Filthy Lucre". *The Daily Mail* threw its hat into the ring with "Four-Letter Punk Group In TV Storm", and the following day's edition featured a stinging editorial entitled "Never Mind Morals Or Standards, The Only Notes That Matter Come In Wads".

This was the first article to actually point the finger of blame at EMI's door by insinuating that the label – having a vested interest in the Sex Pistols – stood to benefit from the group's verbal spat with Grundy as it would benefit from every record the group sold.

But if there was a prize for headlines then it would surely have gone to the *Daily Mirror*[1]* for its catchy couplet: "The Filth And The Fury". And the paper cleverly – or criminally, depending on one's viewpoint – accompanied its front page outrage with a photograph taken of the group leaving EMI's Manchester Square offices having just signed to the label back in October. John, Steve, Glen and Paul – having celebrated the signing with beer and champagne – are grinning like loons, and just as the photographer had been about to snap the shutter John sprayed him with a purloined can of lager, causing the photo to be splattered with flecks of beer foam. The *Mirror*'s already outraged readers – having no idea of where or when the photograph was taken – would have naturally assumed it had been taken as the group were leaving the television studio, and that their obvious ebullience was therefore due to what had just occurred.

While other items made the news in the first week of December, including the assassination attempt on Bob Marley and his manager in Kingston, Jamaica, the scandal surrounding South Africa's decision to enter two candidates – one white and one black – in that year's Miss World pageant, and Patrick Hillery being elected as the new Irish President, the headlines were reserved for the Pistols. The *Mirror*'s coverage was typical: "A pop group shocked millions of viewers last night with the filthiest language heard on British television.

---

1   Ironically, elsewhere in that day's issue of the *Daily Mirror* was a feature on the Sex Pistols as part of its series on the 'Outrageous New Pop Kings'.

"The Sex Pistols, leaders of the new 'punk rock' cult, hurled a string of four-letter obscenities at interviewer Bill Grundy on Thames TV's family teatime programme *Today*.

"The Thames switchboard was flooded with protests. Nearly 200 angry viewers telephoned the *Mirror*. One man (47-year-old lorry driver, James Holmes of Waltham Abbey, Essex) was so furious that he kicked in the screen of his £380 colour TV."

The infuriated Mr Holes told the *Mirror*'s reporter: "It [the television set] blew up and I was knocked backwards. But I was so angry and disgusted with this filth that I took a swing at the TV set with my boot. I can swear as well as anyone, but I don't want this sort of muck coming into my home at teatime. I am not a violent person but I would like to have got hold of Grundy. He should be sacked for encouraging this sort of disgusting behaviour."

It beggars belief that Holmes – as John Lydon pointedly asked in *No Irish, No Blacks, No Dogs* – didn't simply reach for the off button to stop the muck coming into his home, but what is even more surprising is that the *Daily Mirror* chose to lay the blame for Holmes' knee-jerk reaction at the Sex Pistols' door rather than Grundy's for having encouraged their "disgusting behaviour". Even Thames TV's Controller of Programmes, Jeremy Isaacs, was willing to concede that Grundy had

"provoked" the Sex Pistols into using bad language. As the Pistols were an EMI act, Bob Mercer had called Isaacs expecting to have to do a lot of grovelling on the label's behalf, and had been taken by surprise when Isaacs interrupted him to say he'd suspended Grundy for his "inexcusably sloppy journalism".

Another telling indication as to where Thames believed the blame lay came with Mike Housego calling Eric Hall and saying that while the Sex Pistols would never again be allowed to darken Thames' portal, the station wouldn't be averse to playing one of the group's promo videos in the future.

Since people without a television wouldn't need to pay the licence fee on which the corporation depended, viewers trashing their TV sets didn't sit well within the corridors of power at the BBC. With the exception of John Peel – who'd regularly aired 'Anarchy In The UK' on his late-evening show – none of Radio One's other DJs had included the single on their play-lists prior to the *Today* scandal, so a decision to ban the single from daytime rotation was viewed by many – including Peel – as something of a futile exercise.

"I was frankly appalled, because if you took any four or five lads off the street... made them feel important, filled them with beer, put them on television and said, 'Say something outrageous', they'd say something outrageous," Peel said in *Sex Pistols: The Inside Story*. "I rather suspect that – as a middle-class individual of 38 – if they did the same to me, I'd do the same. So for those people then to wring their hands in horror and say, 'This is outrageous', is just bare-faced hypocrisy."

Taking their lead from the BBC, the handful of independent radio stations that hadn't taken offence to 'Anarchy In The UK' on its release followed suit by removing the single from their own play-lists. This supposed "unofficial" ban quickly extended to commercial radio stations such as London's Capital Radio,

Manchester's Piccadilly Radio, and Birmingham's BRMB. Sheffield's Radio Hallam had also recently decided to pull the single from its play-list, but only after conducting a poll among its listeners, while Radio Luxembourg's Tony Prince received a one-night suspension for having had the audacity to send out an on-air invitation to the Sex Pistols to perform live on his show.

It was perhaps unfortunate that the music press, the most likely media outlets to take the side of the Sex Pistols, had already gone to press by the time the group had their date with destiny. It wasn't until the following week that they could present their views as to who was actually at fault, though NME restricted themselves to a straightforward account of the facts: "Repercussions to their [Sex Pistols] TV appearance were widespread. BBC Radio stated they would not play the Pistols' single 'Anarchy In The UK', in its daytime programmes. Aidan Day, controller of London's Capital Radio, said his station would not play the record 'because I don't think it's very good'."

Sounds, on the other hand, laced its report with a bit more colour: "As you will no doubt have noticed Fleet Street went absolutely bananas over the Sex Pistols last Thursday. Ignition point for the biggest press ballyhoo over a rock group since the Stones relieved themselves against a garage wall almost a decade ago was the Sex Pistols' appearance on London Weekend's [sic] *Today* programme, a teatime magazine-format show dealing principally in local news and personalities.

"The furore began when the group delivered a series of four-letter words after being baited by interviewer Bill Grundy, man of 52 summers, six offspring and no little wit.

"Needless to say the TV station's switchboard was jammed with hysterical calls from the moment John Rotten uttered his first muted ruderie.

"Next morning's *Daily Mirror* carried a blow-by-blow account of the 'incident' on its front page, including a literal transcript of the offending dialogue which left only the central 'uck's in the most frequently used adjective missing, *MM*-style. An amusing irony here is that the same issue also carried a feature on the group on page 9, part of a series on the 'outrageous' new 'pop kings'.

"Meanwhile *The Sun* saved the story for its notorious page three, its account of the event and mixed reactions as to who was responsible lying alongside a deliciously exploitative titpic of a doctor's daughter."

The Letters section of the Saturday, December 11, 1976 issue of *Sounds* carried several letters from irate readers, one of which – supposedly from "Roxy Music Followers, Leeds" – sounds very much like the letter Sophie Richmond is seen typing up, and then reading aloud to Malcolm at Dryden Chambers in a scene from *The Great Rock 'N' Roll Swindle*:

Of course, another explanation is that with the scene being recreated for the film, Malcolm and Sophie had a copy of that particular issue of *Sounds* at their disposal, and had simply borrowed from the text. "So the Sex Pistols have now shown television reviewers just how punk rock bands look, dress and speak. I thought punk bands were supposed to be trying to identify with teenagers in order to do away with the Stones, Led Zeppelin etc…

"I'm a 16-year-old female, but if they think I'm going to be taken in by a bunch of bloody loonies, whose manager is just as bad, running a sex shop, they can flaming well piss off and think again.

"I thought we were trying to cut out violence at concerts, football matches and wherever – it's these sick bastards who encourage it – you just have to look at a punk group's audience, I doubt if they've got one O-level between them.

"Punk is supposed to be 'in' is it? Well, if punk is tatty clothes pinned together with last week's porridge, music that makes Doctor Magnus Pyke sound an interesting bloke to listen to, and interviews on television that consist of four-letter words fouling up meaningless sentences, then you can flaming well count me OUT."

On the God Save The Sex Pistols website, Mike Thorne describes a seismic shift in support on the shop floor within EMI towards the Pistols as the "august institution hadn't had so much fun in years", and that the corporation's more reserved employees found it exciting to be involved with "something which was clearly noteworthy and making big waves".

The Sex Pistols' antics were making waves within the music industry as a whole as Thorne's EMI colleague Brian Southall reported in *Sex Pistols: 90 Days At EMI*: "The calls were coming in thick and fast, and just about everybody we knew in the [music] industry called up to say the whole thing had been fantastic and [that] it was one of the great publicity stunts of the decade."

With reporters and photographers from every leading national newspaper having set up camp in and around Manchester Square, and having got wind of Isaacs' actions they were naturally keen to know if EMI and the Sex Pistols were willing to express similar contrition. Since there was little likelihood that EMI's chairman Sir John Read was going to demean himself by discussing the Sex Pistols with reporters, it was left to Leslie Hill – who'd long been advocating that EMI Records should operate as a separate entity – to hold a press conference to clarify the label's position. Due to the relatively small amount of cash involved he hadn't actually been involved in the group's signing to the label, but he decided the best course of action was to call Malcolm and have him bring the group down to Manchester Square so that they could field the majority of the questions.

"He [McLaren] came up to the office, and I remember that he was cagey, strange, he didn't react," Hill recalled in *The Wicked Ways Of Malcolm McLaren*. "He didn't look anything special to create such a sensation, but then people never do. He spoke quietly and slowly, and listened to what I said. I couldn't pin him down on anything. I couldn't get him into line because obviously he didn't want to anyway."

While Malcolm's blasé "boys will be boys" attitude was perhaps only to be expected, it wasn't appreciated by those within EMI who were fielding the flak on the Sex Pistols' behalf, and trying to keep the group on the label. "I got off the bus at Marble Arch and walked round to Manchester Square. The other three guys were already there, hanging out of an upstairs window," Glen recalled. "It was a big press conference. Whether it was Malcolm's idea or EMI twisted his arm I just don't know. But in one way it was certainly an eye-opener for me. For the first time I got first-hand experience of the British gutter press.

"One particular photographer said he wanted to take a group picture of us all together and handed us a couple of cans of beer each. We were all sitting in a line, 'Can you sit a bit closer?' the photographer asked. Steve said, 'I'm not getting any closer to him – meaning John – he's got smelly armpits. I was drinking my beer. I burped and, like any well brought up lad said, sorry, pardon me. The next day in the papers this appeared as: 'They wouldn't move in closer together on account of Johnny Rotten's stinking armpits and, when the bass player was asked a question, he just burped.'"

Paul, too, has vivid memories of his first encounter with the press: "Nothing was different until the next day, when it was all on the front pages," he told *Punk*. "We were still in bed at 1pm, so we missed all the early papers banging on the door. The *Evening Standard* was there, though, shouting, 'Wake up, where are you?' We ran down to our offices [Dryden Chambers] and they were all running after us. People recognised us and were pointing at us in the street. All hell broke loose. Malcolm did his best to control the situation. After that we had security guards and bouncers because the press wanted to get any story that was going."

Open season had been unleashed, with the Pistols as Public Enemy Number One. *The Mirror,* having set the pace with its 'filth and fury' story, continued to pile on the pressure, reporting on December 3: "The punk rock 'nasties' who shocked millions of viewers with their filthy language came out with a fresh barrage of belches and obscenities last night.

"The four 19-year-old members of the Sex Pistols were unmoved by the criticism of their performance on Thames TV's teatime programme, *Today*. They blamed it all on interviewer Bill Grundy. 'He was falling about all over the place,' said leather-clad Steve Jones.

"And the group's manager, 29-year-old Malcolm McLaren, claimed they had been 'goaded' by the interviewer. 'They were set up for all this by Grundy,' said Mr. McLaren. 'They were goaded into saying lots of things that perhaps they did not intend to say. But there are no regrets. These lads were expressing the mood of most kids these days. They want a change of scene.'"

Earlier that morning, Leslie Hill had received a call from Roy Matthews, the manager of the label's Hayes pressing plant, who informed him that the [predominantly female] workforce had gone out on strike and were refusing to handle the Sex Pistols' single. As soon as the press conference was out of the way Hill intended to drive down to the plant to see what might be done to pacify the workers and get them back to work. It was seemingly OK for the women – local housewives, earning some extra pin-money – to work for a corporation that was making millions of pounds from its enormously profitable weapons systems and electronics arms that were killing people by the thousands, but to be involved with a group that dared to swear on television was evidently beyond the pale.

Whereas Brian Southall had only to deal with the music press who published on a weekly basis, and could therefore wait for stories and quotes, EMI's head of PR, Bryan Samain, had the infinitely more voracious dailies to contend with. Indeed, the tabloids had started calling the moment *Today* went off the air, and as watching one of EMI Records' newly signed acquisitions giving a TV interview didn't come under his normal remit, Samain had no idea what the reporters were asking about. Rather than allow himself to become embroiled in anything until he knew all the facts, he simply issued a stock statement along the lines of anything that didn't enhance the behaviour or conduct of the company would be considered disgraceful, and that the relevant parties would be looking into the matter further.

Of course, with the press' clamour for copy escalating out of control, Southall was informed from on high that his office was no longer to deal with any press matters regarding the Sex Pistols.

"I had some personal reservations but as MD of a record company, I felt here we were again with something big," Leslie Hill said in *Mojo*'s 20th anniversary Anarchy Tour retrospective in December 1996.

"It was like another Beatles – 50,000 singles sold in just a few weeks – and we'd been talking for years about finding a new Beatles. It wasn't just the Sex Pistols that were the problem. It was the damage I knew would be done to us in the recording industry at large because, if we let them go, people on the outside would see us again as a fuddy-duddy record company."

Never having heard of the Sex Pistols until that day, EMI chairman Sir John Read also suddenly found himself under fire – this time from the financial press. Though Read was content to allow Hill sufficient rein to deal with the group, he had EMI's 80,000 employees and its shareholders to consider, and there was no way he was going to allow a shoddy rock 'n' roll group to impact unfavourably on EMI's share price. Then there was the matter of Jamie Reid's defacing of the national flag for the Pistols' new single. The poppy-red wreaths commemorating the countless thousands who'd laid down their lives for king and country during both world wars were still on display at the Whitehall Cenotaph, and here was a pop group making a mockery of their sacrifice. While those within EMI whose job it was to promote the single had skilfully avoided a summons to the boardroom to explain that the poster idea had had nothing to do with them, at least one version of Reid's poster did feature the EMI circular logo and the record's catalogue number.

"The pressure was all coming from EMI's corporate side," Bob Mercer recalled. "The feeling was that the last thing we needed in December was a dispute at the factory, because that's when the Christmas singles are being pressed and LP sales are at their highest."

Like Read, EMI Publishing's head Terry Slater – who'd been the first within EMI to recognise the Sex Pistols' worth by offering them a publishing deal – also had the company's disgruntled shareholders to contend with and, in an attempt to diffuse the situation, suggested changing the copyright line on 'Anarchy In The UK' from EMI Music Publishing to Sex Pistols Music Publishing. Read, and EMI's board, however, viewed this as closing the stable door after the horse had bolted, and rejected his idea out

of hand. While Hill was wending his way to Hayes to quell the mutiny, Slater accompanied the group to the Cambridge pub, which, being a short stroll from their Denmark Street HQ, was their preferred West End watering hole.

"For years the record companies have been repackaging this, repackaging that, breaking the odd group here and there, but really when it was something new, when it was there, very few record companies – and I really mean this, and I'd been in the business 20 years – very few record companies would recognise it," he bemoaned in *Sex Pistols: The Inside Story*. "It was there. Once the whole thing got going then, oh, everyone got it. But I feel quite good that I was the one who did recognise it, proved it, by singing the Pistols."

Meanwhile, Bill Grundy had been suspended by Thames TV and reprimanded by Jeremy Isaacs for "inexcusably sloppy journalism", as *NME* reported. "The station has issued a statement of apology: 'Because the programme was live we could not foresee the language that would be used.'" *NME*'s report added that Nigel Watts, a researcher at London Weekend Television, claimed he had warned the *Today* team to expect such behaviour from The Pistols. "Only days earlier, Mr. Watts had worked on a Punk documentary presented on LWTV's *London Weekend Show*, where it was necessary to use a bleeper to cover certain words in conversations. He criticised Thames for not doing the same."

CHAPTER SIX

Who Are These Punks?

> "They wear torn and ragged clothes held together with safety pins. They are boorish, ill-mannered, foul-mouthed, dirty, obnoxious and arrogant. They like to be disliked. They use names like Johnny Rotten, Steve Havoc, Sid Vicious, Rat Scabies and Dee Generate. They are the teenage punks of the Punk rock bands nervously hailed in some quarters as perhaps the most exciting development in rock music for a decade."
>
> The Sun, Friday, December 3, 1976

There was a biting wind blowing up Denmark Street on the morning of Friday, December 3, 1976 – and the atmosphere in the Sex Pistols' rehearsal space wasn't much more accommodating. The so-called "punk solidarity" that had taken root earlier in the summer at the 100 Club had to all intents and purposes withered and died on the bough. Of course, competitive rivalry between bands of a similar ilk was nothing new in the annals of rock 'n' roll with The Beatles and The Rolling Stones being the obvious example. But whereas Mick and Keith had been happy to rub shoulders with John and Paul, as well as borrow the occasional song, aside from the odd personal friendship there wasn't much love in the house as far as the groups spearheading the latest musical craze were concerned.

"I think the press fuelled those rivalries among the bands," Paul Cook reflected in *Rotten: No Irish, No Blacks, No Dogs*. "The press were jealous of the Pistols too. 'Wow! Here's The Clash. They're much better than the Sex Pistols, blah, blah.' They took to The Clash a lot easier than they did to us because The Clash were more accessible. A group like The Damned was just jumping on the bandwagon. The other punk bands would play three-minutes of thrash with no break in it at all. You could say that about The Clash as well."

The Sex Pistols have never made any secret that they viewed The Clash and The Damned – as well as the vast majority of the bands that were gliding in their tailwind – as mere "bandwagon-jumpers", but whereas Steve, Paul, and Glen were always happy to show support by going along to watch the other punk bands performing, John purposely kept the usurpers to his crown at arm's length. His antipathy

was particularly aimed at The Clash's frontman, Joe Strummer, who up until undergoing a Damascene conversion after seeing the Sex Pistols, had been fronting pub-rockers The 101'ers.

It mattered not that Joe had seen the light and stepped into the future, as far as John was concerned he was never going to be allowed to forget his past. Of course, now that Fleet Street had proclaimed him "Prince of the Punks", one word from King John could make or break any up-and-coming group. Steve might well have been the one to call Grundy's bluff and say "something outrageous", but "Steve Jones" was the bloke down the dog track, whereas "Johnny Rotten" was excellent copy. In the 36 hours following their appearance on *Today*, John's ego had swollen to huge levels of inflated self-importance while his relationship with Glen – never harmonious at the best of times – was noticeably worsening.

"I could never bear Glen's simplistic attitude about everything. He just wanted to be nice and not offend anyone," John said in *Rotten: No Irish, No Blacks, No Dogs*. "That's not the way around solving problems. If you're going to play that kind of game, you're never going to get anywhere. Nothing is concluded, and you look wishy-washy. [He] would say things like, 'The lyrics to 'God Save The Queen' have to be changed,' because his mum didn't like it! When someone talks to me like that, I just don't listen any longer."

Glen's introspective recollections about his and John's seemingly never-ending spat had been in circulation for four years by the time John's autobiography hit the bookshelves. "Although I like being in control as much as anybody else, I didn't in fact want to rule the roost in the group," said the bass player. "But what I did object to was the total shift in the balance of power. This change in the group from a democracy to John in charge all the time started as soon as we got press."

Though Glen tended to bear the brunt of John's antagonism, once the Sex Pistols started to get some press no one – with the possible exception of Nils – was totally exempt from his acerbic salvos. Indeed, when the Anarchy Tour bus rolled up at the Derby Crest Hotel none of those on board – again, with the possible exception of Nils – seemed overly keen to share a room with John as Clash bassist Paul Simonon subsequently explained. "The first night we arrived at [the] hotel we all had to pair up in double rooms, and someone said, 'Right, who's sharing with John?' and there was silence," he recalled. "I almost said,

'I will,' cos I liked John. But Mick had teamed with Glen Matlock, so I thought I'd better share with Joe to keep a sense of unity."

The antipathy towards the Sex Pistols' frontman wasn't solely reserved for the English musicians on the tour as Johnny Thunders and Jerry Nolan's drug buddy Eliot Kidd – who'd excitedly boarded the next available flight to London on hearing from Thunders that the Sex Pistols were "awesome" – revealed in *Please Kill Me*: "When I first got to England, I went right to where the Heartbreakers were staying. I'm asking them what the Pistols are like, and since I was a lead singer (with New York glam-power-pop outfit The Demons, from whom Walter Lure had recently been 'lured'), I asked Walter, 'What's Johnny Rotten like?' He [Walter] said, 'He's an asshole.' And he [Rotten] was an asshole, a total asshole, a jerk-off. It wasn't like I just didn't like him; no one liked him. And it wasn't like he was sitting by himself on the tour bus. He was an in-your-face type of guy."

Malcolm has always opined that Glen was simply "too nice to be a Sex Pistol", or as Bernard Rhodes eloquently put it: he was "always eager to please, like a woman wanting to be fucked". With that in mind, it's fair to say that had Glen been just another run-of-the-mill bass player he'd have quickly followed Wally Nightingale out of the rehearsal door – but Glen was far from an ordinary bassist. For all his supposed non-punk foibles such as forever washing his feet, being a dutiful son, and – dare we say – his liking of The Beatles, his musical dexterity was the glue that held the Sex Pistols together, and the understanding that he and Paul developed and nurtured had made them one of the tightest rhythm sections around. There wasn't a group in the land that wouldn't have taken Glen in a heartbeat, but such considerations meant little to John. And so while Steve and Paul were rooming together on the tour, Glen would be rooming with Mick Jones from The Clash.

The comings and goings between the personnel of London's early punk bands was an incestuous roller-coaster of revolving doors that exposes just how small the scene really was and at the same time created rivalries and friendships which impacted on the careers of all those involved, beginning with the Anarchy Tour itself. Though it was external factors that would have the most detrimental impact on the tour, internal factors – the relationships between all those involved – also played a part in scuttling the ship, and it's necessary to look at these relationships, and how all involved came to join the groups they did, to understand the dynamics of the tour.

Mick Jones

Indeed, legend has it that Malcolm and Bernard had contemplated swapping bassists in their respective bands about this time – a supposition subsequently denied by everyone concerned. At first glance, it seems a logical proposition as Glen and Mick shared a love of music while Paul Simonon had all the laddish qualities that made Steve and Paul Cook so endearing. Yet while Glen – whose melodic playing would undoubtedly have augmented The Clash's style – was certainly beginning to ponder a future away from the Pistols, his Clash counterpart had no intention of defecting. Simonon wasn't the only member of The Clash to have been considered a potential Sex Pistol, as 12 months earlier Mick had been only a phone call away from joining the group.

Shortly after the Pistols moved into Denmark Street Paul Cook evidently decided Steve wasn't quite cutting it as a guitarist and announced he was leaving the group. Glen believes Paul was simply stalling for time while he sat his City & Guilds electricians' exam, wanting to get the qualification under his belt in case the Sex Pistols fell at the first hurdle, but in hindsight Glen's claim holds water as he thought he was improving with each rehearsal. In order to placate Paul – and possibly as a delaying tactic of his own – Malcolm agreed to bring in a second guitarist to supplement Steve.

Though they tried out future Rich Kids guitarist Steve New, who at 15 was considered a tad too young, their search came to nought. Having by this time passed his exam to become a qualified electrician, Paul dutifully remained at his post. Nevertheless, Malcolm placed a second ad in the 'Musicians Wanted' section of the *Melody Maker* classifieds, requesting the services of a "Whizz kid guitarist not older than 20 not worse looking than Johnny Thunders" and it caught Mick Jones' disbelieving eye, not least because he'd placed an almost identical ad in the *Melody Maker* classifieds back in July looking for a lead guitarist and drummer with a "great rock 'n' roll image" and influenced by the "Stones, NY Dolls, Mott [The Hoople] etc".

Until they saw Malcolm's ad, Mick and his bass-playing buddy Tony James (a Brunel University maths graduate), had naively believed they were the only musicians in London that were hip to the New York Dolls. The duo had spent the best part of 1975 trying to put their own Dolls-esque group together and were fruitlessly auditioning vocalists and drummers – which ironically included future Clash drummers Terry Chimes and Nicky "Topper" Headon, as well as soon-to-be Damned stalwarts Brian James (Brian Robertson), and Rat Scabies (Chris Miller) – in their dingy basement rehearsal space beneath the Paddington Kitchen Café at 113-115 Praed Street.

Several weeks earlier on Saturday, August 2, Mick and Tony had gone along to the Nashville Rooms in West Kensington to check out an up-and-coming group from Liverpool called Deaf School. Whilst there, Tony had spotted a diminutive, mole-like figure – none other than Bernard Rhodes – who just happened to be wearing the same You're Gonna Wake Up One Morning T-shirt as himself.

"We were thinking we're the only two people in the world who believe there's something else happening out there," Tony James recalled in Pat Gilbert's Clash book *Passion Is A Fashion*. "Then this little guy comes up to us, in a black cap, wearing the same T-shirt. We said, 'Could you stand over there a bit? You're wearing the same T-shirt as us.' He said, 'Fuck off! I fucking designed this T-shirt, you cunts! What have you got going for you?'"

The sartorial stand was soon forgotten as Mick and Tony told Bernard about their ambition to form a radical new group from a stable of like-minded musicians which included ex-Hollywood Brats frontman, Andrew Matheson, Stein Groven (aka Casino Steel) and Casino's fellow Norwegian, Geir Waade, with whom Mick had played in a group called Little Queenie. Despite their decidedly un-punk image – long hair, floral blouses and flares – Bernard was suitably impressed with what Mick and Tony had going for them and offered to manage their embryonic outfit, which they'd tentatively named London SS.

Bernard then told Mick and Tony about his one-time involvement with the Sex Pistols, and it was shortly after Malcolm's second ad appeared in *Melody Maker* that Mick, Tony, Casino and Matheson accompanied Bernard over to Denmark Street to meet – as well as check out – the competition. While this so-called "meeting of minds" didn't lead to anything – primarily because of the seismic difference in the two groups' attire – Mick stayed behind to jam with Steve, Paul and Glen (John was absent owing to Arsenal playing a League Cup tie).

Having succeeded in persuading Malcolm that Mick would be perfect for the Sex Pistols, Glen borrowed his dad's car and he and Malcolm drove round to Matheson's and Casino's flat on London Street to find out where Mick lived and offer him the gig. Fate, however, had another musical course set aside for Mick, and thanks to Casino's obstinacy Glen and Malcolm returned to Denmark Street empty-handed. "I remember a bunch of guys with hair down to their arse. They looked ridiculous," Glen said of his initial encounter with Mick Jones in *Passion Is A Fashion*. "We were all laughing. One of them [Mick], instead of going upstairs, picked up a guitar and started jamming with us, and it would have worked except for the hair. Later we tried to contact him, without Bernard knowing, but at the address we had there was just this Norwegian bloke (Casino) who would only speak to us through the letterbox."

Perhaps not surprisingly, Bernard spent the latter part of 1975 putting his not inconsiderable energies into establishing London SS as viable rivals to the Sex Pistols and, as a result, over the coming months every aspiring musician in London made the trek to Praed Street. Only James, Scabies, Chimes and Headon had the vision Bernard was looking for and the failure to secure a working line-up eventually saw Tony lose faith. Though he and Mick would remain close over the ensuing years – and ultimately work together again with Carbon/Silicon – shortly into the New Year he left to join Gene October's proto-punk outfit Chelsea, soon decamping with Chelsea's equally disillusioned guitarist Billy Idol to form Generation X.

Another reason for Tony's departure from London SS ranks might have been Bernard's belligerent management style: rather than allow Tony and Mick to develop at their own pace, he'd first belittled their lack of understanding of modern art, then compiled a list of books he felt they ought to read to further their education. It didn't end there: shortly before Christmas 1975 he'd called Tony at his parents' home in Twickenham and let him have both barrels of a not-so-festive missive: "The trouble with you, James, is that you're too fucking safe," he'd ranted. "What I want you to do is tell your parents that you're not gonna spend Christmas with them, you're gonna spend it with hookers in Praed Street. And buy a copy of *Gay News* and *Spare Rib* from your local corner shop!"

Although Tony couldn't have guessed it at the time, he'd already encountered his replacement on bass guitar as 20-year-old Paul Simonon – a budding artist who was enrolled at the prestigious Byam Shaw School of Art – had accompanied a friend to Praed Street who was hoping to stake a claim for the London SS drum stool. His subsequent audition – in which he stumbled his way through The Standells' 1967 classic 'Barracuda', as well as Jonathan Richman's yet-to-be-officially released 'Roadrunner' (which the Sex Pistols also happened to be covering), soon exposed his vocal limitations, but he and Mick had kept in casual contact over the coming months.

"The first time I met Mick Jones was in the [Praed Street] basement with the London SS," Paul recalled in *Passion Is A Fashion*. "All I could see was hair. I don't think I even saw his face. He said, 'Sing "Roadrunner"'. I said, 'What's that?' It was a bit of a disaster. There was this bloke in the corner [Bernard], and I said, 'Are you the manager?' And his immediate retort was, 'What's it to you?' And I thought, 'Well, that's fair enough...'"

It was at Bernard's behest that Mick suggested to Paul that he should learn the bass as his looks and attitude would be wasted hidden away behind a drum kit. This proposal came sometime in March 1976, but it wasn't until accompanying Mick, Bernard and Keith Levene (who would quit The Clash in September) to the Nashville Rooms on Friday, April 23, to see The Sex Pistols supporting The 101'ers that Paul set aside his brushes in favour of the bass. This was also the night that the soon-to-be Clash found their frontman. "I told Joe to forget The 101'ers. I told him that he could be great," said Bernard. "The Clash were a great group, but they could have been a truly great group if Joe had been willing to go the whole way. I don't know why he wasn't willing to go the whole way, but he just wasn't."

When the Sex Pistols took to the Nashville stage that night, the rest of The 101'ers – just as they had when the two groups had played together there three weeks earlier – didn't think much about what

was on offer. They looked on aghast when a fight broke out at the front of the stage between some of their fans and the Pistols' following, and John, Steve, and Glen suddenly downed tools and jumped into the mêlée. Joe Strummer, however, had sensed his group was about to get swept away by the fast approaching wind of change.

Joe's first musical venture came with his purchasing a second-hand ukulele so that he could earn a few coppers busking on the London Underground, but it was while studying at the Newport College of Art in south Wales where he began nurturing his self-taught "six strings or none" rhythm guitar style with collegiate rockers The Vultures. On returning to London he'd then put The 101'ers together from among his fellow squatters at 101 Wallerton Road W9 (hence their name), and while The 101'ers had predominantly started out as nothing more than in-house entertainment, so to speak, they quickly gelled into a tight rock 'n' roll combo.

As The 101'ers had recently recorded their debut single, 'Keys To Your Heart', on the independent Chiswick Records[1*], several major labels were finally beginning to sit up and take note, and while Dr. Feelgood and Eddie & The Hot Rods were the pub-rock scene-stealers, the music weeklies had also started to give The 101'ers recognition for their hard-earned efforts.

However, Joe was all too aware of the excitement the Sex Pistols were generating following Neil Spencer's review, and just because *Melody Maker*'s review of their Nashville debut had declared the Sex Pistols to be doing "as much for music as World War II did for the cause of peace", he saw nothing to change his opinion that The 101'ers were "yesterday's papers".

According to Clash legend, Joe first became aware of Mick and Paul sometime the following month as he and Mick stood in line to collect their weekly dole money at the Lisson Grove Labour Exchange. No words were exchanged – possibly owing to Joe being a "name" in Mick's and Paul's eyes – and their being too shy to make the first move. However, their less than subtle eyeballing had not gone unnoticed, and Joe had been convinced that he was under surveillance of sorts. He would later confide that he'd thought they were going to jump him for his dole money the moment he got outside, and that his plan was to hit Paul – the more menacing of the two – before then legging it. "We saw Joe playing with The 101'ers and thought he'd be perfect for our group cos our singer [Billy Watts] didn't cut it and left," Paul Simonon recalled in *Punk*.

Their paths would inadvertently cross again sometime the following week. This time, however, Mick and Paul were accompanied by Glen, whom Joe obviously recognised from the two recent Nashville shows. Glen made the necessary introductions, but even before Joe had the chance to mention their previous encounter Mick let it be known that while he didn't think much of Joe's group, he thought Joe himself was "great".

Now that Mick and Paul had decided on their frontman, Bernard approached Joe at a Sex Pistols show at the 100 Club on Tuesday, May 25. Joe was intrigued enough to give Bernard the telephone number where he could be reached, but when Bernard called the following day his call was intercepted by 101'ers' guitarist "Desperate" Dan Kelleher who, having sensed Joe hadn't been his usual self of late, had pretended to be Joe in the hope he might suss out what was occurring. Bernard, however, twigged it wasn't Joe on the other end of the line and quickly hung up.

"I'd never met anybody like Bernard before, and haven't since," said Paul. "I really liked his aggressive attitude and sort of found him a challenge. I used to go up to his house a lot when the group was moving along, and we'd talk about albums and artwork and posters and all sorts of stuff, so I got on quite well with Bernard. He'd say, 'What do you think about South Africa?' Or, 'What would you do if you had £100?' Unfortunately, the drummers that arrived for the try-outs were subjected to this as well and they didn't know whether they were joining a group or a political party."

---

1   Somewhat ironically, given what was to occur, the two Nashville dates had been arranged by Chiswick to celebrate The 101'ers' deal with the label.

Having decided to wait until he could next approach Joe in person, Bernard – accompanied by Keith Levene – collared Joe backstage after a 101'ers gig at the Golden Lion on Fulham Broadway the following Sunday. Rather than pussyfoot around making small talk, Bernard delivered his ultimatum, giving Joe 48 hours to decide whether he wanted to step into the future or stay mired in the past. Joe, of course, would subsequently opine that "the future is unwritten", but while he readily accepted that Bernard had played no small part in the Sex Pistols' development, he was naturally sceptical as to Bernard's ability to make lightning strike twice. He was only a day into his deliberations about his next step, however, when an impatient Bernard called demanding an answer.

The following morning, Bernard – once again accompanied by Keith – collected Joe from Orsett Terrace in Paddington and delivered him to the squat on Davis Road in Acton Vale where Mick and Paul where anxiously waiting, guitars at the ready. The four spent the afternoon running through Mick's compositions such as '1-2-Crush On You', 'Protex Blue', and 'I'm So Bored With You', which the more politically astute Joe would revise to 'I'm So Bored With The USA'.

Satisfied that he'd made the right decision, Joe duly returned to Orsett Terrace that evening and, having informed 101'ers drummer, Richard "Snakehips" Dudanski, of said decision, asked his friend if he fancied being the drummer in his new group. Dudanski declined.

Having blooded themselves in the public arena supporting the Sex Pistols in Sheffield with drummer Terry Chimes, The Clash marked their London debut with a showcase at their new rehearsal space – Rehearsal Rehearsals – in Camden Town on Friday, August 13, in front of a select audience of prospective booking agents and journalists. "When they started out I gave The Clash a blank canvas: one that didn't have any room for Elvis, The Beatles, or The Rolling Stones," says Bernard. "If you can't be better than what is around at the time, there's no point in bothering."

While the majority of the agents came along – if only to see whether The Clash were worth putting on a London stage – only three of the journalists on Bernard's list thought the occasion worthy of the cab fare. Bernard wasn't overly concerned, as this trio were likely to be sympathetic to the cause. *Melody Maker*'s Caroline Coon and Jonh Ingham from *Sounds* had been shamelessly casting the Sex Pistols in a favourable – some would say biased – light for several months, and could elevate The Clash's position with a single sweep of their pen. Though *Sounds*' Giovanni Dadamo was another Sex Pistols aficionado, he would end his enthusiastic critique of The Clash's 40-minute set with the tagline: "I think they're the first group to come along who'll really frighten the Sex Pistols shitless."

After Keith Levene's departure in early September the truncated Clash really began to gel as a unit. Though they continued to play second fiddle to the Sex Pistols – most notably at the 100 Club Punk Festival that same month – they were keen to make it known they could stand on their own. Indeed, by the time of the Anarchy Tour they had recorded a set of demos for Polydor Records with maverick producer Guy Stevens, and their incendiary live outings – particularly those at the ICA (Independent College of Art) on Saturday, October 23, and the RCA (Royal College of Art) on Friday, November 5 – had seen them build up a steady following in and around the capital.

They'd also been forced to take time out to break in another drummer following Terry Chimes' unexpected departure towards the end of October. Thankfully, however, Terry's rushed replacement, Rob Harper, had already witnessed The Clash's live onslaught having caught them at the Lacy Lady in Ilford on Thursday, November 11, and therefore knew what was required after responding to their ad in *Melody Maker*. "Terry Chimes quit just as we were about to start the Anarchy Tour and we found... Rob Harper," Joe recalled in *The Clash*.

Meanwhile the other act on the Anarchy Tour bill, The Heartbreaks, had arrived at Heathrow where a chauffeur-driven limo waited to ferry them to their hotel. Having lived in resplendent squalour in New York they must have thought they'd landed on another planet. The Americans – particularly Johnny Thunders and his partner-in-rhyme Jerry "Niggs" Nolan – believed their musical pedigree and expertise gave them an edge over the Sex Pistols and the other "Limey" bands on the bill, a cursory listen to the cassette tape of the Dave Goodman demos that Malcolm had sent their manager, Leee Black Childers, having been more then enough evidence that the Pistols had borrowed extensively from the New York Dolls' back catalogue.

"The Pistols loved us," Jerry Nolan said in *Please Kill Me*. "Johnny Rotten would just stare at me and say, 'Niggs – my nickname – you are the fucking greatest drummer I've ever seen. I hate you for it.' I was kinda tickled, but I couldn't really enjoy myself on the Anarchy Tour. The Clash were on the Anarchy Tour, and so were The Damned. But The Damned got thrown off after a couple of gigs, because they were such sissies. The drummer, Rat Scabies, and the guitarist, Captain Sensible [sic], were tough kids, but the others were a bunch of poufs. They wanted to ride in their own bus. The Pistols were a little afraid of us too, but they tried hard not to show it."

Having watched The Clash and The Damned going through their respective paces in Harlesden, the Americans would have noted that the burlesque Damned were equally indebted to the New York Dolls, while The Clash would have been disregarded as being little more than Ramones copyists. The Heartbreakers knew that all they needed to do was to put in a couple of decent performances at Norwich and Derby to get the UK's music press behind them, and the only "Johnny" anyone would be interested in talking to from that point on would be the one from Queens. Thanks to the *Today* interview, however, their aspirations were halted before they'd shaken off their jetlag.

"Malcolm called me from London and asked, 'Do you want to tour with my group the Sex Pistols?'" Leee Black Childers remembers. "At the time I'd never heard of the Sex Pistols, but I said I would call him back after speaking with Johnny. I asked Johnny if he wanted to go on tour in England with the Sex Pistols. Johnny had never heard of them either, but of course, he remembered Malcolm. He said something like, 'He was the weird guy who managed the Dolls for a few months and made us dress like Commies.' But then he thought about things for a minute and said, 'It could be fun. And it's a trip to England. Let's go.' So we did. We arrived on the night of the Grundy show. They [Nils and Sophie] met us at the airport. Nils was in one of those big, fluffy Vivienne Westwood sweaters and had this cute pixie haircut. I thought he was Malcolm's assistant, so I said, 'Hello, you must be Sophie.' That went over really well with Nils."

Leee's faux pas probably didn't go down all that well with Sophie either, but Nils was too caught up with being in the presence of rock'n'roll royalty to take offence. "Everyone loved The Heartbreakers immediately," he later enthused. "Nolan and Thunders' pedigrees are immaculate coming from the New York Dolls, and their manager Leee Black Childers used to work for Bowie."

Though rock 'n' roll royalty might be something of an exaggeration, as Nina Antonia puts it in her New York Dolls biography *Too Much Too Soon*, they were the Bowery butterflies that irrevocably altered the course of rock'n'roll. By the time Malcolm McLaren caught up with them in 1973, they were pretty much burnt out and when the group imploded guitarist Johnny Thunders formed The Heartbreakers with Dolls

Opposite: The Clash

drummer Nolan[2]* and bassist Richard Hell, late of Television, who is the first known musician to perform on stage in a ripped t-shirt and spiky hair.

A group featuring two livewires such as Johnny Thunders and Richard Hell caused plenty of excitement down at CBGBs, but Hell's inability to remain in the background meant that his tenure with The Heartbreakers would prove short-lived. Johnny was happy to allow Hell to take centre stage and sing a couple of his compositions, but he'd spent too long fighting to get out from Dolls singer David Johansen's shadow to ever let it happen again. Hell, rather than concede defeat and accept his role with grace, foolishly approached Jerry with a view to getting rid of Johnny. There was only ever going to be one outcome and Hell's replacement in The Heartbreakers was Georgia-born bassist Billy Rath, who at the time of receiving the call from New York was "working" his way along Florida's extensive beachfront earning his living as a gigolo.

Dave Vanian and Brian James

"The Damned are among us!" reported *Sniffin' Glue* in its review of the group's performance at the Nashville Rooms on Thursday, July 15, 1976. "It was all so obvious at the Nashville. They were only the support group but they realy [sic] turned on the style. It's bands like this that could blow the lid off the London punk-scene and make everybody listen. The Damned just scream out with energy, they are brash, flash and loud!"

Like The Clash, The Damned were also a by-product of London SS. Having eagerly responded to Mick Jones and Tony James' late-'75 *Melody Maker* ad seeking a guitarist into The Stooges and MC5, Brian James joined the fledgling line-up and spent the early part of 1976 fruitlessly auditioning for singers and drummers. "We auditioned people for six months, and no one had a clue what we were on about," Brian recalled for *Mojo* in March 2003. "Out of all the dust, there were a few little diamonds that were into the same sort of stuff and gradually this bunch of like-minded people grew from it."

It was from within this colourful coterie that he gradually rounded up three unlikely characters and moulded them into a group with long-term potential. First was the newly christened Rat Scabies, who despite failing his audition with London SS, did at least receive his lasting punk nom de grrrr courtesy of Paul Simonon. In the months since failing to grab the London SS drum stool, Rat's "dustbin lid drumming" had come on leaps and bounds, and like Brian he was itching to make dynamic music à la mid-sixties Who and Small Faces, rather than merely go through the motions playing with staid mid-seventies outfits.

Somewhat serendipitously, Rat was approached by Malcolm to audition with *NME* journalist Nick Kent – who was also very briefly a pre-Johnny Rotten Sex Pistol – and his on/off American girlfriend, future Pretenders frontwoman Chrissie Hynde, to perform at a Women's Lib festival at the Cardiff Arts Centre. As Kent and Chrissie were experiencing relationship difficulties at the time Kent agreed to let Rat call in Brian and his Croydon Fairfield Halls work colleague Ray Burns – soon to be rechristened Captain Sensible – and called themselves The Subterraneans.

---

2 Nolan replaced original New York Dolls drummer Billy Murcia who died in drug-related circumstances on the Dolls' first visit to the UK in 1972.

According to Kent, the ad hoc outfit purposely went out of their way to antagonise the pro-women's rights crowd by playing macho songs such as the Rolling Stones' 'Under My Thumb', and The Crystals' 1962 hit 'He Hit Me (It Felt Like A Kiss)' which blatantly endorsed spousal abuse. If Kent is to be believed, the group also played Brian's songs 'New Rose' and 'Fish', both of which would subsequently resurface on The Damned's debut album, *Damned, Damned, Damned*.

As there was never any thought of The Subterraneans being anything more than a one-off affair, on returning to London Rat linked up with Chrissie Hynde for another of Malcolm's and Bernard's ad hoc projects, Masters Of The Backside, a.k.a. Mike Hunt's Honourable Discharge. The idea never got much beyond the planning stage, probably because Chrissie objected to playing in a group named – albeit tongue-in-cheek – after vaginal secretion. When Chrissie elected to forge for own career path, the three approached an Alice Cooper-esque singing gravedigger who'd taken to calling himself Dave Vanian, whom Brian and Rat had encountered a few weeks earlier at the Nashville Rooms.

It was Malcolm who actually stumped up the money for the newly formed Damned to begin rehearsing in earnest sometime during April 1976. "Malcolm came and put us in rehearsal for two days and then came down with Helen [Wellington-Lloyd] and Rotten, and all those people," Captain Sensible says in *England's Dreaming*. "They sat down watching us, laughing, and told us to fuck off. No commercial possibilities. Malcolm was good to us: he gave us money and talked sense. Brian and Rat had met Vanian at the Nashville – they thought he looked good. The name 'The Damned' was Brian's idea. We were damned really: everything that could go wrong did."

Malcolm's benevolence towards The Damned reflected his dream of becoming a latter-day Larry Parnes, with a stable of bands under his control. "Rat Scabies will always say that the main reason they [The Damned] were on the [Anarchy] tour was nothing to do with punk solidarity or any ideas of Larry Parnes-style package tours," Glen said in *I Was A Teenage Sex Pistol*. "He says they were on it because Malcolm had realised that they'd already played loads of shows around the country and had proved to be good crowd-pullers."

The Damned played several low-key "test-the-water" shows over consecutive Saturdays at a gay club in Lisson Grove before trumpeting their arrival on the scene by supporting the Sex Pistols at the 100 Club on July 6, 1976. Although The Clash had played with the Sex Pistols two nights earlier, the scene's movers and shakers proclaimed this to be the night punk rock officially broke in London.

Of course, their signing to Stiff Records, and subsequently pipping the Pistols to the post in the "first-punk-group-to-release-a-single" race, coupled with their decision to part company with quasi-manager Andy Czezowski in favour of Jake Riviera saw them expelled from Malcolm's good graces. However, their burgeoning reputation in and around London meant Malcolm had to include them on the 100 Club Punk Festival bill, and if any doubt remained that they were considered "punk personae non grata" it came with the glass-throwing incident midway through their set.

Interestingly, at the time of the incident it was reported that a close personal female friend of the group – supposedly a friend of Dave Vanian's girlfriend – ended up losing an eye after being caught by one of the glass shards. Yet while there's no denying people in the crowd suffered varying injuries, it's hard to believe – in the wake of the media backlash against the Sex Pistols and punk rock – that the girl in question wasn't paraded in public to show the ugly face of punk (again, no pun intended).

Rather than sit around brooding about being given the cold shoulder by the scene's hallowed inner circle, however, The Damned simply got on with what they did best – playing live; especially after the release of 'New Rose' (BUY 6) on Friday, October 22. By the time of the Anarchy Tour, they'd played as far afield as Liverpool, Birmingham, and Manchester.

Though Malcolm's argument was with Jake Riviera, in a classic Freudian instance of displacement – the unconscious transposing of emotion from one subject to another – Malcolm passed his ire onto The Damned by insisting that Stiff Records provide separate funding for its act. He knew full well that the newly formed label – which had been financed with a £400 loan from Dr. Feelgood's frontman, Lee

Brilleaux – was operating on a shoestring budget. This of course, meant that while both The Clash and The Heartbreakers would be enjoying salubrious five-star hotels, The Damned would have to settle for low-rent B&B accommodation. However, rather than have his charges suffer the indignity of having the other bands on the bill crowing over them whilst they traversed the country, Riviera announced that The Damned would also make their own travel arrangements.

That didn't mean they were happy being left to plough a lone furrow. "One night I went to have a drink with The Damned and ended up on their tour bus, going back to their hotel with them," Glen recalled in *I Was A Teenage Sex Pistol*. "While we were staying in expensive five-star places, they were in some bed and breakfast. 'Wouldn't you rather be with us?' I said. 'We would, we would,' they said to a man." "We were signed to Stiff – if the latest [Elvis] Costello record didn't sell, the next Ian Dury record didn't get made," Captain Sensible explained to *Mojo*. "There was no money, so we had to stay in bed-and-breakfast places and travel in a transit van."

Meanwhile the fall-out from the *Today* show refused to go away, and that week's *Record Mirror* carried a useful summary of the situation as it stood on the eve of the tour: "'Were The Pistols Loaded?' screamed the page one headline of Friday's *Sun*. The story was the same for the rest of the popular national press. Punk rock hit Fleet Street. A few four-letter words on the small screen and they went bananas.

"It carried on into Sunday's press, where punk and the Pistols overtook other matters of national importance.

"The media – press, radio and TV – have the power to make or break a cult. With their 'Shock Horror Filth' outrage, they have made sure that punk rock isn't going to leave us just yet. In fact, they have helped to establish the music industry's biggest money-spinner for 1977.

"Fleet Street might have seemed to be outraged, but really they loved it. Tales of sex, drugs and violence sell papers. With the Sex Pistols, Bill Grundy and all the punk ingredients which have surfaced, the papers had a field day.

"But what of the TV programme that started the 'Great Controversy'? It would seem that the outburst of swearing by the Sex Pistols was just what those connected with the programme wanted. Well at least what Bill Grundy wanted? He said afterwards, 'The object of the exercise was to prove that these louts were a foul-mouthed set of yobs.'

"Does such an exercise have a place in a TV programme? Not according to Jeremy Isaacs, Thames TV's Director of Programmes who described the 'feature' as 'A gross error of judgement caused by inexcusably sloppy journalism.'

There was further comment from Grundy: 'There is no way that I can be accused of encouraging offensive language on TV.' Why then did he ask one of the Pistols to repeat a four-letter word which, first time round, was inaudible?

"Getting them to swear live on TV as they did, seemed deliberate.

"It seems peculiar that Bill Grundy, after being judged innocent, was suspended.

"One thing's for sure, when the dust has settled, the Sex Pistols have had more publicity in a few minutes than most bands get in a lifetime."

CHAPTER SEVEN

From Norwich To Nowhere

"The Sex Pistols' first British tour was in tatters this week in the wake of a series of incidents which gave them front page headlines on the national newspapers for five consecutive days.

"As SOUNDS went to press on Monday evening most of the tour dates had been cancelled or rearranged at alternative venues.

"The remaining schedule now reads: Leeds University [sic] December 6, Manchester Electric Circus 9, Bristol University (formerly Colston Hall) 13, Caerphily Castle Cinema (formerly at Cardiff) 14, Dundee Caird Hall 16, Guildford Civic Hall 19, Plymouth Woods Centre 21, London Roxy Theatre Harlesden 26.

"However, the situation is constantly changing and fans should check with the venue before going. An additional date in Croydon is being arranged for December 12."

Sounds, Saturday, December 11, 1976.

The Anarchy tour was indeed in a state of flux. By midday Friday, instead of ferrying the Sex Pistols, The Heartbreakers, The Clash and their retinues to Norwich's East Anglia University for the opening show of the tour, the coach was still standing idle at the kerb on Denmark Street. While the beleaguered Sophie fielded calls from indignant council officials and anxious promoters over at Dryden Chambers, an equally irate Malcolm – sporting a silver-flecked fur coat that he'd purchased specially for the tour – was relating the constantly changing situation to the bemused musicians. He'd just spent the last half-hour or so cooped up in the public phone box outside St. Giles' Church on nearby St. Martin's Lane remonstrating with the East Anglia University's Vice-Chancellor, Frank Thistlewaite, over the latter's decision to cancel the show.

Malcolm's vexation didn't stem from the cancellation itself, but rather Thistlewaite's insistence that he'd reached his decision not because of what had occurred on the *Today* show per se, but rather over fears that the furore now surrounding the Sex Pistols meant that he was no longer fully satisfied that the

concert could proceed peacefully. It seemed the eleventh-hour cancellation had resulted in a sizeable contingent of the university's students threatening to stage a sit-in protest. However, Thistlewaite had assured Malcolm that the demonstration wouldn't be bringing about a reversal in his decision.

The front page of that evening's edition of the *Eastern Evening News* carried a banner headline: 'UEA Shoots Down Sex Pistols Concert' and reported that the university's powers-that-be had acted over concerns for campus safety. The university's Information Officer, Frank Albrighton, said that the decision had been taken because the university was "responsible for the safety and security of persons and property on the campus", and added that the concert wasn't going to happen so there was little point in anyone turning up. However, the cancellation meant there was a distinct possibility that the Student Union would still have to pay the agreed £750 fee. The previous day, the union's president, Aiden Lines, had gone on record saying that he'd wanted to cancel the concert, but that doing so would cripple the Student Union financially. While Lines was conveniently unavailable for comment, the Student Union's social secretary, Paul Heck, having made mention of the Union's forlorn security measures which included speaking with Norwich Police, tripling their own security staff, as well as closing the concert hall bar to prevent the risk of glasses being thrown, stated: "I agree there was a risk, but I don't think it's as great as it's made out to be. I don't know what he [Lines] will do about the money if we have to pay it. We hope the university will pay a fair bit since they cancelled it, but I doubt they will."

Meanwhile, Sally Partington, the Student Union's Publicity Officer, used the newspaper to issue a formal apology on its behalf to those left disappointed by the university's decision: "We wish to make it known that we are disgusted with the manner in which the Vice-Chancellor's decision was taken. It was the result of an impromptu and ill-informed meeting with two representatives of the union who did their best to put the union's point of view to no avail. We feel that the wishes of the union and the students here have been totally disregarded, and we wish to apologise to all those who have bought tickets and will be disappointed – particularly those from Norwich and the surrounding area."

In his book, *My Amazing Adventures With The Sex Pistols*, Dave Goodman claims that the Anarchy Tour defied the "so-called ban" by securing an alternative – undisclosed – venue within the Norwich area, but as no one else connected with the tour has ever alluded to a show that evening, we'll assume he was under the influence of one herbal substance or another while penning his recollections, and that Malcolm simply gave orders for the coach to make for Derby where the bands were due to perform the following evening.

Goodman, of course, had been counting down the days to the tour, because owing to an oversight at EMI Chris Thomas had been inadvertently credited as producer on the 'Anarchy' single's B-side 'I Wanna Be Me', which had in fact been culled from Goodman's own Denmark Street demo sessions back in July. Seeing as Frank Brunger would be acting as EMI's tour liaison, this was the first chance Goodman would have of coming face-to-face with those he deemed responsible.

Following the release of 'Anarchy In the UK' the otherwise amiable sound engineer – who'd been smarting from his having been replaced by Chris Thomas in the first place – had instructed his solicitor to write to EMI's legal department threatening an injunction, while also demanding that the label send out notices to the media and all other interested parties admitting their error and regretting any embarrassment the oversight had caused, and that after the initial 15,000 pressing with the incorrect label had been sold, all future records would bear a label correctly crediting him as producer. Brunger, however, was unwilling to play the role of label fall guy.

"I wasn't responsible for the details on the ['Anarchy In The UK'] label but Goodman did lay into me about us having credited Chris Thomas with both sides," the former Harvest manager said in *Sex Pistols: 90 Days At EMI*. "We got the information from A&R, but as I was there he [Goodman] picked on me."

While EMI had readily acquiesced to Goodman's demands, and put the error down to the teething problems that occurred with a new signing, they might have stopped to ponder that it was Goodman who was indirectly to blame for the unfolding disaster. After all, had he not exhausted EMI's patience by attempting to capture the Sex Pistols' live sound on tape then the 'Anarchy' single would have been released on Friday, November 19, as the label had originally intended. Had this occurred, then in all likelihood the Anarchy Tour would have proceeded a week earlier than subsequently scheduled, with the triumphant London homecoming show at the Roxy Theatre taking place on Sunday, December 19, before everyone concerned headed off to enjoy Christmas with their nearest and weirdest.

This, of course, would have meant the Pistols would have been in mid-tour by Wednesday, December 1, and therefore wouldn't have been available for the *Today* slot. In all likelihood they'd have been enjoying a night off in Manchester looking forward to playing the Electric Circus the following evening.

In the event, the tour party arrived at Derby's elegant 19th century Crest Hotel – which before burning down in suspicious circumstances in 2002 was located in Littleover a few miles from the city centre – to find the lobby swarming with reporters and photographers. Indeed, it's fair to say that the local press hadn't seen so much excitement since Derby County sacked Brian Clough as manager some three years earlier, and though none of the reporters made any mention of the coincidence, Malcolm's forebears – the MacLarens – had marched into Derby beneath Bonnie Prince Charlie's standard during the '45 Rebellion exactly 231 years to the very day the Sex Pistols were set to appear at the Kings Hall.

Rather than face the press after an already taxing day and a tedious journey from London Malcolm elected to order everyone to their rooms. While the musicians readily took advantage of room service to order a never-ending supply of lager and club sandwiches – and the four Heartbreakers making several surreptitious transatlantic calls to their girlfriends – to all intents and purposes, they were under enforced house arrest. Bill Grundy, however – having bleated to the *Daily Mail* that he'd been made a scapegoat of the whole saga – had reportedly taken his wife and kids abroad for a fortnight's holiday.

Speaking from the family home in Cheshire prior to heading for Manchester airport, Grundy said how he hadn't been involved in the decision to have the Sex Pistols on the show as such decisions were usually made at the morning conference which he wasn't expected to attend. Despite denying any

Paul Simonon, Dave Goodman, Steve Jones and Johnny

knowledge of the supposed two-week suspension imposed on him by his bosses at Thames TV, he did admit to having received a telephone call late Wednesday evening from Jeremy Isaacs who'd informed him that he wouldn't be doing the following Wednesday's show. The interview ended with Grundy boldly declaring that he would be most surprised if he were to lose his job over what had happened, and that he believed the Sex Pistols had deliberately set out to swear on his programme in order to guarantee maximum publicity for themselves and their new single.

Having packed her suitcase, Grundy's wife, Sheila, also provided the *Mail* with a damage limitations interview which had appeared in the previous day's edition in which she said that it was completely out of character for "her Bill" to encourage bad language when he knew that young children could be watching the programme.

"It's not like Bill to encourage bad language, especially at a time when children could be watching," she told the paper. "I know that with the boys in the pub after a few drinks he uses some pretty strong language, but he's never allowed swearing in his own home because he hated it, and the family were never allowed to indulge."

Grundy's 29-year-old daughter, Dorothy – a schoolteacher by profession – also leapt to her dad's defence, insisting that he'd never sworn in front of either her or her five brothers and sisters. She told *The Sun*: "My father hasn't spoken to me about this, but it seems to me he is in an invidious position. It was a live programme and he had to keep it going until the end."

On arriving in Derby Malcolm discovered that Sunday night's show at Newcastle City Hall had been cancelled by Tyneside City Council in the interests of protecting its children. Although Derby's elected officials didn't quite feel their own youth was in peril from the latest rock'n'roll rebellion, the city's Leisure Committee issued a proposal whereby the show at the Kings Hall would only be allowed to proceed on the strict proviso that the Pistols consented to perform a private matinee show in front of the committee in order to determine whether the group's stage act was indeed appropriate for public consumption.

The understanding was that should the Sex Pistols be deemed unsuitable, then the other three groups on the bill could still go on as scheduled. However, whether a truncated three-group bill with The Damned installed as headliners for the evening would have had the same appeal quickly became a moot point as The Clash and The Heartbreakers closed ranks behind the Pistols and refused to play. "We were told we had to audition for some fucking council," Walter Lure told *Punk*. "All of us, especially Johnny and Jerry, thought, 'Fuck this shit.'"

On the Saturday morning – the same day that half-page advertisements for the 'Anarchy In The UK' single and the accompanying tour appeared in the match-day programmes for the (old) First Division football matches Bristol City v Leeds, Manchester City v Derby County, and Ipswich Town v Liverpool – the *News Of The World*'s Wendy Henry had shamelessly offered Malcolm £500 cash for an exclusive interview. To his credit, Malcolm declined her offer as at the time he was under the impression that the Derby show was still going ahead. However, on subsequently learning of the council's proposal, he'd set off in search of Ms Henry with the intention of giving the interview, banking the £500, and then telling the council where it could shove its proposal. Unfortunately, the word "perseverance" didn't seem to feature in the reporter's lexicon as she was nowhere to be seen.

Nevertheless, the *NOTW* was promising something to titillate its readers the following morning, a trailer that night stating: "The Sex Pistols disgusted and enraged viewers with their foul behaviour – Punk Rock? We say Punk Junk! – You'll be shocked by the report on Pop's new heroes. Only in the *News Of The World* this Sunday."

Fleet Street's rabid refusal to let sleeping dogs lie was certainly an eye-opener for Mike Thorne, who was in Derby in an unofficial capacity. "I went to the hotel [the Derby Crest] just outside Derby where everyone was staying," he recalled for the God Save The Sex Pistols website. "We were jammed in one tiny room with the phone going every few minutes and the press literally banging on the door. Good money was offered for a story, but none changed hands as far as I know. One tabloid scribe had a Sunday double-page spread reserved for his story and was getting really desperate. He probably made it all up when he couldn't get anything real. Most of them did. It was a shock to me to see how venal, dishonest and cynical many of these journalist characters were."

He added: "Vivid memories remain of an almost empty hall in Derby on an unseasonably warm afternoon. Empty except for the promoter, Dave Cork, who was watching his business quickly disintegrate, and was right on the edge of falling apart. Derby didn't hear music that night. The mayor and council had asked for a private performance so that they could judge whether to grant permission or not. Piss off. Malcolm was probably more politely elegant in his communications with them."

As The Damned were holed up in a B&B on the opposite side of town, they were obviously unable to keep abreast of unfolding developments. The last they'd heard was that Malcolm had consented to the Leisure Committee's wishes and so their tour manager, Rick Rodgers – little realising the implications of his actions – issued a statement to the press saying there was nothing offensive about The Damned's stage act, and that they would be happy to perform for the committee. It was here that Malcolm most definitely conjured up some of the Machiavellian mischief which ultimately became his byword, because while he was plotting how best to snatch victory from the jaws of humiliating defeat at the hands of the Leisure Committee, The Damned were probably pondering how best to occupy their time until the soundcheck. Having decided that the Sex Pistols weren't going to be held to ransom, all Malcolm needed to do was have Nils call Rodgers and have him get The Damned the hell out of Dodge and arrange a rendezvous at one of the M1 motorway services for the following day while they were all en route to Leeds.

Of course, Malcolm had also undoubtedly realised he'd been presented with a gilt-edged opportunity to settle old scores for The Damned's past transgressions, such as their boasting to the *Melody Maker* about their being better than the Pistols, and their playing the European Punk Festival – not to mention it allowing him to put Jake Riviera in his place. By purposely keeping Rick Rodgers out of the loop The Damned would – albeit inadvertently – hoist themselves by their own petard.

"McLaren and Rhodes said their bands wouldn't do it, and if we'd have been there we'd have said the same thing," Captain Sensible told *Mojo*. "But our tour manager, Rick Rodgers, said that we would do the audition; there was nothing offensive about our act and we'd be happy to play for the council. When he told us we were just devastated, couldn't believe it. As a result, we got booted off the tour."

Brian James, however, chose to put a different slant on things: "When Malcolm McLaren put the Anarchy Tour together, he and Bernard Rhodes needed to bring in some better known names like us [The Damned] and The Heartbreakers," he said. "After all, the Pistols had really only played the odd art college, and The Clash hardly at all. Of course, the Grundy show changed all that and Malcolm suddenly realised they didn't need us.

"He tried to push us into supporting the other bands rather than giving us equal billing. We told him where to go and left the tour. We didn't agree or care about politics – we just wanted to play our music. It was only rock'n'roll."

Unaware of these matters, Derby Council's Leisure Committee issued a statement about the issue: "I have spoken to the manager of the group who tells me the Sex Pistols will not perform before the councillors unless we're prepared to come here this evening and see the whole of the show, which we are not prepared to do. The Committee have decided that the concert of the Sex Pistols, they will not perform here tonight. But we are quite agreeable that the other three groups that have already been booked will go on."

While the Committee's carefully worded statement made it appear as though they were simply vetting the Pistols' stage act in light of recent events, it was nothing short of an autocratic action expected in countries living under the Communist yoke but not in a country that supposedly espoused democracy. As The Clash astutely pointed out in their 1982 single 'Know Your Rights', it's only when we attempt to put our supposed fundamental right to freedom of speech into practice that we realise its judicial limitations. It also didn't go unnoticed that although the special matinee performance was supposed to take place behind doors, the Leisure Committee thought to invite the press along to document how the upstanding folk of Derby had neutered the foul-mouthed Sex Pistols.

"The group [Pistols] were asked to audition at one joint in Derby, and they could only play if the councillors approved of what they were doing," Nils said in *Punk*. "Malcolm quite rightly said, 'Fuck off.' I'm not sure if this is true now or not, but The Damned tried to team up with The Clash to do the tour without the Pistols. (I've heard that Jake Riviera claims it isn't true)."

Sounds reported: The [Sex] Pistols were due to perform at 3.30pm and the place was awash with national newspaper reporters and cameramen as well as a large contingent of police outside in case of any rumoured demonstrations by the National Front or irate parents (neither demonstration happened).

"But by 4.30pm the group had not arrived and councillor [Len] Shepley [sic] announced that the group had refused to appear at the preview unless the committee would also attend the show that evening. But the committee refused to agree and the show was cancelled. At one point it was suggested that the other groups on the tour – the Damned, the Clash, and the Heart Breakers [sic] – might appear without the Pistols but no sooner had the committee agreed than the managers of the other bands said that their groups would not appear without the Sex Pistols.

"Bernard Rhodes, manager of the Clash, said: 'We don't agree to the terms we have to perform under. It's ludicrous that people who are 102 years old should be passing judgement.'

According to *NME* – as reported in the paper's December 11 issue – the National Front intended to make its presence known outside the Kings Hall, and a spokesman for the ultra right-wing party was telling anyone willing to listen that it was intent on aligning itself with the Sex Pistols. It was also rumoured that a local Hells Angels chapter was planning on coming into town to create a little anarchy of their own. Though there's no evidence that Malcolm was aware of either potential disturbance, in hindsight it makes sense as to why he appeared to be acquiescing to the Leisure Committee's demands because if the Pistols were seen to be willing to perform and yet being denied the opportunity, then the local promoter

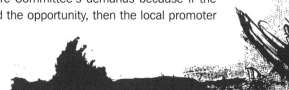

would be contractually obligated to pay half the fee. He even had Nils arrange for the road crew to go down to the Kings Hall and set up the group's equipment on stage, but this was also a ploy to throw the salivating press hounds off the scent, as while it was great seeing his charges on the front page of every newspaper, having a microphone or camera thrust in his face every time he stopped to draw breath was beginning to wear a bit thin.

"Finally, at about four minutes to three, the Mayor and lady Mayoress walked in accompanied by the Chief Constable," Dave Goodman recalled in *My Amazing Adventures With The Sex Pistols*. "They took up seats laid dead centre in the hall. They were wearing their full dress of office – complete with 18th Century hats and silver chains – and made quite a sight. I took up position behind the mixer and a deathly hush fell. There was a large clock above the stage ticking away the seconds. Everyone was expecting the Sex Pistols to walk on stage at 3 o'clock sharp. At two minutes to, the roadies switched on the amps and the glow of red lights made it seem as if something was going to happen. "

Nothing happened because Malcolm's scheme had – albeit unwittingly – already been sanctioned by EMI. For although it was a Saturday afternoon, and there was no one of any significant rank at Manchester Square, Frank Brunger was occupying one of the rooms further along the hall. "EMI [had] sent me on the tour in case there was any trouble. I was the point of contact if there were any major incidents," Brunger said in *Sex Pistols: 90 Days At EMI*. However, as he had no real authority, all he could do was call his Harvest boss, Mark Rye, who was the next link in EMI's chain of command, to get consent to supply Malcolm with Paul Watts' home telephone number. Watts was understandably reluctant to get involved, but with the Sex Pistols being an EMI act, he had little option but to agree to Malcolm's demands and call the Derby Crest to say that EMI would cover any outstanding bills.

The hapless Brunger would also be called upon to stand in Malcolm's corner in his fight with the Leisure Committee. "Malcolm argued about censorship, said his group was a group of the people and told the council they had no right to ban them, and then he got me to do my bit," he explained. "I told them that EMI was a reputable company and that we didn't want any trouble, but it made no difference."

Thanks to Watts' benevolence, however, Malcolm no longer cared what the committee thought, and while Derby's Mayor and Lady Mayoress, dressed in their civic robes and chains of office, the city's Chief Constable, and councillors Edith Wood, Les Shipley and Richard Wayman sat waiting patiently for the Sex Pistols to make their humbled appearance on stage, the group was back at the Derby Crest with The Clash and The Heartbreakers readying themselves for another evening of free-flowing booze courtesy of EMI.

The group's official statement, issued by EMI, read: "The Sex Pistols feel that it is unreasonable to expect their performance to be judged by people unconnected with, and unfamiliar with their music. They prefer to be judged by those who see their concerts and listen to their records."

CHAPTER EIGHT

Sex Pistols Will Play

> "As a manager, Malcolm could have tried a little harder. What was the point in setting all this up, calling it a tour, and then sending us up north, to drive from town to town, spend two nights in a hotel, do one gig, then drive around for a week with nothing to do? I think we have a concert at – no cancelled, next town. There were no escape hatches or alternatives and again, no money. It's difficult when two hundred journalists with cameras are following you around."
>
> John Lydon

When they'd last played Leeds – at the Fordham Hotel back in September – the as then relatively unknown Sex Pistols had been free to go about the city as they pleased. Now, however, just as they had in Derby, the tour party arrived at the Dragonara Hotel[1*] where they would be based during their two-night stay to find the five-star hotel's gleaming foyer teeming with both local and national press – all of whom were seemingly determined to continue, or even exacerbate the on-going witch-hunt against the Pistols.

Once again, everyone had to remain on the coach while Malcolm and Nils went inside to take care of the reservations. And having entrusted Nils with getting everyone to their respective rooms while keeping them away from the press, Malcolm went straight up to his room which he was sharing with Dave Goodman to confer with Sophie. Despite it being a Sunday, Sophie was at the Glitterbest office rapidly running out of fingers with which to plug the crumbling dam that was the Anarchy Tour. For while Thursday's show at Manchester's Electric Circus would definitely proceed as scheduled, Tuesday's show at Bournemouth's Village Bowl and Friday's show at Lancaster University were both now definitely off.

The Village Bowl came under the auspices of Rank Leisure Services, and a company spokesman had told reporters that it was – in a mirror action of East Anglia University's Vice-Chancellor Frank Thistlewaite – pulling the show owing to "anxieties over the security aspects" of staging a Sex Pistols concert, before hinting at the underlying factor behind the decision by saying Rank Leisure Services wasn't particularly keen to be associated with the Sex Pistols at the present time. The show at Lancaster University – where future Clash road manager Johnny Green was enrolled studying Arabic and Islamic Studies – had fallen foul of a group of feminist students belonging to the Student Union who were decrying the Pistols and every other punk rock group as being "sexists". Although replacement bookings had been tentatively

---

1   Now the Hilton Leeds City hotel.

arranged in Sheffield and Preston respectively, there was no guarantee that either of these would actually go ahead.

The Liverpool show, too, looked more and more unlikely, as the *Liverpool Echo* reported on December 7: "An outraged Liverpool Councillor to-day called for a boycott on punk rock group Sex Pistols – who vow to sidestep a ban on their city concert.

"Councillor Doreen Jones plans to demonstrate outside the club where they are to play in a bid to dissuade youngsters from seeing the group.

"'Let's show the rest of the country Liverpool is too good for this sort of rubbish. We don't want them here,' she said."

On discovering the Saturday, December 11, show at Liverpool Stadium had also been cancelled, Malcolm had called Roy Adams, the owner of the Cavern Club, to sound out the possibility of restaging the show at the legendary subterranean venue made famous by The Beatles. However, despite Adams himself having no objection to staging a Sex Pistols show, local councillor Doreen Jones had called on her colleagues on the Liverpool City Council to place a special banning order that prevented any venue in the city – including Eric's, where the Pistols had played back in October – from staging a punk rock concert that weekend.

Back at the Dragonara the press had set up camp en masse in the hotel's bar and were refusing to budge until being given something of note for their respective editors, all of which prompted Malcolm to gave an impromptu press conference in the foyer. After fielding by now run-of-the-mill questions about the tour cancellations, as well as being asked for his thoughts on EMI's impending AGM (Annual General Meeting) set for the coming Tuesday afternoon in which the Sex Pistols were sure to feature, he gleefully informed the gathering that the highlight of the following evening's show at the polytechnic would be the Sex Pistols' new song 'No Future' with its opening couplet: 'God Bless the Queen and her fascist regime.' Learning the Pistols had penned a song which likened the British Establishment to Hitler's Nazis was enough to send most of the reporters rushing for the hotel's phones. This titillating revelation, however, wasn't enough for the *Daily Mirror*'s hack, who – having espied two Sex Pistols sneaking into the bar – took muck-racking to its true literal sense.

Despite Nils' best efforts, Steve and Paul had managed to slip the net, and were heading for the hotel bar when the *Mirror* man – having no doubt recognised Steve as being the one who'd called Bill Grundy's bluff on TV – cajoled the two Pistols into throwing a few ornamental plants around the foyer. Of course, what the subsequent article neglected to mention was that before approaching Steve and Paul,

the enterprising hack had slipped the Dragonara's bemused manager £25 to cover the cost of replacing the ornamental plants and having the carpet cleaned. Needless to say, judging by the *Mirror*'s screaming banner headline of the following morning anyone would have thought the Sex Pistols had embarked on a wanton rampage akin to the Chapeltown Riots which had occurred in the city the previous year.

The following day's *Daily Mirror* reported: "The Sex Pistols were busy making a nuisance of themselves again yesterday. The four-man Punk Rock group wrecked the lobby of a luxury hotel, uprooting ornamental plants, hurling pots around the room and scattering soil over the carpets.

"The vandalism at the four-star Dragonara in Leeds was the prelude to a Punks' concert in the city tonight. Ten shows scheduled for other towns have been cancelled by worried managements since the foul-mouthed group angered millions of TV viewers last week.

"A *Mirror* man who watched the group go wild at the Leeds hotel said: As they walked away they shouted, 'Don't blame us. That's what you wanted. Send the bill to EMI' – their record company."

The report concluded with Malcolm's quote: "The group's manager, Malcolm McLaren, said that the high spot would be a song that opens with the words, 'God Bless the Queen and her fascist regime.'"

"In the foyer of the Dragonara Hotel, Leeds, a TV reporter asked if I was anything to do with the group," Ray Stevenson recalled. "He said he'd been waiting for an hour and wanted to talk to Mr McLaren or the Sex Pistols. I told him it was unlikely, but I would tell 'Mr McLaren' that he was here. I asked if I was also to tell 'Mr McLaren' that he would like some swearing for his TV show. The TV reporter smiled at me."

Though Bob Mercer – having spoken with Frank Brunger, as well as the Dragonara's manager after reading about the Pistols' plant-throwing antics – was happy to accept the *Daily Mirror* reporter's culpability, he decided that the task of keeping the group in line was perhaps too much for one EMI man to handle. "I thought it was all beginning to get out of hand. So I appointed Graham Fletcher [from EMI International] to go on group watch – to go with them anywhere they went and to make sure things didn't go too far."

Back in September, the Sex Pistols had performed for the inmates at Chelmsford Maximum Security Prison, and having spent the past two days holed up in their hotel rooms they now had some understanding of what it was like to be incarcerated against one's will. There were others among the tour party who were also feeling the strain, particularly The Heartbreakers who hadn't travelled some 3,000 miles just to sit staring at four walls.

While Malcolm lay in his darkened room ruminating over the well-worn adage of "buts and ands being pots and pans", the majority of his charges headed into Leeds city centre in search of some action; hopefully to happen upon some members of the opposite sex who'd be willing to show them where said action might be found. With it being a Sunday evening – and a cold, miserable one at that – the only females to be seen were those that would want financial recompense for their company. Indeed, the only one to get lucky was the tour's in-house security guy, who, owing to his weighing in at 18 stone, was affectionately known to one and all as "Fat Freddie".

Having been on the road with various bands over the years, Freddie had learned one or two tricks in his time, and having already clocked the receptionist's "bored-with-it-all" expression, he'd excused himself from accompanying the others into town then homed in on his target and enticed her up to his room. However, if Glen is to be believed, the hapless Freddie inexplicably got himself and the unfortunate receptionist wedged in his bathtub.

Before departing from Derby, Mike Thorne, who was tagging along in an unofficial capacity, had called Paul Watts to give an unbiased report on the Leisure Committee situation, as well as suggest it might be good for morale if EMI picked up the tab for a nice relaxing dinner at the Dragonara as this was something the label did with every other artist on their roster during a tour.

"We were probably 24 around the table which I had guaranteed to the hotel," Thorne recalled. "There had been an incident earlier where Steve [and Paul] had naively consented to smash a plant pot for a gentleman of the press, but we had avoided the flash point that would give the hacks another shock/horror opportunity. Everyone settled down comfortably, some more than others as Jerry Nolan and Johnny Thunders repeated and repeated their orders for triple vodkas on the rocks.

"The mood was great, upbeat and positive, and Malcolm and I had to implore everyone to hold it down only once every 15 minutes or so. But there was a queasy feeling in the stomach when the [bread] rolls started flying. At the back of the dining room – not far from the hovering gang of the press corps, were two Leeds city councilmen. The silent prayer that they wouldn't get struck on the head worked nicely."

Rather than break communal bread at the Dragonara, or accompany the others on a boozy pub crawl, Glen and Mick opted to venture out into the night to see what gastronomic delights Leeds city centre had to offer two discerning Londoners. Their gourmet options were somewhat restricted, however, owing to it being a Sunday evening, coupled with Mick's recent decision to become a vegetarian.

These days, one can find vegetarian options on any menu, but back in the mid-seventies – and especially out in the Shires – vegetarianism was something of a rarity. It's worth remembering, too, that as vegetarianism was associated with the Haight Ashbury hippie movement of the late-sixties, which punk rock was openly deriding, Mick was leaving himself open to ridicule – especially from Johnny Thunders and the other Heartbreakers – as a meal without meat was anathema to most Americans.

The staff at the Italian restaurant they'd decided on were equally bemused at finding themselves waiting on a vegetarian – so much so, they dropped their faux-Italian accents. All they could offer the Jones was something from the fish menu, and though far from thrilled, Mick eventually settled for the grilled trout. However, when the food arrived he was horrified to find the trout was still in possession of its head; its glazed eye staring accusingly up at him from the plate. Mick understandably insisted that the dish be taken away and the trout's head removed. The waiter did as instructed, only to return again a minute or so later with the freshly severed head still nestled amid the garnish with a solitary lettuce leaf separating it from its body, and though Mick and Glen were both starving by this point, they got up and walked out.

As if there weren't enough problems on the tour, though neither Glen nor Mick realised it at the time, their closeness was causing friction in both bands, largely because Johnny Rotten and Joe Strummer were barely on speaking terms.

Though 20 years have passed since Leeds Polytechnic was promoted up the educational ladder to university status – the Leeds Metropolitan University, no less – it will forever be synonymous with the Sex Pistols for staging the default opening date of the Anarchy Tour. It also has the dual distinction of not only being the sole site still standing where the bands actually got to tread the boards during the tour, but also the only venue to stage a show featuring all four groups.

On the afternoon of the show, while the four bands and their entourages gathered in the polytechnic's sports hall during the soundcheck, a Yorkshire Television film crew was interviewing the polytechnic's bemused chancellor, Dr. Nashenter:

Interviewer: *Dr. Nashenter, how come that the Sex Pistols, with their extraordinary reputation, are playing at Leeds Polytechnic tonight when they've been banned virtually everywhere else?*

Dr. Nashenter: The only people who can really answer that is the Student Union, which organises these kind of events. You may think this odd, and there are times when I do, but by the constitution and the articles of the government of the polytechnic, I have no authority over what the Student Union… I mean, it is very carefully controlled, I may say, but the Student Union is an autonomous body which handles its own affairs and its own money. So, if they want these people here – who, ah, about whom I know nothing, but they sound to me, you know, as puerile and disgusting as most of these people do.

Interviewer: *By some extraordinary coincidence, you're performing the Messiah in Leeds Polytechnic tonight, also.*

Dr. Nashenter: Yes, that actually is strange and even more odd is, ah, such financing as the *Messiah* needs, it does in fact come from the Student Union. But the *Messiah's* being performed actually in another building in the polytechnic, and the staff and students, there's quite a big crowd, about 80 or 90. It's been rehearsing all yesterday afternoon, and...ah, it will do actually rather a good performance of most of the *Messiah*. The extraordinary thing is that I suppose by the evening, there will be two great sort of streams of prayer going out from Leeds Polytechnic. One, upwards, and the other, I suppose, down or maybe sideways.

Although it was too late to do anything about it at this juncture, Dr. Nashenter's unassuming comment about the polytechnic's Student Union being an "autonomous body which handles its own affairs and money" certainly calls into question the high-handed actions of Nashenter's East Anglian counterpart, Frank Thistlewaite. If the good Dr Nashenter was powerless to cancel the Sex Pistols' show, Thistlewaite must have surely been in breach of his mandate in riding roughshod over Norwich University's own student body.

Having satisfied themselves with the polytechnic's chancellor, the Yorkshire TV film crew then headed over to the Dragonara Hotel intent on interviewing the Pistols. Malcolm, however, had other ideas, and insisted that while he was happy for the group to appear on camera, he would be the only one doing any talking. And while this wasn't exactly what the film crew had in mind, interviewing Malcolm was better than no interview at all. The interview was conducted in one of the Dragonara's function rooms with Malcolm sitting at a table while the Sex Pistols – already changed into their stage gear – were loitering in the background looking suitably bored for the camera:

Interviewer: *People say that you're sick on stage, you spit at the audience, and so on. I mean, how can this be a good example to children?*

Malcolm: Well, people are sick everywhere. People are sick and fed up of this country telling them what to do.

Interviewer: *But not getting paid for it.*

Malcolm: Pardon?

Interviewer: *But not getting paid for putting on that sort of show.*

Malcolm: Well, nor are we. We ain't even being allowed to play.

Steve: It makes you sick, dunnit?

Interviewer: *In fact, you're acting as spokesman for the group today.*

Malcolm: Yes, indeed.

Interviewer: *Have you stopped them from talking to us?*

Malcolm: Not at all. They're just so disgusted by our having to answer so many questions about something so simple.

Interviewer: *Do you feel the publicity following the Thames Television interview has been damaging? Or do you think it has helped you?*

Malcolm: I don't think it's been damaging; far from it. Whether it's helping us is another matter. The point is people are getting very disappointed by the fact that kids who have bought and purchased tickets of these venues that are now being cancelled, are having to travel further afield to see the group of their choice.

Interviewer: *What sort of future do you see a*

group like the Sex Pistols having? A long future?

Malcolm: I do indeed. I think… I think at least they're standing up and, um, not tolerating any form of censorship in their act. And in that sense it's exhilarating a lot of young kids around the country, and giving them confidence to stand up and say what they want.

Interviewer: *Would you not agree in any way, that the packed halls which you're playing to, wherever you get a concert launched, are entirely due to the bad publicity that you've had?*

Malcolm: Not at all. Many dates were sold out long before.

Interviewer: *How do you react to the reputation that your group is the most revolting in the country?*

Malcolm: Look, our group is creating a generation gap for the first time in five years in this country and a lot of people are feeling genuinely threatened by it. If the kids wanna buy the record it's called 'Anarchy In The UK', it's out in the shops and they can make their own decisions. And their mothers, they can ask them to equally make their decision about it. And if the mothers care anything about their young kids they should be up in arms about having councillors – of which they are paying taxes to – to tell, to be angry with them about not allowing their kids to go in the concerts and making their own choice.

Interviewer: *But let's be absolutely frank about it. Do they [pointing across to the group] enjoy being known as a revolting group?*

Malcolm: Every young kid is, is ah… is ah… finds enjoyment in being known as revolting.

Despite Bernard Rhodes' repeated protestations about his group being better than The Damned, it was The Clash who finally got the Anarchy Tour underway. As stand-in drummer Rob Harper wasn't one of the gang, he was allowed to wear whatever he pleased, but Joe, Mick, and Paul were all dressed to impress. Joe took to the polytechnic's stage sporting a green shirt emblazoned with the stencilled slogan 'Social Security £9.70' – his weekly dole stipend – while Mick and Paul both wore their customised Jackson Pollock-esque paint-splattered shirts, replete with matching armbands.

Though the Sex Pistols were the headliners, and the name on everyone's lips, it fell to The Clash to give the Leeds crowd a taste of what punk rock was all about. However, neither Joe's opening Orwellian gambit about his having spent the previous 48 hours thinking Big Brother was really upon them, nor the group's opening number, 'White Riot', failed to make much of an impression on the largely apathetic audience. Indeed, had it not been for the on-going media circus surrounding the Pistols many of those gathered in the hall would have surely opted to spend the bleak Monday evening ensconced in the Student's Union bar, or sat at home watching *Coronation Street*.

Someone who was suitably impressed with what was happening on stage, however, was *NME*'s young gunslinger Tony Parsons, who opined: "Clash opened up the evening with a great set. Hard, committed, loud, brash, violent rock music. I got the impression they expected nothing from the audience or anybody else, so they didn't have the same problems as the Pistols."

While The Clash weren't expecting any favours from the audience, neither were they willing to give any quarter in return. With Harper providing a rock-steady beat, the "three Eddie Cochrans" – as the drummer would later liken Joe, Mick and Paul's stage act – gave vent to their pent-up frustrations at having spent the last few days either confined to their hotel room or traversing Britain's motorways, with a blistering 30-minute set that included 'I'm So Bored With The USA', 'Career Opportunities', 'Protex Blue', 'Deny', 'Cheat', 'Janie Jones' and their apocalyptic curtain-closer '1977'.

The consenting opinion of those who witnessed The Clash's live debut in Sheffield six months earlier was that their return visit to Yorkshire was rather well received. "I was a Brummie, at Leeds Uni, in my second year," Terry McCarthy recounted for BBC Yorkshire's 30th anniversary feature on the Anarchy Tour in December 2006. "Me and my girlfriend went along after the Bill Grundy thing and after the national press outrage. Prior to the gig, a guy from Watford told us, 'Forget the Pistols – watch out for The Clash'. I was never subsequently particularly into punk but have since become a huge fan of The Clash."

Another student who'd found the hors d'oeuvres more appetising than the main course was Nick Haigh: "It was the support bands that were the best bands, especially The Clash who really got you pogoing! The Sex Pistols were a bit of a let down. I remember it as a very tense atmosphere in the hall," he told Yorkshire TV. "Best song on the night was 'White Riot' by The Clash and 'New Rose' by The Damned. I had originally gone to see Johnny Thunders who used to be in the New York Dolls, this being a good chance to see one of my heroes."

By the time Nick's hero came out on stage the audience had swollen considerably in both number and volume, as those preferring to remain ensconced in the adjoining Student Union rather than sample what The Clash had to offer, weren't going to pass up the chance to see punk rock New York style – and The Heartbreakers were not about to disappoint. The elegantly wasted Thunders was the epitome of guttersnipe cool, and he and Jerry held an unassailable advantage over the English bands in that they could draw on years of stage experience from their time with the Dolls. Thunders' only half-joked query as to whether there were "any junkies in the house" served as the perfect prefix for their opening number, 'Born To Lose', and while his leather motorcycle jacket, drainpipe jeans, and winkle-picker boots ensemble risked being a little clichéd on New York's Lower East Side, it brought a little piece of rock'n'roll celebrity to warm the hearts on a cold December Monday evening in West Riding.

The sound was slightly distorted due to Goodman being slightly worse for wear – having spent most of the afternoon getting wasted with Roadent and Heartbreakers' roadie/guitar tech-cum-soundman, Keeth Paul[2*] – but The Heartbreakers were sufficiently long of tooth to know how to work a lethargic crowd, effortlessly building up momentum with songs like 'Baby Talk', 'All By Myself', 'Get Off The Phone', 'One Track Mind', and 'Pirate Love', before bringing their set to a climax with the heavily drug-referenced 'Chinese Rocks'. If Dave Goodman is to be believed, however, The Heartbreakers only talked the talk when on stage:

"The Heartbreakers posed around with fags hanging out of their mouths, looking like junkies, and they definitely liked a bit of blow," he told *Mojo* in 1996. "But when they'd come off stage all they wanted was a cup of tea."

With little or no fanfare The Damned walked out on stage and launched into 'New Rose', which aside from being their debut single was undoubtedly the most explosive song in their canon. The pasty-faced, kohl-eyed Dave Vanian was again decked out head-to-foot in Bela Lugosi-black and prowled about the stage like an undernourished ghoul. At the song's end – as if further proof was needed that he was anything but sagacious – the beshaded Captain

---

2   In 1978, Paul would find himself equal billing with Jerry Nolan
      when the pair played and recorded together on the single
      'When I'm Bored' by female singing duo Snatch.

Sensible sprayed those gathered at the front with lager, which in turn provoked a retaliatory barrage of beer and spittle from those caught in the deluge. Although the beer fight was meant as a harmless bit of fun and an attempt to liven up the proceedings, the Captain was inadvertently playing into the hands of the handful of journalists standing at the bar to the rear of the hall.

Under Brian James' guidance The Damned had come on leaps and bounds since making their shaky debut supporting the Sex Pistols at the 100 Club back in July, and the fusion of new material such as 'Neat, Neat, Neat', 'Problem Child', 'Stretcher Case' and a souped-up version of The Beatles' 1965 UK number one 'Help' – which was also the accompanying B-side to 'New Rose' – together with their kitsch stage act, brought a favourable response from the crowd.

Mike Thorne was equally impressed: "With the tension building I had to follow the bandwagon to Leeds," he said on the Stereosociety website. "Although permission had been debated at length in the mayoral chambers, the first gig of the tour had been given the go-ahead, and would be a resounding success. I vaguely remember the Pistols' performance – although it was The Damned who were the standouts that night."

Surprisingly, given that he was something of a Damned aficionado, Tony Parsons confessed to feeling somewhat underwhelmed by the performance as his subsequent missive to *NME* HQ in London reveals: "I had eagerly awaited the appearance of the dole queue supremos, but they turned out to be the biggest disappointment on the night." Having put their "lacklustre performance" down to the frustrations of the cancelled gigs, their having to play a truncated set, as well as what he furtively describes as "behind the scenes problems", he goes on to tellingly add that the group won't need telling that their performance was below par before then assuring the readers that Rat, Brian, Dave and the Cap would soon be back on top form and "playing at the heights we expect from them and they expect from themselves."

Though Parsons' review hints at backstage backbiting between the bands, as The Damned departed the beer-sodden stage they were blithely unaware that "behind the scenes" Malcolm had decided to expel them from the tour in retaliation for their having supposedly consented to the demands of Derby's Leisure Committee. Whilst the Captain and Co. had been out front entertaining the crowd, Rick Rodgers had been backstage pleading with Malcolm to accept that their acquiescence had come during the time frame when it had seemed Malcolm was giving in to the council's demands. Seeing as their having to travel separately from the other bands was due to his ongoing spat with Jake Riviera, they could hardly be blamed for being incommunicado when the coach unexpectedly departed for Leeds. However, Rodgers' pleas fell on deaf ears, and The Damned had little option other than return to London.

"The Damned released 'New Rose' before the Pistols had put anything out, and there was a row between us over punk solidarity," Joe Strummer said in *The Clash*. "It was the Pistols who were banned from playing because they'd sworn on television and we weren't going to play anywhere the Pistols couldn't. The Damned decided to play anyway and that caused a rift. Soon everyone was at each other's throats."

Despite the three support acts having done their all to liven up the proceedings, the Sex Pistols walked out on stage to somewhat stilted applause and some derogatory heckling. John – looking like an "amphetamine corpse from a Sunday gutter press wet dream" in his bondage trousers, vermillion-red SEX waistcoat, white shirt and skinny black tie, ambled up to the microphone – can of Tartan Ale in hand – and stood surveying the audience while casually running his fingers through his ginger-dyed spiked coiffure. He continued to stare trance-like into the void whilst Steve busied himself tuning his Les Paul, and it was only when the guitarist – sporting a decidedly un-punk ensemble of leather biker's jacket and leather jeans – started grinding out the spine-tingling G/F/Em/D/C intro to 'Anarchy In The UK' that he was suddenly galvanised into action. The self-professed anti-Christ and anarchist didn't know what he wanted, but he knew where to get it. And he wanted to destroy the passer-by...

"Something thrown from the audience hits him [Rotten] full in the face," reported *NME*. "Rotten glares at the person who did it, lips drawn back over decaying teeth. 'Don't give me your shit,' he snarls,

'because we don't mess…This first number's dedicated to a Leeds Councillor [Bill Hudson], Bill Grundy and the Queen – fuck ya.' And straight into a searing rendition of the Blank Generation anthem 'Anarchy In The UK', done even better than the single which just charted at 43 [in the *NME* chart]. The rhythm section of Cook on drums and Matlock on bass are tighter than tomorrow, fully complimenting the pneumatic guitar work of Steve Jones and Rotten's deranged dementoid vocal."

At the song's finale John grabbed up another can of Tartan Ale and – ignoring the heckling and catcalls – raised it aloft in acknowledgement of the small coterie of fans who were in ecstasy at finally being able to see their heroes in the flesh, and who had braved the weather regardless of the group's newfound infamy. He'd been looking forward to engaging his supposedly educated audience in a bout of verbal sparring, and he was just getting into his stride when Steve – having now discarded his leather jacket to reveal another of Malcolm's and Vivienne's SEX creations, a white string/black mohair jumper with hangman's noose string collar – powered into the single's B-side 'I Wanna Be Me'. The song, which perhaps more than any other song of the era encapsulated punk's plea for individuality, has featured in

the Sex Pistols' set since the summer, and as with everywhere else they played outside of London, the break towards the end catches out most of the audience.

"You ain't wrecking the place," John spat derisively as the song comes to an end. "The *News Of The World* will be really disappointed!"

The taunt got a reaction from certain sections of the audience, but whereas most bands at the polytechnic are happy to play, get laid and come back another day, the Sex Pistols – especially John – thrive on audience interaction. So when their cover of '(I'm Not Your) Steppin' Stone' – which was first recorded by Paul Revere & The Raiders in 1966, before giving The Monkees a surprise US Top 20 hit that same year – failed to win the crowd over, John finally lost patience and let them know that if they don't like what's on offer then they "know where the exit is".

Next up was 'No Future', with its much-vaunted inflammatory lyrics about the Queen. Given that Malcolm had already alerted Fleet Street to the as-yet-unreleased song, it's a wonder why the reporters present – one of whom was thrilled to get "two fucks and a shit from Johnny Rotten" – made no mention of the Sex Pistols supposedly calling Her Majesty a "moron" in her Silver Jubilee year. Similarly, given the adverse publicity surrounding the Pistols' every move, it's also a wonder why Lanchester Polytechnic's Student Union – having refused to pay the group on account of the "fascist" lyrical content of 'No Future' just a few days prior to their appearance on *Today* – didn't grab their Warholian 15 minutes of fame by alerting Fleet Street to the song?

'Substitute' followed but, again, the cheers from those there to see the group were lost in the vast, high-ceilinged auditorium. Seeing those gathered at the front continuing their "so-show-us-what-you've-got" attitude, John derided the audience by asking if their continued show of apathy was due to the local

council having perhaps imposed a ban on handclapping? This jibe brought yet another barrage of catcalls, with one wag shouting out for the New York Dolls. However, instead of launching into 'New York', with its acerbic put-down of the New York music scene – and the New York Dolls in particular – the group stuck to the script by launching into 'Pretty Vacant', before bringing their set to an end with 'Problems'. Although they returned for an encore, a plod through The Small Faces' debut single 'Whatcha Gonna Do About It' and The Stooges' classic 'No Fun', there was a sense of anti-climax and the Pistols disappeared from the stage for good.

It's ironic, given that this was the only occasion that all four bands on the Anarchy Tour billing graced the same stage, that "No Fun" should be the general consensus amongst those filing out of the hall. Then again, how many of those left unmoved by the musical fare – particularly the Pistols' performance – would have ventured out had it not been for the events of five days earlier?

"The truth is that outside of London we didn't have much of a fan base," Glen opined in *I Was A Teenage Sex Pistol*. "This was the tour that was going to carry the punk thing out of London, but in Leeds most of the kids had come out of prurient interest, generated mostly by the Grundy thing."

Former *Yorkshire Evening Post* journalist Howard Corry recalled for BBC Yorkshire about the night he went along to Leeds Poly to capture the mood for the *YEP*'s readers, whilst under strict instructions from his editor to "remember that the majority of those readers were not taking too kindly to foul-mouthed, bin-bag clad, spitting, anarchical yobs with safety pins through their ears and chains dangling from their noses!"

Having made mention of how a sizeable contingent of the audience had fled the hall long before the end, and how those who remained did so only to jeer the Sex Pistols, Corry goes on to recall the music being "amplified to distortion [whereby] it was hard to distinguish chord changes – any of the three would have done! – let alone individual notes." He also remembers the lyrics being "screamed at such a volume that again it was hard to pick out more than a word at a time."

Corry's *Post* colleague, photographer Steve Riding, was equally taken aback by the spectacle: "All I can remember was everybody was jumping up and down, spitting and throwing beer and generally causing mayhem," he said. "I'd done other bands like Bowie and Roxy Music, but I'd never seen anything like this in my life. I thought, 'Christ, what's this all about?'"

Another photographer left wondering what all the fuss concerning the Sex Pistols was about was Robert Matheu: "I was dragged to this show by some friends on my first visit to the UK, and I hated them," the American said of the Pistols in *Punk 365*. "I hadn't heard any of their stuff yet, and I was just starting to listen to The Ramones. And being a huge fan of The Stooges and MC5, I really didn't understand the anger that was projected at the gig."

Even *Record Mirror* gave the Pistols a thumbs-down. Beneath the headline: 'Pistols Fire Big Blank', it reported: "The Sex Pistols were met with jeers on the first night of their troubled-hit tour, at Leeds Polytechnic.

"Scores of fans walked out and lead singer, Johnny Rotten yelled at those that remained: 'You're just a load of dummies – you're dead!' But in fact it was punk rock that was in danger of dying. The group was met with hoots of laughter as they tried in vain to whip up excitement.

"They kicked off with a swipe at Bill Grundy and the Queen, and then they broke their manager's orders by using a string of obscenities. Their music was predictably loud and crude but alas it was also dismally disappointing – relentless and unimaginative.

"When the group waited among cat-calls to do an encore, Rotten turned on his fans and snarled: 'Has the council banned you from clapping? If you don't like us, you know where the exit is.'

"The Pistols, who have stirred up so much controversy with their four-letter tirade on TV, were left dejected and antagonistic by their brusque departure. Certainly the show 'Anarchy In The UK' left much to be desired and the unanimous opinion of the northern fans was, 'What a load of rubbish!'"

We Are Ruled
By None

> "We were public enemy No. 1, but also national heroes to a lot of people as well, you know, to a lot of kids. They loved it. They loved what we were doing especially – it split, really split down the middle. It was one group of people that totally hated us and wanted to kill us, and then there was another group who were totally behind us and everything we were doing, the music, the image, the whole thing, the subculture, you know – everything."
>
> **Paul Cook**

The Anarchy Tour had finally passed "Go", and collected a much-needed £698 in takings. However, the following evening's replacement show at Sheffield University still hung in the balance and Wednesday – somewhat ironically under the circumstances – had been designated a rest day so as to allow the bands to recharge their batteries. Unless Malcolm could find someone willing to provide sanctuary from the political storm then the money accrued from the Leeds show would be frittered away on everyday living expenses before the next confirmed show at Manchester's Electric Circus. As far as the musicians were concerned – with the obvious exception of The Damned – the polytechnic show had been a good night all round, but any hopes of their being allowed to celebrate in style in the Dragonara's bar were dashed on finding the hotel's foyer once again teeming with reporters. Yet again everyone had to settle for making merry in one of the rooms.

"The major memory of the tour is boredom," wrote Glen in *I Was A Teenage Sex Pistol*. "We spent most of our time hanging around hotels, just waiting. As gig after gig was cancelled, we had no idea of what would happen next – or what was happening at the time. We'd just sit around hoping they could find somewhere we would be allowed to play. That's probably why the whole tour is a bit of a blur in my mind."

As luck would have it, Glen and Mick's room was the one designated as 'Party Central', so while the Dragonara's beleaguered night porters were kept busy ferrying up a steady supply of drinks, Dave Goodman – having procured a sizeable lump of Lebanese black for the tour – took it on himself to set the ambience by rolling one of his special 12" on-the-road spliffs. Not everyone was interested in partaking, which meant the foot-long spliff should have gone around the room many times over, but John, who considered himself something of a cannabis connoisseur due to his friendship with soon-to-be-resident Roxy DJ Don Letts, wasn't only content with hogging the headlines, and refused to pass the kouchie on his left-hand side. Indeed, the spliff had to be prised from his grasp and his protestations at being manhandled by his sidemen and other "lesser beings" were so vociferous that he woke those trying to get some sleep in the adjoining rooms.

One of these happened to be Jerry Nolan, who was so incensed at being wrenched from his drug-induced slumber that he kicked a sizeable hole in Glen and Mick's door while trying to get at Rotten. "Two weeks before we had left New York, I'd gone on a methadone programme to try to clean up. But I didn't know how heavy methadone was," the drummer said of his chronic condition during the Anarchy Tour in *Please Kill Me*. "They started me on 30 milligrams, got me up to 50, taking it for two or three weeks. And I was still shooting heroin."

While their respective charges were partying the night away, Malcolm, Bernard, and Leee were also burning the midnight oil, busy revising the tour schedule. Malcolm had summoned The Clash and Heartbreakers' managers to his room to inform them of his decision to throw The Damned off the tour over their perceived insubordination in agreeing to perform in front of Derby's Leisure Committee.

According to Glen's autobiographical recollections, while The Damned had been out on the polytechnic stage Malcolm had been busy playing devil's advocate by surreptitiously asking for opinions as to The Damned's worth. "Don't you think they spoil it?" he'd asked Glen. "The Clash and The Heartbreakers are great, but The Damned are awful, they're bringing it all down."

While Bernard and Leee both knew that Malcolm's case for dismissing The Damned from the tour was thinner than a politician's election campaign promise, neither raised any objections to Malcolm's high-handed decision. Bernard's antipathy towards The Damned was hardly a guarded secret and he'd been objecting to his group having to open the proceedings ever since Malcolm had invited The Clash onto the tour, and while Leee had nothing against The Damned per se, eliminating them from the billing meant that The Heartbreakers would get a larger percentage of the door takings.

"My boys wouldn't audition for some jumped-up council, not in a million years. We wouldn't go against the grain. We were in it together," he recalled. "So we went along with the Sex Pistols and The Clash, and The Damned went back to playing in dreary pubs in north London. The rest, as they say, is history. The Damned were all very nice boys, though."

An official statement was released by Stiff Records: "Following reports that the Sex Pistols have fired The Damned due to various oblique reasons, confirmation is given that The Damned will not be appearing at any more of the Pistols' dates. No further dates are planned at the present for the group. They will instead return to the studio to complete their first album with producer Nick Lowe, which Stiff plan to release early in the New Year."

Contrary to popular belief, rather than sack The Damned outright, Malcolm — knowing it was a humiliation they would not suffer — forced the group into tending their resignation, as Brian James explained in *The Clash: Last Gang In Town*: "Malcolm suddenly shoved us to the bottom of the bill, and it was because Bernard was in cahoots with him. Malcolm never did anything for Bernard unless it suited his own purposes, and his juggling with the running order was intended solely to humiliate The Damned and provoke a confrontation, which it did."

"When they [Sex Pistols] asked us to do the tour, they needed us. We had been gigging a lot, so we had a reputation and a following," Captain Sensible told *Mojo*. "After the Grundy incident, the Pistols were the big deal and really didn't need us to help sell tickets, so they dumped us."

On the Tuesday the coach then headed back down the M1 to Sheffield. Whether the university's faculty would have followed Dr Nashenter's line in allowing the Student Union to make their own decision re the concert was rendered something of a moot point when news came through that the van carrying the PA – having inexplicably taken a wrong turning en route to Sheffield – had broken down somewhere in Berkshire. So while everyone else sought refuge in the university's subsidised Student Union bar, Malcolm spent a futile hour on the phone trying to cajole Dr. Nashenter into booking a second show at Leeds Polytechnic for the following evening.

Even if Nashenter had given his blessing for a second date, playing two shows within three days in the same city was surely tempting fate as the first show had been far from a sell-out – and playing to a near-empty hall would only provide the press with more negative ammunition. Another factor to consider was that with Malcolm having unceremoniously expelled The Damned, there was no guarantee that the polytechnic's cash-conscious students would be willing to hand over the same admission price for a truncated billing. Then there were the remaining dates to consider – or at least those that were assured of escaping third-party intervention. For while Malcolm had long-since been assured by the promoter in Manchester that Thursday night's show at the Electric Circus would definitely go ahead as scheduled, those fans that had already purchased tickets would have done so expecting to see The Damned on the bill.

That Manchester would welcome the Sex Pistols with open arms was never in question seeing as the group had already made three successful forays to the city, but the confusing events of the last few days paled into insignificance compared to the bombshell awaiting them on their arrival at the Midland Hotel where they were given the news that EMI would be withdrawing support and finance for the tour. Ignoring the reporters that were besieging him for a response, Malcolm went straight up to his room. Having first conferred with lawyer Stephen Fisher, he'd called Leslie Hill who informed him the story was indeed true. Hill then reiterated what he'd already told Fisher, in that he himself had not been party to EMI's decision before advising Malcolm it was perhaps time to cut his losses and return to London.

Returning to London had seemed the only sensible course of action, but his next call to Sophie had changed everything for a sizeable cheque from EMI Publishing had fortuitously arrived at Dryden Chambers that very morning. Bolstered by the unexpected influx of cash he decided to thumb his nose at Manchester Square and carry on regardless. As long as the tour continued then so would the publicity, and publicity – be it good or bad – meant more record sales which was the whole point of the tour. Having again conferred with Fisher, he'd then put in a second call to Leslie Hill to inform him of his decision to carry on with the tour.

There was a certain irony in the fact that EMI's money would allow Malcolm to keep the show on the road and this wasn't lost on Hill but, like Paul Watts, he had to accept that no matter how distasteful he found the Pistols personally, the group was signed to EMI. "There were a number of strands running through my head," he explained in *Sex Pistols: 90 Days At EMI*. "Personally, I didn't like what they were doing, but running a record company meant this was what could happen and I was prepared to defend them [the company] against the group's attitude."

What made the situation all the more distasteful for Hill was that he had found himself in Fleet Street's firing line over EMI's perceived lack of contrition regarding the Sex Pistols' behaviour on the *Today* show. Someone with an axe to grind on EMI's corporate side had wilfully supplied the *Daily Mail* with Hill's address and home telephone number. The *Mail*'s scurrilous reporters had descended on Hill's home in leafy Gerrards Cross, Buckinghamshire, and having canvassed Hill's bemused neighbours about the "evil man behind the Sex Pistols", they arrived on Hill's doorstep. And when Hill's wife refused to come to the door the hacks literally set up camp in the front garden.

To Malcolm, the possibility of EMI dropping the Sex Pistols was mortifying in itself, but if the label instead chose to sit on the group – as it was perfectly entitled to do under the contract – whilst simultaneously refusing to release any more records, it would effectively reduce the group to a live act. The mere thought of the Pistols being shackled at a time when The Damned were making plans to record their debut album for Stiff Records was simply more than he could bear.

Hill must have sensed from Malcolm's tone that he was close to breaking point, and tried to sooth his frayed nerves by confirming his continued personal support for the Pistols. He also promised that he would do everything within his power to ensure that the group went into the studio with Mike Thorne as soon as touring commitments allowed. Hill then proceeded to give Malcolm an outline of the brief he'd presented to the AGM which, aside from outlining said plans for the group to go into the studio with Thorne to record a second single scheduled for release in early February 1977, followed by an album with a scheduled release date for either March or April 1977, also included mention of Graham Fletcher's appointment as EMI's on-the-spot representative for the remainder of the tour. Hill had attempted to further assuage Sir John Read and the rest of the board by bringing attention to the undeniable fact that – regardless of what was being reported in the tabloids – the Sex Pistols had visited Manchester Square on at least 10 separate occasions within the previous three weeks and that nothing untoward had ever occurred.

In his memo to Sir John Read on December 6, he wrote: "Regarding the supposed problems at the Dragon Noria [sic] Hotel in Leeds, I understand that the hotel was only concerned about the fact that there were so many press men in the lobby being a nuisance. In the absence of any of our representatives and indeed the Manager of the Group himself, the Group were asked to destroy a plant for the benefit of a *Daily Express* photographer. This they did and then paid the £25 cost of the plant to the hotel without any trouble of any kind."

Hill also attempted to play down the plant-throwing incident at the Dragonara Hotel by saying the whole sorry episode had been wilfully engineered by a reporter from the *Daily Mirror*, and that the Dragonara manager's chief concern had not been about the Sex Pistols' supposed reputation, but rather the behaviour of the reporters who were constantly hanging around the lobby causing a nuisance to his other guests. The EMI Records MD concluded his brief by exonerating Eric Hall, whose decision it had been to book the Pistols onto the *Today* show, while attaching sales figures to date for 'Anarchy In The

UK' in the hope that they might help sway any corporate decision on the label's future relationship with the group.

Nick Mobbs had also gone on record as saying he felt that the violence aspect surrounding the Pistols had been blown up out of all proportion, and that it was certain sections of the group's audience who were responsible for the purported flare-ups at their concerts; although he had been willing to concede that such instances could rub off on the performers themselves.

"There was a rather complicated administrative arrangement in the way EMI handled the Pistols," Frank Brunger explained to *Mojo*. "The Pistols had always said they wanted to be with a label which had no identity. Having both Cilla Black and Queen on the label, EMI apparently qualified. McLaren, however, was astute enough to have insisted that they should be worked by the Harvest team, because we understood the marketing of cult bands."

Although keen to stress that he wasn't looking to lead a crusade against the Pistols, Sir John Read was equally determined to do what was right by the EMI Corporation as a whole. As its chairman he believed it was his job to safeguard EMI's interests as well as protect its share price on the financial market; in other words, he wasn't about to allow a smutty pop group to besmirch the company's reputation.

Despite EMI Records' worldwide music business having reported profits of more than £27million in the financial year 1975-76 (some 42 per cent of the company's total profit), Read and the rest of the sixth-floor suits holding sway in the boardroom wouldn't have known a Beatle from a Bay City Roller if he'd tripped over one, and were of the collective opinion that defence was the jewel in EMI's corporate crown. Having said that, Read was painfully aware that the AGM was open to investors and shareholders, who would no doubt want to voice their concerns – as well as demand answers as to what EMI intended to do with regard to the Sex Pistols – and so for the first time in EMI's proud and distinguished history, its chairman was forced to discuss the merits of a pop group.

So it was that Sir John Read, as Chairman of EMI, found himself obliged to comment on the issue. His statement of December 7 read as follows: "The EMI Group of companies operates internationally and has been engaged in the recorded music business for over 75 years.

"During recent years in particular, the question of acceptable content of records has been increasingly difficult to resolve – largely due to the increasing degree of permissiveness accepted by society as a whole, both in the UK and overseas. Throughout its history as a recording company, EMI has always sought to behave within contemporary limits of decency and good taste – taking into account not only the traditional rigid conventions of one section of society, but also the increasingly liberal attitudes of other, perhaps larger, sections of society at any given time.

"Today, there is in EMI's experience, not only an overwhelming sense of permissiveness – as demonstrated by the content of books, newspapers, and magazines, as well as records and films – but also a good deal of questioning by various sections of society, both young and old, e.g. what is decent or in good taste compared to the attitude of, say, 20 or even 10 years ago?

"It is against the present-day social background that EMI has to make value judgements about the content of records in particular. EMI has on a number of occasions, taken steps totally to ban individual records, and similarly to ban record sleeves, or posters, or other promotional material which it believed would be offensive.

"The Sex Pistols' incident, which started with a disgraceful interview given by this young pop group on Thames TV, last week, has been followed by a vast amount of newspaper coverage in the last few days.

Sex Pistols is a pop group devoted to a new form of music known as 'punk rock'. It was contracted for recording purposes by EMI Records Ltd in October, 1976 – an unknown group offering some promise, in the view of our recording executive, like many other pop groups of different kinds that we have signed. In this context, it must be remembered that the recording industry has signed many pop groups, initially controversial, who have in the fullness of time become wholly acceptable and contributed greatly to the development of modern music.

"Sex Pistols have acquired a reputation for aggressive behaviour which they have certainly demonstrated in public. There is no excuse for this. Our recording company's experience of working with the group, however, is satisfactory. Sex Pistols is the only 'punk rock' group that EMI Records currently has under direct recording contract and whether EMI does in fact release any more of their records will have to be very carefully considered. I need hardly add that we shall do everything we can to restrain their public behaviour, although this is a matter over which we have no real control.

"Similarly, EMI will review its general guidelines regarding the content of pop records. Who is to decide what is objectionable or unobjectionable to the public at large today? When anyone sits down to consider seriously this problem, it will be found that there are widely differing attitudes between people of all ages and all walks of life as to what can be shown, or spoken, or sung.

"Our view within EMI is that we should seek to discourage records that are likely to give offence to the majority of people. In this context, changing public attitudes have to be taken into account.

"EMI should not set itself up as a public censor, but it does seek to encourage restraint.

"The board of EMI certainly takes seriously the need to do everything possible to encourage the raising of standards in music and entertainment."

Such moral posturing was, of course, only to be expected as no one with a vested interest in EMI wanted a repeat of the previous Wednesday. Yet while making it clear that EMI would do everything within its power to restrain the group's public behaviour, Read readily admitted this was an area in which the company had no real control. Though he was careful to avoid making any mention of terminating the Sex Pistols' two-month old contract, neither did he appear willing to confirm the label would be standing by the group. However, for those who knew how to read between the corporate lines, Read's ambiguous comment as to whether EMI would release any more Sex Pistols records left little doubt that the group's days at the label were numbered.

This, at least, was the line taken by *Record Mirror* which headlined its story 'EMI To Drop Pistols?' "Following the Sex Pistols' controversial TV appearance last week EMI are debating whether to sever their connections with the group and their planned UK tour has been drastically reduced

"Answering a call by shareholders to end the Pistols' contract Sir John Read, EMI Chairman said at a meeting last night (Tuesday): "They are the only punk rock group under direct recording contract to us. Whether EMI release any more of their records will have to be very carefully considered."

"Told of the latest upset during their performance in Leeds, in which they insulted the Queen, Sir John added: 'This will obviously influence the board's decision on whether or not the contract was ended.'"

It was left to *NME* to rally the troops: "The kids played at revolution in the Sixties and failed because they thought they could change the world without damaging people. Everyone can see now that if no one gets hurt then nothing is going to change. The [Sex] Pistols are coming to your town soon; are you going to make sure they're allowed to partake in the fable of free speech of this democratic country or are you going to sink back into stupor for another decade?

"The fascists are in the council chambers, not on the stage."

CHAPTER TEN

A Day At The Circus

> "Then it was that whole thing like being banned in this town and being banned in that town. And it really wasn't about us playing any more, it was about this controversy, like we were throwing up onstage and spitting and… the *Sun*, the *Daily Mirror*, and all of them papers, just took it a lot further for selling papers' sake – for shock value… they, you know, they started inventing things they thought people wanted to read. To sell papers, I mean, we really wasn't as outrageous as they were saying at all."
>
> Steve Jones

That the Electric Circus Show was the only occasion following The Damned's expulsion from the Anarchy Tour that Malcolm thought to invite a replacement act onto the bill goes some way to showing the regard he held for Buzzcocks. While some might argue that he did so simply to repay the Mancunians for orchestrating the two Sex Pistols dates at Manchester's Lesser Free Trade Hall during the summer, he had already repaid those particular favours by inviting Buzzcocks onto the billing for both the Screen On The Green Midnite Special, and the 100 Club Punk Festival – and as everyone knows, Malcolm wasn't known for his altruism. Then again, of course, had it not been for Neil Spencer's *NME* review of the Pistols' chaotic showing at the Marquee back in February, there might never have been a Buzzcocks – at least not in the guise the world came to know and love.

While there's no arguing that Spencer's "Don't look over your shoulder" headline caught the eye of many a disillusioned youth up and down the country, the vast majority probably did nothing more than make a mental note to keep an eye on *NME*'s gig guide for when the Pistols might come within train fare range of their town. Howard Trafford and Pete McNeish, however, weren't prepared to wait and headed up to London to find out more.

"*New Musical Express* came out in Bolton and I kind of flipped through it, gave it to Pete," Howard Devoto said in David Nolan's book *I Swear I Was There*. "He looked through it and handed it back to me and said, 'Did you see that?' [Spencer's February 21 review of the Sex Pistols' Marquee show] The Stooges were mentioned in there and 'We're not into music, we're into chaos.' Well it clicked with me."

At the time of their life-changing odyssey, Howard and Pete were aspiring musicians enrolled at the Bolton Institute of Technology. Howard was floundering in the second year of a Humanities degree when, seeking a distraction from his academic failings, he stuck a "Musicians Wanted" ad on the college's notice board. "I mentioned the name of The Stooges in the advert and 'Sister Ray' (Velvet Underground) and stuff like this," Howard recalled. "He [Pete] wasn't the only person [who answered that advert], but he was the only person I kind of stuck with."

Though Pete was three years younger than Howard, he was already something of an old hand having played guitar in bands whilst attending Leigh Grammar School. The fledgling outfit messed around playing Stooges, Brian Eno, and Brian Jones-era Rolling Stones numbers, but by February 1976 neither Howard nor Pete was under any illusions that it was going anywhere. As luck would have it, one of Howard's housemates had allowed him the use of their car for that coming weekend in return for a favour, and having collected their friend – and soon-to-be Buzzcocks' manager – Richard Boon from his home in Oxford en route, they made their way to London.

Arriving in the capital they bought a copy of London's weekly entertainment guide, *Time Out*, but finding no mention of the Sex Pistols they called *NME*'s offices and spoke with Neil Spencer. Spencer was unaware of what – if any – shows the Sex Pistols had coming up, but he did at least point them in the right direction by informing them that their manager ran a sex shop on the King's Road. Howard would later say in *I Swear I was There* that they'd set off from Sloane Square tube station up the King's Road vaguely expecting to find an "Ann Summers type shop".

Though the duo had made the 250-odd mile journey to London totally on spec, their luck was in as the Sex Pistols were playing that very night supporting Screaming Lord Sutch at the High Wycombe College of Higher Education. And though there'd been no mention of the Sex Pistols in *Time Out*, it did feature an article on a new ITV show *Rock Follies*[1*] which carried the tagline: 'It's the Buzz cock!' And a group was born.

While the High Wycombe show was marred by violence, the Sex Pistols more than lived up to Howard's and Pete's expectations. So much so, in fact, they decided to stick around to see them play another support slot in Welwyn Garden City the following evening, and it was there that Howard approached Malcolm with a view to the Sex Pistols coming up to Bolton to play at their college. While Malcolm was more than happy to have the Sex Pistols make the foray up the M1, it transpired that the powers-that-be at the institute were unwilling to chance wasting a potential money-making Friday evening by staging an unknown group from London. Having already been made aware of the Sex Pistols' aversion to playing pubs, Howard and Pete booked the group to appear at the Lesser Free Trade Hall in nearby Manchester on Friday, June 4.

Of course, the idea behind bringing the Sex Pistols to Manchester was for Buzzcocks to act as support. But although Howard and Pete – who would soon change their surnames to Devoto and Shelley respectively – managed to find two like-minded souls to perform at the 'Textile Students Social Evening' at their college on Thursday, April 1, 1976, it proved something of a fool's errand. And like the Sex Pistols' debut at St. Martin's, they had the plug pulled from under their feet.

As Buzzcocks weren't ready to fulfil their support commitment when the Sex Pistols made their now

1   *Rock Follies* was a Bafta-winning series about the ups and
       downs of a fictional all-female rock group, the Little Ladies,
       starring Rula Lenska, Judy Covington and Charlotte Cornwell.

legendary first appearance at the Lesser Free Trade Hall, Howard had to content himself with the task of floor manager for the evening – which meant running around ensuring everything was going according to plan, while Pete had the rather more sedate job of manning the ticket booth.

Having had to call on one of Howard's one-time work colleague's group to fill in as support on the night must have been exasperating, but as Pete subsequently explained in *I Swear I Was There*, serendipity was about to play a hand: "We didn't have a bass player or a drummer, [but] Howard had a phone call that afternoon from somebody who left a message, saying they were a bass player and Malcolm overheard this," he explained. "Later, he'd gone outside, got talking to a bloke… 'Sex Pistols, inside, do you want to come and see them?' this bloke says no, 'I'm waiting to meet someone.' Malcolm said, 'Are you the bass player?' He said, 'Yes.' 'Oh, they're inside.' He [Malcolm] came in and said, 'Here's your new bass player,' and [that's how] I met Steve Diggle."

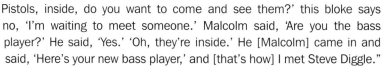

Having recruited drummer John Maher in the more time-honoured tradition of the *Melody Maker* classifieds, the four-piece set to working up a set in time for the Sex Pistols' second Lesser Free Trade Hall showing six weeks later. "Punk was very underground in Manchester at this time. Basically just us and Slaughter & The Dogs, and neither of us were really Manchester bands anyway," Pete Shelley told *Mojo*. "Malcolm phoned me up and asked us to come round to the Midland Hotel. We walked into reception and saw Glen [sitting] there on his own. It didn't occur to us at the time, but he was probably on his own because he was on his way out already."

Aside from making the two forays up to London to play with the Pistols, by the time the Anarchy Tour rolled into Manchester Buzzcocks had made a dozen or so appearances in and around the city. They had also acquired a burgeoning reputation – no doubt aided and abetted by the major music weeklies' reviews of the second lesser Free Trade Hall – and so were in a position where they could actually pick and choose whether to accept Malcolm's offer. Having thrashed out the finer details of lending their weight to the Electric Circus billing, the deal was sealed with another venture to the long-since demolished Tommy Duck's pub on nearby East Street.

Tommy Duck's – or Tommy Duckworth's as the pub would have been known had the signpainter not dropped a clanger – has since passed into Manchester folklore due to its interior décor which consisted of a priceless collection of Victorian theatre and music hall posters, a skeleton within a glass lidded coffin, and a ceiling covered with a fine collection of ladies' knickers, ranging from the skimpiest pieces of lace to capacious bloomers. The group had availed themselves of the pub's delights on their previous visits to Manchester, and were well up for another visit.

"It was a place where women donate their underwear and it gets stuck to the ceiling," Pete Shelley recalled for *Mojo*. "They [Sex Pistols] seemed quite taken by it. John [Rotten] told a funny story about one day when he couldn't find any Vaseline for his hair so he used Vick's instead. When he went outside it was so cold he reckoned it froze his brain."

But of course, the pain the Vick's Vaporub had caused John was nothing compared to the headaches awaiting Malcolm with the following morning's headlines. Though Liverpool Councillor Doreen Jones' on-going determination to keep Liverpool Sex Pistols-free had received a setback in that the acting Chairman of Liverpool Education Committee, Councillor Geoff Walsh, had refused to intervene in her bid, as reported by *Liverpool Echo*, other papers were focusing of the Pistols' situation with EMI.

. 'EMI May Drum Out Pistols' proclaimed *The Guardian*; 'We'll Try To Muzzle Pistols Pledge EMI' said the *Evening News*, while the *Evening Standard* went with 'EMI Give Group A Week To Improve: Sex Pistols – Ultimatum'. But if there was anyone within EMI Records still clinging to the belief that the situation could be resolved amicably then all bets were off with the *Daily Mail*'s banner-headline: 'Sex Pistols Give EMI Chief Four-Letter Reply', the chief in question being Sir John Read, and the four-letter reply being John's retort: "Tell him to go **** himself!" upon being informed by the paper of EMI's intention to restrain the Sex Pistols' behaviour in public.

Another unnecessary headache came that same morning when – having no doubt already been unnerved by tabloid tales of the Sex Pistols' plant-throwing escapades at the Dragonara – the latest batch of muck-raking headlines proved all too much for the Midland's manager who revoked the tour party's reservations. Having to find alternative accommodation was the last thing Malcolm needed with everything else going on, but he managed to solve the problem by procuring rooms at the Belgrade Hotel in nearby Stockport. On their arrival at the hotel, however, the tour party discovered that the Pistols' bad press had preceded them, and the manager – no doubt relishing his moment in the media glare – was actually posing with his arms outstretched within the hotel's entrance for the benefit of reporters.

With the wheels having again fallen off the tour bus, Malcolm – armed with a handful of two-pence pieces – entrenched himself in a nearby phone box and painstakingly went through the hotel listings in the local *Yellow Pages* in search of an eleventh-hour replacement. Yet despite there being several hotels with similar creature comforts to those at the Midland within a 10-mile radius, he found the money in his wallet wouldn't be considered legal tender if being spent on the Sex Pistols.

Just when it seemed the tour party would be forced to spend the night either on the coach or the Electric Circus' dressing room floor, he finally struck lucky by securing a block-booking at the slightly less salubrious Arosa Hotel in Withington.

The Electric Circus, a former cinema and variety club whose halcyon days were but a sepia-toned memory, stood like a stark sentinel opposite a triangular patch of derelict wasteland, overlooked on all sides by monolithic tower blocks, in Collyhurst, a mile or so away from the bright lights of Manchester's city centre.

Collyhurst had once played a significant part in Manchester's history. Much of the red sandstone which served to give the city its renowned red-bricked facade was hewn out of the local quarry, but like the Electric Circus itself, Collyhurst had seen better days, with many of those living within the nearby

high-rises now largely dependent on benefit. In recent years, however, the community spirit had slowly been put asunder as the tightly packed terraced houses gave way to the tower blocks which had themselves become a fertile ground for football hooligans.

It's fair to say that many of those who'd attended one or both of the Lesser Free Trade Hall shows would have been filled with trepidation on seeing the Electric Circus listed as the venue for when the Anarchy Tour rolled into town. While the Electric Circus could easily accommodate twice as many punters as the Lesser Free Trade Hall, those Mancunians making their way up the Rochdale Road knew it wasn't going to be much of a fun night out.

Though many of the disaffected residents in the high-rise blocks might very well have agreed with what the Sex Pistols were saying about the state of the nation, to the "Red Devils" – as Manchester United's notorious hooligan army had taken to calling themselves – the Pistols were a bunch of jumped-up cockneys invading their territory and they, and anyone associated with the group, were going to be in for a warm reception.

With the surrounding locale resembling something of a J.G Ballard novel, after the four bands had run through their respective soundchecks, there was little to do other than loiter about inside the venue until showtime, but as darkness descended outside, the surrounding wasteland slowly came to life with shouts of "kill the punks" and "get the bastards" growing ominously louder.

Through gaps in the cramped dressing rooms' boarded-up windows the musicians watched on as a sizeable contingent of yobs began congregating outside, many of whom began pounding their fists against the boards as though trying to gain entrance. Within a matter of minutes Collyhurst Street had degenerated into a bad night on the Bogside as mounted police fought a rearguard action to keep the yobs at bay while the club's bouncers shepherded those there to see the show through the door. For the four Buzzcocks this was an ordinary night out in Collyhurst, but everyone else connected with the tour stared out in amazement as the ever-growing mob pelted the entrance with bricks, bottles, and anything else that came to hand. Even Johnny Thunders and Jerry Nolan, no strangers to street-gang violence, must have wondered what they'd let themselves in for coming onto the tour.

Punk rock may have found fertile ground in Manchester, but not everyone attuned to what the Sex Pistols were doing was strutting round in bondage trousers, and as such a number of thugs managed to slip past the harried bouncers into the hall. "Some loonies were going around the hall asking people whether or not they were punks," Dave Goodman later recalled. "And if the answer was yes, they would punch them! I felt as if the mob were victims of propaganda. The mass media had told them [the general public] that the Pistols had insulted them and now they were taking their revenge. We became very worried about the bands' vulnerability. There were no side exits and the only way onto the stage was through the crowd."

Frank Brunger – who would describe the first Electric Circus show as being "easily the most terrifying concert I've ever been to" – had cajoled his fiancée Diane Wagg to accompany Mike Thorne and Nick Mobbs up to Manchester for what could best be described as an A&R artist relations exercise. Though Wagg had accompanied Mobbs to see the Sex Pistols perform at Doncaster's Outlook Club back in September, seeing the group in full flow and playing to a fiercely partisan crowd had a galvanising effect on the prim ex-grammar school girl.

Reported *Sounds*: "To turn up to a Sex Pistols' show nowadays is to make a statement to the world that you care about rock'n'roll and don't give a Bill Grundy what the yellow press thinks. And enough kids in Manchester, God bless 'em, were prepared to do just that, almost filling the Electric Circus. However, once there, they weren't quite sure what to do."

"The group were great, the best group on the bill and the crowd were really into them," said Wagg in *Sex Pistols: 90 Days At EMI*. "They [the crowd] were pogo-ing and gobbing, the group were gobbing back and beer was being thrown everywhere. It was before plastic cups, so glasses were being thrown about – it was like a war zone and we went to the back of the hall to get out of the way."

While seeing the bands in their natural habitat proved invigorating, spending eight hours or so in their company as the tour bus wended its way back to London was somewhat unnerving. "The bus was filthy with beer cans and there were all these messy, rough, working-class boys – the Pistols, The Clash, and The Heartbreakers. They behaved themselves, probably because I was on the bus with a record company tag, but Johnny Thunders was eyeing me up although I was much too shy to do anything about it."

Though it was less than five months since Buzzcocks made their "official" live debut supporting the Sex Pistols at the Lesser Free Trade Hall back in July, Howard was already disillusioned with the so-called punk scene; he knew the frenzied tabloid exposés in the wake of the Pistols' appearance on the *Today* show would see the floodgates open and allow a wave of "Johnny Wannabes" proclaim themselves to be punks, which could only negate what the Pistols had set out to achieve. Even the prospect of being able to bring forward recording their four-track EP with the money Malcolm was giving them for tonight's show failed to lift his despondency. He knew he had some soul-searching to do in the days ahead, but for now he had a show to do.

When all was ready, Pete Shelley brought his hand down against the strings of his "Woolworths" guitar, and Buzzcocks launched into their opening number 'Breakdown', a catchy tune which soon had those gathered at the front of the stage leaping about in time to the music. Their singer might have been suffering from a bout of musical melancholy, but Shelley and Diggle – adeptly accompanied by the fresh-faced John Mayer on drums – were determined to make the most of this unexpected opportunity to participate in a tour that was drawing national press coverage at every turn – and could only enhance their own reputation. Since supporting the Sex Pistols they had played a sizeable number of shows in and around their home city and songs such as 'Friends Of Mine', 'Time's Up', 'Orgasm Addict', 'You Tear Me Up' and 'Love Battery' had already become crowd pleasers.

Pete Silverton, who was firing back missives from the tour front for *Sounds*, however, wasn't overly impressed with the Mancunians' efforts. He'd seen Buzzcocks performing at the Midnite Special and while making mention of their rendition of The Troggs' "hoary chestnut" 'I Can't Control Myself', churlishly opined that his second viewing served only to reinforce his belief that they were little more than a "second-rate, provincial Pistols copy". The kids gathered at the front – though predominantly there for the Pistols – cared little for the opinions of journalists and leaped about in tandem to the music. Indeed, such was their enthusiasm that the group remained on stage for an encore.

Buzzcocks might have been considered newcomers to the scene, but they were old-hand enough to know that an opening act – regardless of it being their home turf – should never outstay their welcome, and brought their 30-minute set to a frenetic finale with a new song called 'I Love You, You Big Dummy'.

"I thought we played really well," Pete Shelley told *Mojo*. "It was the last time we ever played with the Pistols, and the last time I saw them play. The Electric Circus had previously been a heavy metal club, but the Anarchy gig turned it round and started punk in Manchester."

Next up were The Clash, whose burgeoning reputation seemed to have preceded them for they received a rapturous welcome from the sweaty massed Mancunian ranks huddled in anticipation at the front of the stage[2*]. Joe, Mick and Paul, who were once again dressed in their customised paint-splattered stage gear, were determined on making a good impression to stand them in good stead for when they returned to the provinces under their own banner. Paul might still have had to rely on Mick to tune his bass for him in-between songs, but like Joe and Mick, he was clearly imbued with a self-belief in what The Clash were doing.

After a brief pause while Joe let rip at whoever was responsible to tone down the over-the-top "Amsterdam-esque" psychedelic lighting, they thundered into 'White Riot' which was rapidly becoming something of a call to arms. They had a spring in their step now that they'd been relieved of having to open the proceedings, and they'd also obviously learnt from watching The Heartbreakers in Leeds, for they no longer charged through the songs like amphetamine-fuelled lunatics.

The *Sounds* reviewer certainly liked them: "Mick Jones bust strings on his guitar, Paul Simonon flashed off his bass with the notes painted on the frets so he knows where to put his fingers and Rob Harper, drummer for the tour, beat hell out of his kit and had lots of fun. The Clash did the greatest hits of their, so far, short career: 'White Riot', 'I'm So Bored With The USA', 'Janie Jones' and the sparkling new 'Hate And War'. Their weakest, most strained song '[1-2] Crush On You' coming as an encore to a splendid set."

Some of the more partisan cockney-hating locals were intent on making life difficult for the London bands and during a brief interlude they began their petty barracking. Under normal circumstances Joe would have tackled the hecklers head on and attempt to either win them over, or at least educate them on the error of their ways. Tonight, however, he was under strict instructions from his manager to refrain from doing anything which might antagonise the crowd as they would have to pass through the audience when returning to the dressing room.

The Clash's energy-charged performance was akin to a souped-up Ford Cosworth V8 engine with Joe's left leg acting as the rev-counter as the group skilfully continued to build up momentum so that by the time they brought the set to a climactic end with '1977', the majority of the audience was demanding more and they were obliged to remain on stage for not one, but two encores.

Joe Strummer

---

2   Amongst the audience was the cartoonist Ray Lowry, who would accompany The Clash on their "Take The Fifth" US tour, and would co-opt the cover of Elvis Presley's 1956 debut album for the artwork on the group's seminal third album, *London Calling*.

Interviewed for the God Save The Queen website in January 2010, Pete Silverton said that it was on the Anarchy Tour that The Clash – as with the other groups – first began to envy the Sex Pistols over their imbued self-assertiveness in the wake of the Grundy furore, and realised that if they were ever going to be held in similar high regard then they would have to "become their own special".

It was due to his being friends with Glen and Joe – whom he'd known prior to his days with The 101'ers[3*] – that Silverton was commissioned by *Sounds* to link up with the Anarchy Tour in Manchester to provide the paper with an inside track. Glen was all too happy to oblige and invited him onto the coach, whereas Joe was uncomfortable with sitting alongside a reminder of his pub-rock past and tried to get Silverton evicted – an incident Glen thought worthy of inclusion in *I Was A Teenage Sex Pistol*: "On the coach Joe started a big ruck about not wanting a particular journalist [Silverton] to be on there with us. At that stage, The Clash had no clout. If Strummer had looked like Rotten then what he said would have carried some weight. But he didn't, he looked like what he was, someone who'd just left the 101'ers."

The New York Dolls were now regarded as punk's "elder statesmen" by New York's musical cognoscenti, and the regulars at CBGBs and Max's Kansas City where The Heartbreakers had cut their teeth recognised that the leather-clad quartet were never going to be a punk group in the true sense; and not only because Johnny and Jerry had a preference for needles over safety-pins. Indeed, the more musically astute members of the Electric Circus audience – though surely never having heard Johnny and Jerry's new outfit unless having made the trek over the Pennines to Leeds three days earlier – knew that with two former Dolls in the line-up The Heartbreakers were going to play good old-fashioned 4/4 time rock 'n' roll. Of course, as Malcolm could all too readily testify, Johnny's and Jerry's penchant for putting drugs before duty had been the ruin of many a Dolls show, and with Walter and Billy more than willing to help Johnny and Jerry party the nights away, The Heartbreakers were going to be no different in that respect.

In *Sounds*, Silverton would describe The Heartbreakers as being "like The Ramones [only] with songs that have beginnings, middles and ends... in that order".

He also recognised that the Americans differed from the English groups on the bill as they "played straight-forward rock'n'roll". Tonight, however, unlike their barnstorming performance of three nights earlier, they appeared disjointed and lacklustre, and – as Silverton duly noted – they didn't really get into their stride until two thirds into their set. This in turn elicited little more than stilted applause, and unlike Buzzcocks and The Clash they were allowed to depart the stage without an encore.

"The Clash sort of looked up to the Pistols on the tour, but the Pistols were arrogant bastards who didn't give a shit about anyone," Roadent said in *Punk*. "Thunders was amusing because he thought he was better than everyone else and simply couldn't be bothered."

It was at the Lesser Free Trade Hall back in July that the Sex Pistols had debuted 'Anarchy In The UK', and as the crowd surged forward in tune to the

The Clash

---

3   Silverton had stood beside Joe while the Sex Pistols were on stage at the Nashville Rooms back in April.

music John swept the microphone stand up into the air and screeched out the opening salvo. He had to screech in order to hear himself above the backline because the monitors didn't appear to be working, but the audience didn't care and leapt about en masse punching the air in time to the anthemic chorus. As the song drew to a close John attempted to berate Goodman over the faulty monitors, but his protestations were instantly drowned out as Steve launched into the new single's accompanying B-side, 'I Wanna Be Me'.

The song's lyric was a diatribe against self-styled "Typewriter God" Nick Kent in response to his not-so-thinly veiled attacks on the Sex Pistols over their supposed lack of musicality. Yet, while John was content to spit out the lyrics, he was not happy about being spat at and launched a tirade against the small minority – who'd no doubt been brainwashed by the tabloids into believing this was how punks were supposed to salute their heroes – that gobbed at the stage. He told those responsible – as well as the rest of the audience should they be thinking of joining in – that if the gobbing didn't stop immediately then the show would.

Steve was having problems readjusting the tuning on his Gibson SG, and some of those massed over by the bar area took advantage of the lull in the proceedings to hurl abuse at the stage. John, who normally thrived on verbal sparring with hecklers, appeared strangely reticent to take them on and instead turned his back to the audience and spent the enforced interlude chatting to Paul.

Once Steve was satisfied with his fine-tuning he thundered into 'Seventeen', but while his guitar was in tune, he and the rest of the group seemed to be somewhat out of sync; strangely ill at ease with their surroundings, their performance suffered as a result, though *Sounds* gave them the benefit of the doubt: "They [Sex Pistols] were well below maximum power – getting thrown out of two hotels before lunchtime does sap your energy somewhat. But anyone who can, as Johnny Rotten did, rejuvenate the tired lines of 'Substitute' when he's evidently exhausted, has got to be one hell of a rock 'n' roller."

During 'Substitute' Steve was forced to bring the proceedings to another temporary halt as he was still not happy with his sound and set about giving the Gibson another retuning. This latest interruption triggered another wave of heckling from those at the bar; even the kids at the front were beginning to grow restless at the seconds ticked by. Steve finally appeared satisfied with the tuning and though The Who's classic was completed at the second time of asking, John still had to scream at the top of his lungs, putting a terrible strain on his throat – and this time he signalled for Steve to stay his strumming hand until he vented his frustrations at Goodman's inability to sort out the monitors.

During the prolonged lull the hecklers – having tired of hurling insults – began pelting the stage with bottles. Though John was the obvious target, Glen was the first to fall victim when a Newcastle Brown Ale bottle struck him squarely on the forehead, almost knocking him off his feet. Steve, already frustrated by the group's sloppy performance, lost his rag after being soaked in beer and challenged the perpetrator to come up on stage and face him like a man. The mood within the hall was darkening with each passing second, and the bouncers – fearing that someone in the crowd might decide to accept Steve's challenge – rushed toward the front of the stage to form a human barrier as the group launched into 'Liar'.

The barrage of abuse and bottles continued into 'No Future', but thankfully the perpetrators' collective alcohol intake was affecting their aim and the majority of the projectiles crashed harmlessly against the PA. The Sex Pistols then brought their set – and the evening – to an end with the highly appropriate 'Problems', and while a section of the crowd continually shouted out for 'No Fun', there would be no encore this evening.

"They were really sloppy. The Sex Pistols were still good, but with John the playfulness had gone," Buzzcocks' manager Richard Boon said in *England's Dreaming*. "Some of the sharpness was still there, but something had happened. Life was being made very hard for them."

This view was also reflected by *Sounds*: "It was the end of a great gig but it was also the mark of the unease in the Pistol's set. They lacked a degree of certainty and concentration just as the crowd were unsure how to pogo. But, no matter, it's shaping up to be an all-time classic rock'n'roll tour. The sort

that'll have your grandchildren asking you: 'Where were you when the [Sex] Pistols, The Heartbreakers and The Clash were doing the rounds?'"

The show may have been over, but the hate mob gathering outside the venue was showing little sign of dispersing – and with nary a policeman in sight Malcolm feared that anyone even remotely connected to the Sex Pistols risked being strung up from the nearest lamppost. With this in mind, he had Dave Goodman – who, with his Richard Beckinsale hairdo and flared-denim dungarees had the disarming appearance of a *Play School* presenter – go outside and sort out the transport. Having bundled John, Joe and Mick, as well as The Clash's soundman, Mickey Foote, into the last remaining taxi, Goodman scrambled in beside the anxious driver. No sooner had they got moving, however, when they were set upon by a gang who pelted the retreating taxi with bricks before giving chase in their own vehicles.

Indeed, it was only after a Sweeney-esque high-speed chase through Manchester's dimly lit cobbled streets that the cab driver finally managed to shake off his punk-hating pursuers. All the excitement had given those ensconced in the rear an appetite, and so rather than return to the hotel they had him take them to the city's Chinatown district.

No sooner had they given their order to the waiter, however, when several heavy-looking-types came in and occupied the table nearest to the door. At first the newcomers showed little interest in their fellow diners, but it wasn't long before one of them recognised John from the newspapers and the insults began to fly. The musicians, having already survived repeated barrages of bottles and stones, were not about to let a few insults bother them, but as the abuse grew more and more antagonistic Goodman slipped away to implore the owners to allow him to make a phone call. The bemused waiters were bringing out the food when the restaurant's door almost came off its hinges as Fat Freddie came bursting in, grabbed up a chair, and planted his bulky frame between his charges and their tormentors. Though John and the others were ravenous, they readily heeded Freddie's call and high-tailed it out of the door and into the van.

However, on arriving back at the Arosa, the five were stunned to learn that not only had they been denied their supper they were also to be denied a much-needed night between the sheets. It seemed the hotel's manager – having spent the last 24 hours being plagued by the press for having dared offer shelter to the vile Sex Pistols – had waited up to inform Malcolm that he was cancelling their booking.

"I have booked them in for one night. They [the tour party] seem like decent people and I will expect decent behaviour from them," the Arosa's manager had told the *Manchester Evening News* the previous afternoon. However, in the following day's edition – after the ejection – the put-upon manager grumbled that the musicians had made too much noise, upset other guests, and had had girls in their rooms. "They were filthy and their language was filthy," he said.

Tony Wilson had been at the Electric Circus, but as he hadn't had a chance to speak with Malcolm at the venue, he'd set off for the Arosa in his own car: "I found out they [Sex Pistols] were staying at the Arosa Hotel in Didsbury," he told *Q* magazine. "But when I got to within 50 yards of the place, there was

a ring of police cars with their lights flashing, circling the place. The Pistols were being hounded around the country."

If the Sex Pistols were suffering from fatigue and disorientation, then they would now have four days to recuperate. Since Monday night's show at Bristol's Colston Hall had seemingly gone the way of Bournemouth, Lancaster and Liverpool. the tour calendar was blank until the following Tuesday. While the mooted replacement at Bristol University had since fallen through, Malcolm had at least managed to salvage something from the wreckage by arranging a booking at Caerphilly's Castle Cinema through local promoter Andy Walton to replace the cancelled Cardiff Top Rank date. As there seemed little point in running up hotels bills in the interim, the tour was put on temporary hiatus and the coach returned to London.

The following morning – despite having endured a gruelling overnight coach ride back to London – Malcolm headed over to Manchester Square to find out if anyone at EMI was still fighting the Sex Pistols' corner. He also hoped to persuade Leslie Hill that the label should honour its original commitment and provide funding for the tour which had thus far run up losses in the region of £8,000, but it seemed that everyone within EMI's Record Division, from Hill down, was suddenly unavailable. "You could have cut the atmosphere with a knife. I noticed an in-house memo on Tom Nolan's desk, signed by Leslie Hill, which said that the Press Department were no longer allowed to speak on any subject concerning the Sex Pistols," Malcolm said of his visit to EMI in *England's Dreaming*. "That was from the top. Meanwhile Nolan [EMI Press Officer] was collecting piles and piles of press cuttings; he'd never seen anything like it in his life.

"John Bagnall [EMI A&R rep], who had been artistically into it to the extent that he'd started to wear safety-pins in his V-necked jumper and his jeans started to be rolled up, had changed. His jeans were flared again, he was wearing high-heeled shoes and his hair was more Beatle-ish than before. Nick Mobbs wasn't really available for comment; Mike Thorne was out. Leslie Hill wasn't available for comment either; he was in trouble after the press stories about his house in Gerrards Cross."

Malcolm's claim that EMI's press department was no longer allowed to deal with any matters relating to the Sex Pistols was subsequently backed up by Brian Southall: "All the national press coverage – including one or two inappropriate off-the-record quotes from people within EMI – had brought forth another official reminder that I was to be the only point of contact within the Record Division for all media enquiries. Every request for 'a statement or an opinion' was to be transferred to me so I could then refer them upstairs to EMI corporate. I was in the picture but somehow still outside looking in."

Having been made to feel as welcome as the Ghost of Christmas Future in Scrooge's bedroom, Malcolm headed across town to Dryden Chambers, only to find even more bad news waiting. The show at Dundee Caird Hall on Thursday, December 16 – which had survived longer than Glasgow – had finally fallen through while another replacement show at Lafayette in Wolverhampton had also fallen foul of the local council. Sheffield's council had now also joined in the free-for-all, as had its Cumbrian counterpart by scuppering Malcolm's attempts to book a replacement show at Carlisle's Market Hall. The Southend Kursaal show for Saturday, December 18, had been cancelled a few days earlier, but now the replacement at Maidenhead Skindles was also off.

To complete his misery, an alternative venue would need to be found for the end-of-tour London homecoming as the Roxy Theatre had now rescinded its invitation. "We were huge, but we couldn't play anywhere, so we couldn't earn any money. Nobody wanted to release our records," John said in *Rotten: No Irish, No Blacks, No Dogs*. "We were quite literally paupers – well, some of us! You tried telling anyone that and they would not believe it. They thought we were all millionaires. To be a millionaire you have to work and earn something."

Among those keeping tabs on their plight was Stephen Morrissey, of King's Road, Stretford, Manchester, as yet unknown to the world, who wrote to *Melody Maker* that week and had his missive published in the paper's December 18 issue: "The likes of the Sex Pistols have yet to prove that they are only worthy of a mention in a publication dealing solely with fashion. And if the music they deliver live is anything to go by, I think that their audacious lyrics and discordant music will not hold their heads above water when their followers tire of torn jumpers and safety-pins."

CHAPTER ELEVEN

Sinners At The Cinema

"As Americans, we didn't realise how much power the British tabloids carry, and how intensely they can work with the populace into a frenzy. On the Anarchy In The UK tour, we would be met at the town borders by the mayor and the entire constabulary refusing to even let our bus enter the town. In freezing cold, blazing-winter blizzard weather, they would not even let us go to our hotel, much less play our show. I think we probably ended up doing six dates out of the eighteen or so that we booked. And with the press it was cover your head and run – photographers chasing you, flashes going off."

Leee Black Childers

After the enforced five-day layoff, the Anarchy Tour got underway again with the replacement show at the Castle Cinema in Caerphilly. However, while The Clash and The Heartbreakers had been left with little to do other than kick their collective heels until departure day, the break had been quite productive for the Sex Pistols as on the Saturday afternoon they'd gone into EMI's eight-track basement studio at Manchester Square with Mike Thorne to record some demos for the mooted second single. This was the first opportunity Thorne had had to work with the group since remixing Dave Goodman's version of 'Anarchy In The UK' some six weeks earlier, and while the label's resident in-house engineers weren't overly happy about Thorne being in the studio unsupervised, they were even less thrilled about coming in on a Saturday so Thorne had free rein of the consol.

Under normal circumstances – with the possible exception of Glen – the Sex Pistols would have been equally unwilling to waste a Saturday afternoon's precious drinking time at the office so to speak. These, however, were far from ordinary circumstances, and the group was just happy to be out of the media's glare, and Thorne later recalled how the opportunity to focus on something other than the tour cancellations had ultimately made for a relaxed mood and a productive session.

"I arrived an hour before the session, since I was running it alone and needed set-up time," says Thorne. "Manchester Square seemed deserted. The security guard let me in, then lowered his voice and adopted a confidential stance. 'Orders from above. They told me to lock all the doors off the staircase [the very staircase where The Beatles had their first album cover shot taken]. No reflection on you, Mike.' Thanks, mate. Off to make sure that the set-up was completed well in advance of them turning up.

They [Glen and John] were often irritable with each other, and I didn't want to give further excuse or to be seen wanting in what I had to do."

Of the four tracks recorded that day – 'Pretty Vacant', 'No Feelings' (instrumental only), 'Problems', and 'No Future' – it was the radio-friendly 'Pretty Vacant' that Thorne earmarked for the follow-up single. Of course, EMI had wanted this song to be the debut single, but while 'Vacant' remained a favourite with the fans, 'Anarchy In The UK' had become something of a Sex Pistols' standard-bearer and was the obvious choice.

For Glen, the afternoon would prove to be interesting in more ways than one, for while Thorne's having called the group into the studio went some way to settling his anxieties about whether EMI would keep the Pistols on its roster, the engineer had surreptitiously let it be known that while he and everyone else at Manchester Square who were involved with the group were hoping he and John could sort out their differences, if he should decide working with John was too much of a cross to bear, then EMI – recognising that he was the group's tunesmith – would be happy to listen to any projects he had in mind. As he later explained in the introduction to Brian Southall's *Sex Pistols: 90 days At EMI*: "I was 19-years-old, not the happiest bunny in the world, getting grief all the time from John while Malcolm was stirring things up – I'm thinking, 'This is interesting'."

On the Monday afternoon, seeing as Glen, Steve, and Paul were loitering about the office like spare parts, Malcolm decided to bring them up to speed on his dealings with EMI. According to Sophie's diary accounts, what started out as a gentle conversation turned into a full scale discussion on whether the group should stay with EMI or seek another label? It also provided the three group members with an opportunity to voice their opinions and concerns about the ongoing tour fiasco. Like Glen two days earlier, the afternoon had proved surprisingly revelatory for Malcolm as Sophie had inadvertently overheard Steve – whom Malcolm had always perceived to be his strongest ally within the group – questioning his managerial methods to John. He was surprised to discover that Steve suspected him of having contacted the promoters at various venues and purposely frightened them off in order to keep the headlines rolling in.

"You could see that all that swearing and saying this and that and the other had created all this excitement, and Malcolm was trying to think of more ways to do that. New schemes; stunts to pull," Steve explained in *The Wicked Ways Of Malcolm McLaren*. "Like those gigs what we was getting banned from… I got the feeling he'd called up the gigs and said, 'It's going to be fucking hell there,' and then they would get scared and not put us on."

While Malcolm was undoubtedly surprised that it was Steve and not John who'd voiced the accusation, he was nonetheless secretly thrilled that the guitarist would think him capable of carrying out such an audacious caper. Being the manager of a pop group was certainly a lot more trouble than he'd first envisaged when agreeing to take the group under his wing, and he could only begin to imagine how difficult it must have been for Larry Parnes, who'd had a whole host of temperamental stars on his Tin Pan Ally roster. Then again, none of Larry's acts would have ever dreamed of calling a well-known television presenter a "fucking rotter" – at least not whilst the cameras were rolling.

Ever since the fractious court ruling of February 1986, which saw John metaphorically get "his wallet back" from Malcolm after seven long years of legal wrangling in the high court, the Sex Pistols have individually and collectively derided their former manager's (mis)management style. Yet it's worth remembering that at no point – at least up until their signing on the dotted line at Manchester Square – did Malcolm benefit from being their manager. True, their being human mannequins of sorts brought their fans to SEX to peruse the shop's range of titillating T-shirts and other wares, but the shop had been doing very nicely thank you long before Steve and Paul crossed its threshold, and with the possible exception of the second Lesser Free Trade Hall outing in July, the group would consider themselves fortunate if they broke even – let alone make a profit from their shows.

The managerial contract that Malcolm and Stephen Fisher had drawn up prior to the Sex Pistols signing with EMI was proved a long-standing bone of contention – particularly where John is concerned. However, if he or any of the others were unhappy about the terms, then all they'd needed to do was collectively insist that a clause be added whereby the contract would be considered null and void should an independent legal advisor find fault with any of the other clauses therein. After all, EMI were interested in signing the Sex Pistols, not their manager, and had Bill Grundy played it safe and simply asked the group a few mundane questions about their new single and forthcoming tour, in all likelihood Malcolm would have opted to remain behind in London and oversee the renovations to the shop whilst they went out on the road.

The group were also quick to point the accusatory finger in Malcolm's direction when the tour – which Malcolm had painstakingly put together – fell apart in the wake of their appearance on *Today*. Again, this was a simple case of Freudian displacement, because Malcolm wasn't the one who swore on live television and while there's no arguing that Grundy had wilfully goaded the group, they had to take some responsibility for what subsequently occurred. Indeed, if there's one thing the Sex Pistols are collectively guilty of, then it's their failure to recognise that Malcolm's laissez-faire attitude didn't merely apply to their development – it was his approach to every aspect of his life.

Meanwhile the Castle Cinema in Caerphilly show was causing the usual wringing of hands at the local council chamber where legal advisors had told Rhymney Valley District Council that it could not take any court action to stop the concert. Reported the *Guardian*: "Publicans in the area have said they are considering closing their doors until after the concert. The vice-chairman of the council, Mrs. Madeleine Ryland, said last night that the public outcry against the group's appearance had forced the council into considering a high court action. 'But we have been told that there is nothing we can do legally to stop the event because it had been arranged at such short notice after the concert had been cancelled in Cardiff,' she said."

Two weeks had passed since the coach had first departed from Denmark Street, and in that time all those on board could have been forgiven for thinking they'd suffered every metaphorical sling and arrow, and so arriving at the Castle Cinema to find a sizeable portion of the local populace were staging an anti-Sex Pistols rally in the car park opposite the cinema must have been something of an eye-opener. Rather than be gracious in defeat, Rhymney Valley District Council's vice-chairman, Madeleine Ryland, had tried to do a "Doreen Jones" by refusing the Pistols entry into Caerphilly. Then, on being informed by the council's legal advisors of the futility in her seeking a court injunction against the Pistols owing to the cinema date having been arranged at such short notice after the original date at the Cardiff Top Rank had been cancelled, Ryland and her council cronies elected to voice their displeasure by setting up stall in the car park.

Ryland – who was no doubt an advocate of the government's Devolution Bill that was set to go before parliament within the next few days – told reporters that the people of Caerphilly had been horrified at reports of the Sex Pistols' previous concerts in Wales[1]*, and that she and her fellow councillors felt their constituents shouldn't have to be subjected to such treatment. Indeed, it's a wonder she and her colleagues didn't think to form a human chain across Offa's Dyke, the 8th century linear earthwork separating England from Wales.

Another indignant dignitary determined to exact his pound of Sex Pistols flesh was local Labour Councillor Ray Davies, who, along with opposite number Tory councillor, Colin Hobbs, assisted Ms. Ryland in organising the car park protest after being approached by the town's concerned parents.

At the time, Davis was furious that the children of Caerphilly might have their "minds vandalised and prostituted" by the Sex Pistols, who would be bringing "all the dope peddlers and filth peddlers in their wake". But it would appear that the road to Damascus passes through Rhymney Valley as Davis – who is still a Caerphilly councillor at the ripe old age of 81 – has since revised his opinion on both the Sex Pistols and the protest. Having first thought to apologise on air for his folly when being interviewed by BBC Wales in December 2006 as part of its 30th anniversary Anarchy Tour retrospective, he subsequently penned a letter to the Sex Pistols Experience – which appears in full on the God Save The Sex Pistols website – when politely declining their invitation for him to attend their restaging of the landmark tour in December 2011: "On the night I led a protest carol concert in the car park opposite the cinema/concert hall, and felt very proud of myself until I watched the stragglers go into the concert," he said. "As all the opponents of the punk concert left the car park, I stood alone looking at the entrance

---

1   Caerphilly was the Sex Pistols' third visit to Wales having played the Cardiff Top Rank on Tuesday, September 21, 1976, and then at the Circles Club in Swansea two nights later, both of which passed without incident.

and the last young person that was entering the hall turned and stared me straight in the face. It suddenly dawned on me – what right did I have to stop young people from enjoying their new-found inspiration, when I myself back in the early fifties was an enthusiastic rock and roller, fan of Bill Haley & The Comets, and had won competitions for the Twist."

Davis, who can be seen conducting the carol singers in *The Great Rock 'N' Roll Swindle*'s Caerphilly footage, told BBC Wales said: "When I look back now and see the couple of young people creeping in there [the Castle Cinema] I feel absolutely and thoroughly ashamed of myself. I've got some great regrets when I look back at it because who am I, a fuddy-duddy councillor, to tell young people what they should listen to, what they should enjoy and how they should conduct themselves and their lives? We should try and put a plaque there to the Sex Pistols to commemorate the event that took place in Caerphilly and I would be prepared to unveil it."

Aside from BBC Wales, several other news crews were on hand to capture Caerphilly's choral protest led by the good Pastor John Cooper – whose biblical fire and brimstone speech would also be forever immortalised in *The Great Rock 'N' Roll Swindle*:

Pastor John Cooper: [With the aid of a megaphone] We hope this will get to the press, to let Wales know, to let the people of this town know, that we do protest and that it is by no fault of ours that this thing has come to Caerphilly. We have done everything humanly possible to ban this thing and to stop it. And as we've not been able to, we have done the last thing possible, to stand here in open protest to let you know that we are responsible, and we are doing all that we can to set an example in leadership and every other way, to a clean living, holy living and pure living."

Interviewer: [Inside the venue] *How do you feel about the crowd opposite?*

John: They're entitled to do what they want.

Steve: The thing is they're outside freezin'. We're in here, we're all right.

Commentator: *Caerphilly didn't quite know what to expect so it took no chances. Pubs and cafés*

were closed before and after the concert. On decibels points the Sex Pistols won. On numbers, it was a victory for the carol singers.

Interviewer: [Outside on the street] *Excuse me, sir, can I ask you why you're here tonight?*

Protestor: Because I'm, well... I'm recognised as a Christian.

Female Protestor: Never mind about Christianity. I think it's dis... well, it's degrading and disgusting for our children to hear and see such things.

2nd Male Protestor: I've got teenage daughters and youngsters. I'd let them out to see Rod Stewart, but I wouldn't let them go to see this rubbish.

Female Protestor: If I thought one of mine was in there [pointing towards cinema], I'd go in there and drag them out. Terrible, I think it is. I think it's disgusting, it's, well, it's lowering the standards of our people in Caerphilly.

The Castle Cinema's proprietor, Pauline Uttley, was rather more pragmatic and told reporters that she was perfectly willing to offer shelter to the Sex Pistols simply because there had been no reports of trouble when the group had played in Cardiff and Swansea back in September. Alas, Ms Uttley's was to be the sole voice of reason in Rhymney Valley as aside from the planned council-led protestations, Caerphilly's shopkeepers and publicans – having held a special meeting to consider their options – decided to close their establishments until the punk rock battle bus was across the border and back on English soil.

"The Welsh village of Caerphilly held a demonstration and tried desperately to stop all the local kids from getting into one of our concerts," John recalled in *Rotten: No Irish, No Blacks, No Dogs*. "The campaign worked effectively because there was practically the entire parenthood of Caerphilly at the doorsteps of the concert hall. Sure, it was deeply silly, but I did think it was excellently silly."

On discovering that Rhymney Valley Council had been stymied in its attempt to take its anti-punk petition to the high court, one upstanding member of Caerphilly's Christian community – a John L. Birkin – decided to act. Birkin was so offended that the vile Sex Pistols were being allowed to defile his hearth and home with their odious presence that he took it upon himself to compose the following missive which was printed up in flyer form and handed out on the night along with the hymn sheets and hot chocolate. "I was 30 at the time and a member of the local church leading the singing of Christian songs outside. I also wrote the leaflet distributed on that evening," Birkin told BBC Wales in 2006. "It is amazing that Glen Matlock should be surprised at being termed a 'sinner'. Their [Sex Pistols] own advertising explicitly spoke of their being 'antichrist'. Hardly the stuff of saints!"

IS ANARCHY THE ANSWER????

Does the Sex Pistols' Anarchy in the UK tour offer the real answer to the needs of Youth? What is the meaning of this latest controversial trend in the pop world? Oddly enough, this group's own reported use of the word 'antichrist' indicates the answer.

This term describes the essence of the spirit of rebellion against all that God stands for. Even though apparently just a passing fad, therefore, such trends are clearly in part fulfilment of Jesus' prophecy that before His return to earth, wickedness would multiply beyond all previous limits. The rise of such rampant evil is a direct result of national rejection of God. Scripture warns when this happens He abandons men to vile affections, dishonouring their own bodies.

So great becomes the degeneration that, although fully aware of God's righteous judgement that they who do such things deserve to die, they not only do them themselves, but actually approve and applaud others who practice them. The iniquity of this day will culminate in the worst period of judgement ever known in human history. When God arises in wrath, the very ground we stand on will shake. The Bible says it will be so terrifying that men will actually pass out at the thought of the things which are coming. But there is hope: not for the Earth, but for individuals. They who turn from their wicked ways, and experience the amazing grace which transforms the heart will escape the wrath to come. The power of Christ breaks unclean thoughts and habits. Jesus is the friend of sinners:

He died both to forgive our sin and to offer His life to overcome tyranny. 'The vilest offender who truly believes, that moment from Jesus a pardon receives.'

Come and join us at the Elim Church, St Fagan's St, Caerphilly, this Sunday at 6.30 p.m. (Tel: 883007). Meet young people who can testify further of the reality of God's power to break the hold of sinful habits, and to satisfy without needing modern trends.

Although the long-since demolished 650-capacity Castle Cinema would suffice as a makeshift venue, with nothing concrete showing on the calendar until Sunday and a return to Manchester's Electric Circus – which had been hastily arranged to replace the Guildford Civic Hall date – it was a long way to travel for what was to all intents and purposes a one-off show. While the £400 fee for the Caerphilly show provided some much needed ready cash, Malcolm had again been forced to dip into the Sex Pistols' rapidly dwindling EMI advance to cover the outlay for the trip. However, as far as Malcolm and the group were concerned it was no longer a question of money. Keeping the Anarchy Tour wheels rolling had now become something of a point of honour, as journeyman journalist Brian Case was about to find out.

Case, a sometime *NME* contributor, had come along to cover the show as part of a special feature on both the Sex Pistols and punk rock in the wake of the Grundy incident for the *Observer* magazine.

"It's a piss off, but we're not going to give up," John informed Case prior to going on stage. "We're now bankrupt. But if we give up, no new group will get a chance to play again – ever!" And when asked for his thoughts on the demonstrators outside, John added: "I think they're very bored people who just need something to entertain their drab lives, and we're the excuse. It's pathetic the way people can be swayed like that. How places can have their licences revoked by some sod who's never seen us – just goes by what the papers say. Everybody knows the nationals are liars."

Knowing that his editor would make mention of the Bank Holiday clashes between Mods and Rockers on Brighton Beach during the sixties, Case posed the question of the supposed violence at Sex Pistols shows, but before John could reply Malcolm interjected: "If we're violent, all I can say is people don't know what violence is all about," he retorted. "The violence of the Sex Pistols is basically in celebration of themselves and of whatever reaction occurs in the audience to that fact. Rock'n'roll is a violent music – assertive. But it's violent to see those guys – the demonstrators – trying to prevent young kids from making their choice. Violence is kids being out of work on the streets with nothing to do – that's society being violent." Having clambered up onto his soapbox, he then carried on with his invective: "In the fifties and sixties kids had a little more to do, more access to things. They overtook the music business, the music papers; you had new disc jockeys, pirate stations, Swinging London. That's all gone. Commercialisation and big business have taken that over. These kids had to find expression and rock 'n' roll seemed an adequate means. They can't turn around and say The Who's Pete Townshend is great. He's old enough to be their father."

Paul Simonon

Brian Case's opinions of the Sex Pistols furore would appear in the *Observer* magazine's Sunday, January 30, 1977 issue. "Against the improbable backdrop of the town's thirteenth century castle, a classic generation gap stand-off was enacted," he wrote. "Inside the old Castle Cinema sat the Sex Pistols. In the car park opposite, bundled up against the pre-Christmas cold, stood a coalition of local councillors and Pentecostal Chapel members in a last-ditch protest. Attempts at getting an injunction had failed so they were staging a carol concert as a rival attraction and a beacon."

As *The Observer* was one of the mainstream's preferred broadsheets, Case didn't just settle for interviewing the group and Malcolm, and having taken several snaps of the Sex Pistols' colourful coterie huddled together in the cheap seats he gave the fans their chance to speak. "They face the realities of life," 18-year-old Jill Taylor from nearby Cwmbran responded on being asked why she had latched onto the Sex Pistols. "They understand people on the dole, and they play especially for us. We play closer to them than to people like Rod Stewart and famous stars with all their swimming pools and things. The Sex Pistols don't treat us like dirt like top stars do."

Whilst no doubt bemused by the eclectic punk ensembles on display – ranging from studded leather, ripped T-shirts adorned with chains and safety-pins – Case felt compelled to question

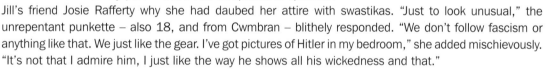

Jill's friend Josie Rafferty why she had daubed her attire with swastikas. "Just to look unusual," the unrepentant punkette – also 18, and from Cwmbran – blithely responded. "We don't follow fascism or anything like that. We just like the gear. I've got pictures of Hitler in my bedroom," she added mischievously. "It's not that I admire him, I just like the way he shows all his wickedness and that."

Had Jill and Josie been speaking to a reporter from *The Sun* or the *Daily Mirror* then their comments about appreciating Hitler's "wickedness" might well have ended up on the following morning's front pages. However, while the two Welsh punkettes – and indeed the vast majority of the audience – appeared genuine in their appreciation of the Sex Pistols, and hadn't merely dressed up for the occasion, Case was savvy enough to recognise their clichéd comments for what they were. Malcolm, of course, would subsequently say in *The Great Rock 'N' Roll Swindle* that punk was aimed at kids who liked to "dress up and mess up", but the *Observer*'s rather more highbrow readership would – having seen past musical fads come and go – expect said dresser-uppers and messer-uppers to at least have an understanding as to the meaning of punk. Yet those kids to whom Case posed the quixotic question appeared at a loss and could alas only "repeat phrases in yesterday's newspaper columns".

One such case in point was Noddy, another disenfranchised teenager whose past musical experimentations included soul, reggae and glam rock, before swearing allegiance to the latest craze. Having followed Jill and Josie's line in eschewing the pop stars of the day in favour of the Sex Pistols because he can at least see his new heroes playing live on stage, he readily confesses to having little idea as to what the Sex Pistols are singing about.

"Well, I don't find much meaning in all that myself because they're new bands and they're singing all this, and we don't know the words ourselves really. Only what we can just about pick up," he responded to Case's question about liking the Sex Pistols' lyrics. "We know really from the write-ups in the press what they're on about. The words of 'Anarchy In The UK' they don't give you no clear view."

It wasn't only *The Observer* that was there on the night. The short-lived local music magazine/ fanzine, *Buzz*, was on hand to capture the Sex Pistols' foray to Caerphilly for its less discerning readership

and managed to corner John and the usually tight-lipped Paul into sharing their thoughts on finding themselves in the eye of the hurricane. Their report, headlined 'Anarchy Is The Answer' is below:

One cold Tuesday evening last December, the Anarchy in the UK tour consisting of the Sex Pistols, The Clash and Johnny Thunders' Heartbreakers came to the Castle Cinema, Caerphilly. Inside the cinema were several TV crews and dozens of newspaper reporters, outside were over 300 people singing carols in protest at the concert, large numbers of police and almost 100 kids who had come to look at the whole spectacle. During the six hours we were at the Castle we recorded over an hour's worth of conversation with various parties; for our part we're not going to pass an opinion on the concert except to say that we didn't enjoy the music – the rest is up to you.

Scene: Johnny Rotten, Sex Pistols' vocalist, and Paul Cook, drummer, before the start of the concert.

Interviewer: (Pointing towards carol singers) *How do you feel about all this?*

John: Well, I'm just surprised that so many grown-up adults can behave so ludicrously childish. Don't they know their papers tell lies, I don't think they do – they live in a twilight zone. That's all right, they can be happy in their own way, but I don't think they've got the right to interrupt my way; each to his own, God loves all kinds.

Interviewer: *That's the only reason that these council officials want to stop this? I mean, they just don't know.*

John: No, it's probably because they don't offer the young generation of Caerphilly anything. They offer them nothing and along comes an alternative and it makes them look foolish. While they've been in office they've done sweet FA for anybody except themselves. There are people getting blown up and they have the nerve to come and complain about this – ridiculous.

Interviewer: *How do you feel about the reaction you've had from the national and musical press?*

John: I don't really care what they get up to. I mean, I've known for years that the national press is squalid and that any cheap rumour – they just love it. Yes, and the music press is even worse. Hypocrisy? They live for it. Well good luck to them, that's fine, they can play their games all day and night. It's when people start taking notice of them it becomes offensive.

Interviewer: *How about the Bill Grundy affair?*

Paul: We just done it on the spur of the moment, it wasn't premeditated or anything it just happened, you know? We forgot about it the next day, but I couldn't believe it when I woke up.

Interviewer: *Does the fact that a lot of universities, who are supposedly open-minded people, pulled out of dates surprise you?*

John: Oh no, universities have proved to be the worst. They went on about us being fascist and rubbish like that. Students have proved that they're not open-minded, they've got closed minds; they're a closed shop.

Interviewer: *Do you think of yourselves as part of a passing phase?*

Paul: People can say that – we're not worried; we're not in it to make thousands of pounds, we're just in it 'cos we wanna do it and we're doin' what we wanna do.

Interviewer: *Where do you get your roots from as a rock group?*

John: Just basic honesty. There's been no honest bands for years, it's all big moguls and twenty thousand tons of equipment.

Interviewer: *What do you think of Clapton and Townshend?*

Paul: They're finished.

Interviewer: *Some bands are doing things by Townshend, things like 'Substitute' for instance.*

Paul: Yeah, it was all right then.

Interviewer: *You think they should have packed it in then?*

John: No, they could have carried on but they just covered it up in bullshit and hype. They became out of touch, and you can't like go up to Pete Townshend and say "Hello Pete", he's become distant, he's not even a human being any more. I doubt if it's him on stage, he's like a puppet in the distance.

Interviewer: *Do you think there's a lot of snobbery in rock music?*

John: Yeah, there has been for centuries. Some of the biggest snobs are rock musicians.

Interviewer: *Is it all that important that you can play really good music?*

John: No, I don't think it's essential; it's your attitude that counts. If you can express something to someone, that's it, you've got it.

Interviewed by a reporter from the *South Wales Echo & Western Mail,* Malcolm attempted to put the blame for the trouble in Manchester and at other recent shows down to "the curiosity value from sightseers". He then went on to opine that the car park demonstration and pub ban on the fans were the most extreme reaction they'd thus far experienced on the tour, before going on to say that it wasn't only the God-fearing adult populace of Caerphilly who were anxious to distance themselves from the Sex Pistols. "Even the bus driver bringing us to Caerphilly was told by his company to leave us on the edge of town and let us walk because they did not want to be associated with us," he bemoaned.

Asked by the same paper if he regretted the group's use of bad language on the *Today* show, John replied: "We were goaded into it. They wanted a scandal and that's what they got and then they couldn't handle it."

Julien Temple, who would subsequently go on to direct *The Great Rock 'N' Roll Swindle,* as well as *The Filth & The Fury*, was serving as the Anarchy Tour's official documenter. Having graduated from King's College, Cambridge, the previous year, the then 19-year-old was enrolled at the National Film and Television School in Beaconsfield. The aspiring filmmaker had originally intended to make a film about The Kinks for his senior film thesis, but had abandoned the project after accidentally happening on the

London punk scene and had readily accepted Malcolm's invitation to base his film on the Sex Pistols. The underlying factor in this arrangement, however, was not due to Temple's talents as a filmmaker, but rather because he had free and unlimited access to his school's equipment.

Prior to embarking on the Anarchy Tour, Temple had spent more time filming The Clash than he had the Sex Pistols, but as he says on the God Save The Sex Pistols website it soon "became very clear that the Sex Pistols were a lot more original, and a lot more threatening and interesting than The Clash could ever be".

He'd already filmed the Sex Pistols – both on and off stage in Leeds and Manchester and his footage of the Pistols on stage at the Electric Circus is featured in *The Great Rock 'N' Roll Swindle* – but only on the understanding that he filmed partial clips of the group's performances and didn't actually record a full song. Malcolm had been quick to realise that although the Sex Pistols had been plastered across every newspaper in the land, there was – at least as far as the British public was concerned – still an air of mystery surrounding the group. He may have been powerless to prevent members of the audience from making secret audio recordings to sell on the black market, but he was determined that there would be very little in the way of visual footage and limiting Temple's access to the group was one way of ensuring this.

"The Sex Pistols were absurd anarchist theatre on the dates they actually managed to appear. I was travelling with the camera and we shot the Labour councillors at Derby announcing the ban on the gig in real trade union style," Temple said in *Punk*. "Once the Pistols got to play, finally, at Leeds, there was this huge pent-up volume of gob because everyone by that time had read about spitting at punk groups. There were these volleys of spit and the group were just leaning into it, letting it go over them. John looked fantastic with all this snot and gob all over his hair."

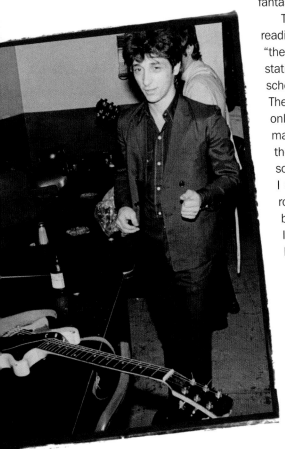

Temple's opinion of the Pistols was not shared by a *Record Mirror*-reading Rolling Stones fan who admitted to being out of sync with "the latest punk rock craze". He or she wrote to the paper that week stating: "As far as I can make out it seems to entail a crowd of art school dropouts dressed in plastic bags kicking hell out of each other. The music is very poor quality and incidental to their image. Fans only seem interested in seeing who can wear the silliest clothes, and maiming as many people as possible. In a recent television interview, the Sex Pistols' manager said that kids today want violence and would sooner have a bottle smashed over their heads than watch television. I don't want this and I know many more who feel the same. Punk rock seems totally concerned with stupidity and violence. It can only be enjoyed by ignorant morons who like making fools of themselves. If punk rock is going to take over British music, then I'll join the Foreign Legion."

Back in Caerphilly, when the time came for The Clash to take to the stage the cinema wasn't even a quarter full, but the 120 or so kids that had defied their parents and run the God squad gauntlet outside make up in enthusiasm what they lack in numbers. As he plugs in his Gibson SG, Mick – in recognition of what some of these kids have gone through simply just to be there – salutes the audience before slamming into opening number 'White Riot'. Joe is again wearing the shirt bearing the stencilled Social Security slogan as a means of communicating with the audience to show that while £9.70 may not seem much with which to live on, it was enough to get a group started –

The Heartbreakers, left to right: Walter Lure, Jerry Nolan, Billy Rath and Johnny Thunders

enough to spark a musical revolution. "The first group as I remember were The Clash, who, up until that moment I'd never been that keen on but they blew the place to bits," Chris Sullivan says in *Punk*. Despite the group's efforts, however, the audience – though appreciative – remains seated throughout. Chris and his friends – who'd been travelling to London to catch the Sex Pistols wherever they might be playing – were equally appreciative of The Heartbreakers who "just rocked us and everyone else to pieces".

Having the Sex Pistols and The Clash coming to Caerphilly was an exciting prospect in itself, but having two former New York Dolls in town had the valleys atrembling with anticipation. And Thunders looked the epitome of rock 'n' roll chic in his leather pants and biker jacket.

"On the Anarchy Tour The Heartbreakers really were a good time rock'n'roll group. Everybody appreciated that," Nils said of the Americans. "Some of their subject matter was a little controversial of course, such as 'Chinese Rocks'. In fact, Johnny Thunders wanted to change the name of the group to The Junkies. The Pistols weren't like The Heartbreakers at all. They were difficult, and were there to bury rock'n'roll, yet they were part of the same movement. It was very confusing."

One of those who wasn't confused about what The Heartbreakers were doing of course, was their manager. "Basically, on that tour, The Heartbreakers just blew everybody else away," Leee opined whilst sharing his Anarchy Tour recollections. "They were a great rock 'n' roll group. They had their roots in good old solid rhythm 'n' blues. While the rest of the bands were still getting their act together, The Heartbreakers would just step on stage and kick ass. When you've got a great bass player, Johnny Thunders on guitar and Jerry Nolan on drums, what you have is great rock'n'roll, and there ain't no way round that. The audiences, of course, went crazy."

While The Heartbreakers wowed the majority of the audiences on the Anarchy Tour and beyond, none left an impression on Leee quite like the kids from Caerphilly: "Do you remember when some people used to fake putting a safety-pin through their nose or their cheek? Well, a lot of these Welsh punks had done it for real – their noses were all sort of green and scabby. It was horrible."

While The Clash and The Heartbreakers lived up to their billing, the subdued mood which had marred the Sex Pistols' performance at the Electric Circus had not lifted. John, however, looked resplendent in Malcolm's and Vivienne's straight-jacket-esque creation, the "bondage suit", which had first been unveiled in Paris when the Pistols performed at the opening of a new nightclub at the beginning of September. Those do-gooders still gathered in the car park across the way were of course oblivious as to what John was wearing on stage, but the opening couplet to 'Anarchy In The UK' where he declares himself both an "anti-Christ" and an "anarchist" would have served to confirm their worst fears. "As a performer Johnny Rotten is a cross between Richard III and Pinkie in Graham Greene's *Brighton Rock*," wrote Brian Case in the *Observer* magazine. "Hobbled at the knees with a curious strap and buckle device, spiky with safety-pins, he winds himself into glaring white-faced rages."

The kids huddled in the front rows immediately respond to John's barbed challenge for them to get off their "fuckin' arses and fuckin' dance!", but the group's onstage lethargy has transmitted to the rest of the audience who remain in their seats. On seeing the recently arrived Border Television film crew setting up to capture the colourful spectacle for the viewers at home, several of those leaping about in the centre aisle engage in a gobbing fight, yet even this appears to be half-hearted.

Wayne Nowaczyk, who was there covering events for the *Rhymney Valley Express*, told BBC Wales in 2006 how he'd gone along to the Castle Cinema expecting a "small demonstration", and had been shocked to find some 150 petitioners massed in the car park opposite and police swarming about the place: "I thought the whole thing was less about the Sex Pistols and more of a comment on British society and media at the time. People were quite sheltered and easily shocked and the Sex Pistols were prepared to ride the media storm."

Former Caerphilly resident Kevin Dicks also contacted BBC Wales: "It's difficult to comprehend now but back then people really believed it was the end of the world and the Sex Pistols were responsible," he said. "I went to the gig along with several mates from Nelson, some out of curiosity and some looking for a dust-up."

Contrary to news reports on the night itself, Caerphilly's pubs and clubs seemingly didn't close their doors as Dicks and his pals – on finding the cinema doors locked – "listened to the bands through one of the fire exits down the side of the cinema before having a few beers in the pubs located on either side of the cinema.

"It's a shame the Castle Cinema is no longer there or the pubs for that matter," he concludes wistfully. "It was an interesting evening which has passed into punk folklore and I'm glad to say I was there and part of it, however over the years, I've regretted not getting there earlier to see the show."

One local who did get to see the show was 17-year-old Steve "Strange" Harrington, who would go on to become a face on the new romantic scene, and enjoy a modicum of chart success with the group Visage who would score a Top 10 hit in January 1981 with 'Fade To Grey'. "No sooner had I arrived [in London] than the Sex Pistols set off on the famous Anarchy Tour, or at least what was left of it after so many dates had been cancelled. I couldn't get enough of them and started following them to gigs," he says in *Blitzed: The Authorised Biography Of Steve Strange*.

"One of the few remaining shows was in Caerphilly. When we got there people from the local church were protesting outside the gig saying the Sex Pistols were evil. A vicar was shouting through a loudspeaker that Satan would enter the body of anyone who went to see this vile group."

The tone of the *South Wales Echo & Western Mail's* report on events certainly seemed to echo the vicar's feelings. Under the heading 'Punk and Protest...And Victory Goes To The Carollers', its reporter wrote: "Five hundred and seventy empty seats out of 630 showed what South Wales teenagers thought of Punk Rock last night. And across the road Christmas carols were sung by a packed protest in the open.

"All the ballyhoo about the Sex Pistols rock group failed to produce the expected capacity crowd for the first live concert at the Castle Cinema, Caerphilly, and only 60 fans turned up.

"The big snub went further – the police said their only problem was preventing interested onlookers blocking the pavement.

"But if the Sex Pistols leader, Johnny Rotten, sang to an empty auditorium the rival protest concert of carols did not.

"A large crowd, including councillors of all parties, turned songs of praise into songs of protest.

"District Councillor Lindsay Whittle said today: "The young people of the valley deserve high praise for the way they literally ignored punk rock.

"And the carol singing was just great. It was nice to see councillors from all political groups side by side for a change."

CHAPTER TWELVE

Our Friends Electric

> "I threatened EMI with a 48-hour ultimatum, which was that they must come out into the open and say that they would support the Sex Pistols. And we wanted this statement to come from the Managing Director, if not from [Sir] John Read himself. We were not willing to suffer his insults saying he might censor the Sex Pistols or any other pop music. It left us in a state where we didn't seem to be in a position where we were going to be promoted too much. At that point there was no message coming through from EMI, and it didn't look like it was [going to]. Just before Christmas, EMI delivered a hamper from Fortnum & Masons to Dryden Chambers, and that was all."
>
> **Malcolm McLaren**

The fast-changing uncertainties surrounding the Anarchy Tour left the weekly music press floundering in their wake, for by the time they reported on events the itinerary had changed or concerts cancelled after they went to press, thus leaving their readers unsure what was happening. This was doubly unfortunate as the music press was, by and large, sympathetic towards the Pistols while the daily press – which could keep up with events – was almost uniformly dismissive of both the group and punk rock in general.

So it was that on December 18, under the headline 'Six Pistols Latest: London Gigs Are Off – Only Four Dates Left', *NME* reported that the tour "had been further decimated by more cancellations, and now only four gigs remain in their itinerary. Biggest blow is the scrapping of their two major London concerts, which should have opened at the new Roxy Theatre in Harlesden on December 26 and 27.

"And with The Damned now out of the package, the current bill consists of the Pistols, The Clash and Johnny Thunders' Heartbreakers. Remaining dates are at Birmingham Bingley Hall (December 20), Plymouth Woods Leisure Centre (21 and 23) and Paignton Penelope's (22).

"However, at press time there was still some doubt as to whether the Heartbreakers would fulfil these bookings, as Thunders told *NME* at the weekend that he is 'thinking of going home'.

"Pistols' manager Malcolm McClaren [sic] told *NME* he was 'thoroughly disgusted' with the attitude of people involved in the British music scene, who wanted to suppress the new wave of punk bands. He claimed that, if the Pistols capitulated now, it would deter emerging young talent. This, he added, would kill rock 'n' roll."

The paper spoke to Terry Collins, licensee of the Roxy Theatre, who explained his decision to pull out of the Pistols dates. He told *NME*: "They booked rehearsal time at the Roxy, so I went along to assess them, and I was horrified by their attitude which was absolutely disgusting. I may say that this was before their infamous TV interview."

Collins also alleged that they had caused "considerable damage", and added that he finally cancelled the Pistols gigs because he "did not want to condone their attitude."

Of course, by the time *NME* had gone to press that week, its "Sex Pistols Latest" was in serious need of updating. Monday night's replacement show at Birmingham's Bingley Hall had since been pulled, but as the original date at Birmingham Town Hall had fallen foul of official interference, it hadn't come as too much of a surprise when the second city's councillors put the mockers on the Sex Pistols entering their domain. While the *NME* had mistakenly alluded to two Roxy Theatre dates having now been cancelled, the homecoming Boxing Day date was indeed off. Terry Collins, the Roxy's manager, cited the Pistols and the other groups having wantonly defaced the theatre's toilets whilst rehearsing there prior to going out on tour as his excuse for cancelling the date. As he'd allowed the group a place to rehearse, and had – albeit unwittingly – allowed them to continue with their rehearsals on their return from the Thames TV studios, his rant to the *NME* was probably little more than a damage limitations exercise.

Though a last-minute replacement for the Bingley Hall date had been found in the unlikely setting of Cleethorpes' Winter Gardens, Malcolm had thus far failed to find an alternative London venue to stage what was supposed to have been the Pistols' triumphal return to the capital after having conquered the provinces.

"Malcolm's attitude – and I agree with it to this day – was that we couldn't just knock it on the head, turn round and go back to London," Glen said in *I Was A Teenage Sex Pistol*. "That would look like we'd been defeated by all those arseholes round the country. So we had to stay out there, which we did. Nearly a month of hotel bills with just three gigs to show for it. But we'd still dutifully turn up for the next gig expecting – well, hoping – to play."

As might be expected, that bastion of middle-class values the *Daily Mail* had stooped lower than most of its rivals and somehow ambushed Paul Cook's mother, Sylvia, "at her two-up two-down council house in Hammersmith" to obtain her opinions on the issue. Her son, the paper reported, was unlikely to be welcome when he returned home. "His mother, 44-year-old Mrs Sylvia Cook, is heartily fed up with Punk Rock in general and The Sex Pistols pop group in particular," according to the *Mail,* which went on to quote her as stating: "For four years my bedroom has been full of drums. I wouldn't mind if he played tunes, but it's just bang, bang, bang. My hall is full of Sex Pistols' dirty washing and my husband has temporarily left home because he can't stand the rows. It's rotten."

The *Mail's* attitude contrasted sharply with *NME*'s editorial stance. "Fleet Street have [sic] revealed by the way they handled the Pistols' tour publicity that their integrity when it comes to rock music is mostly gutter level," it commented. "At the Leeds gig, one reporter from one very well-known London paper had actually received orders from his editor to write a 'front page hatchet job.' Luxembourg DJ, your royal ruler, Tony Prince was suspended for one night from the airwaves for inviting the Pistols on his show. The witch-hunt goes on and on and on… If this is democracy, what else can you show me?"

While Paul might have been getting grief at home, he and the other Sex Pistols could at least rely on their weekly £25 stipend from the EMI advance, whereas the guys in The Clash and The Heartbreakers weren't so fortunate – as they were both as yet unsigned, if they didn't play they didn't get paid.

The Clash were the better off of the two bands as Bernard was willing to put his hand in his pocket to provide sustenance and guitar strings, but even this munificence failed to lift Joe's spirits. On returning to London following the Caerphilly show he discovered that renovators had forcibly gained access to his squat – a former ice-cream factory on Foscote Mews, just off the Harrow Road in Maida Vale – and had unceremoniously dumped all his worldly possessions into a skip. With little hope of finding another unoccupied abode so close to Christmas, he'd been forced to move into Rehearsal Rehearsals and share its meagre accoutrements with Paul Simonon and Roadent.

The second enforced five-day lay-off was a particularly hard pill for The Heartbreakers to swallow as being non-UK residents meant they weren't even entitled to claim the £9.70 dole stipend, which Joe had been championing throughout the tour. They were holed up in a low-rent B&B in Earl's Court wondering where their next meal was coming from. Being picked up from Heathrow in a plush, chauffeur-driven limo must have seemed like a distant memory.

Indeed, had it not been for Andy Czezowski inviting them to play the second trial opening night at his new London punk venue the Roxy on Neal Street in Covent Garden on Wednesday, December 15, they might well have been reduced to throwing themselves on the mercy of the American consulate. "Those were very hard times financially," Leee Black Childers recalled. "Each member of the group was allowed only one treat a day. For Jerry Nolan it was a Granny Smith apple, for Johnny a tube of Smarties. Of course, somehow the drugs were always present."

Tony James' new outfit Generation X – whom Andy Czezowski had recently taken under his wing – had played the Roxy's unofficial opening the previous night with Siouxsie & The Banshees serving as support. Ever since witnessing the Sex Pistols' debut at St. Martins, Czezowski had watched from the sidelines as the nascent London punk scene had slowly taken root, and despite having had The Damned nicked from under his nose by Jake Riviera, he still wanted to be involved and was hoping the Roxy would take over from the 100 Club as London's premier punk venue, and securing a known group like The Heartbreakers would go a long way to realising those ambitions. Hastily printed flyers advertising what would be The Heartbreakers' London debut had been handed out to those punters who'd braved the December cold to see what Generation X and Siouxsie & The Banshees had to offer. And while 120 or so paying guests – which was pretty much the Roxy's fire-safety capacity – was an indicator of the club's potential, the flyers – coupled with the resultant word of mouth – saw 300 queuing up along Neal Street the following night.

Czezowski had hit upon the Roxy – a former gay bar – while trying to find venues for his friend Gene October's then unknown group Chelsea. Though it lasted just 100 days, thanks to Don Letts' *Punk Rock Movie*, the Roxy has gone on to become synonymous with the UK punk scene, but the truth is that the tiny nondescript club was totally unsuited for staging live music, the most glaring hindrance being that it was on two levels which meant those queuing at the upstairs bar were missing out on the stage action downstairs. However, Czezowski and his business partner Barry Jones shared Malcolm's view that punk was all about imperfections. Having brought in Don's brother Des and his pal – future Big Audio Dynamite bassist, Leo Williams, to man the bar, and Glen Matlock's current squeeze, Celia Parry, to oversee the paperwork – the pair got down to business.

The Roxy's official opening was set to be New Year's Day, and Czezowski had initially contemplated booking the Sex Pistols and The Damned as a double-billing. This was subsequently revised to a Sex Pistols/Clash double-header following The Damned's fall from Malcolm's graces, and on learning that the Anarchy Tour's Boxing Day date at the Harlesden Roxy was a no-go, he'd approached Malcolm with the view to extending the New Year's Day invitation to include The Heartbreakers.

Though Malcolm initially appeared enthusiastic to Czezowski's proposal, he would ultimately change his mind, which left The Clash to usher in The Roxy's 100-day reign.

The Roxy wasn't the only punk-affiliated entity set for a grand reopening, as Malcolm and Vivienne had chosen New Year's Day to ring in the changes at 430 King's Road, and while the latest lay-off was hamstringing the Sex Pistols – both physically and financially – it did at least enable Malcolm to concentrate his energies on overseeing the latest renovations.

Seditionaries, as the shop was to be rechristened, would be the shop's fourth incarnation in as many years. When Malcolm and Vivienne had first started trading at 430 King's Road back in October 1971 they'd named their enterprise Let It Rock, and had cashed in on the early seventies rock'n'roll revival selling drapes, zoot suits, brothel creepers, and other mid-fifties ephemera.

In keeping with the merchandise the shop's interior had an authentic fifties theme, replete with flock wallpaper and furniture of the period. By the spring of 1973, however, drapes and suede had given way to studded leather, and in keeping with the shop's new sixties Americana biker culture theme Malcolm and Vivienne changed the shop's name to Too Fast To Live Too Young To Die in homage to the actor James Dean who'd been killed at the wheel of his Porsche Spyder sports car on September 30, 1955.

By April 1974, however, Malcolm, having become hopelessly enamoured with the New York Dolls, decided on the infinitely more radical makeover to SEX, decking the interior out in wall bars draped with pink Lurex and rubber gauze, while selling leather and rubber S&M fetish wear that was hitherto the reserve of the back pages of porn magazines.

"The interior of Seditionaries was high tech, more pristine, more Spartan," Malcolm subsequently enthused in *England's Dreaming*. "The wall bars were kept, but they were polished and placed in the centre. On the walls there were these huge photographs of Dresden being bombed in the war. Then I thought of a fun thing: Piccadilly [Circus]. We put it upside down. Then to still have that bomb look we just bashed a hole through the ceiling. David Conner – the designer charged with bringing Malcolm and Vivienne's dreams to reality – built this lovely little table with a live rat in a cage."

The surgical bed had also been consigned to the dustbin, to be replaced with more modern fittings such as sixties-style futurist nuclear chairs made from fluorescent-orange plastic, while the floor was fitted with a rugged-grey industrial carpet. And just as he had when insisting that EMI issue 'Anarchy In The UK' in a plain black bag so that only those looking for the record would know to find it, Malcolm was determined that only those seeking out the shop would cross its threshold.

"For the front, we had the glass milked so you could have light coming in," he continued. "It was a frosted white light so you couldn't look in. We wanted to keep the street outside and the photographs separate. Outside we just had a fluorescent light. Onto the glass we screwed in a brass plaque that said 'Seditionaries'. People were terrified of entering the shop. You couldn't see in, so once you were in you were totally on edge. You were being watched. That was the point."

When Malcolm wasn't concentrating on the shop, he could more often than not be found playing devil's advocate by dropping hints to the music weeklies that EMI was intending to drop the Sex Pistols in the coming year when all the brouhaha surrounding the group's appearance on the *Today* show had subsidised. Despite the fact that Mike Thorne and the rest of

the label's A&R team were working on 'Pretty Vacant' as the follow-up Pistols single, which was to be released around the time Malcolm was claiming EMI would be tearing up the contract.

"I don't know what is going on," he bemoaned. "We think the EMI Group might be trying to quietly remove us from the label in January or February when the fuss dies down."

While much of what Malcolm said around this time regarding EMI's attitude towards the Sex Pistols can be put down to Machiavellian mischief, evidence of his prescient comments about the internal grumbling within Manchester Square came with the December issue of the corporation's monthly in-house magazine, *EMI News*.

Like everyone else in the country, workers employed at EMI's other divisions would have formed an opinion of the Sex Pistols in the wake of the *Today* scandal, and this was the first occasion they'd had to voice their displeasure at being associated with the group. According to Brian Southall, the most vociferous complaint came from 26 disgruntled staff at EMI's Radar and Equipment Accounts Department (part of EMI Defence Weapons & Systems) who were outraged that "so-called 'pop stars' be allowed to offend the general public with such vulgarity and be paid good money into the bargain", while sincerely hoping that EMI wouldn't consider arranging "any further contracts with these so called 'entertainers'."

That these two dozen or so upstanding men and women could vilify the Sex Pistols for muttering a few expletives on tea-time TV whilst spending their working week perfecting lethal weapons systems that were ultimately sold to questionable regimes around the world beggars belief. Not surprisingly, there were internal grumblings within EMI Records itself, and one unnamed act [a precursor to the Rick Wakeman/A&M episode of March 1977] went so far as to put their protests in writing. The leader of this disgruntled outfit that was signed to Harvest opined that by signing the Pistols – "the foremost exponents of this new <u>low</u> in music [punk rock]" – EMI was "making it almost impossible for bands with genuine musical finesse and bona fide ability [such as themselves, of course] to be taken seriously."

The unnamed group claimed they had signed with EMI/Harvest because they felt EMI was a "respectable label that proffered for sale to the public worthwhile music", yet it was – in their eyes – in the process of turning into a "JOKE!"

That these purveyors of "worthwhile music" recorded two albums and released two singles between

1976-77, all of which failed to trouble the UK charts, goes some way to explain why the author wished to remain anonymous.

Interviewed for *Sex Pistols: The Inside Story*, Laurie Hall denied there was any pressure from other artists on EMI's roster: "I wouldn't say there were any pressure inasmuch as a number of artists may have expressed slight displeasure but none of them really felt very strongly," he said. "And in fact, there were other artists who were right behind us and certainly felt that we should resist the media pressures and stay with the group."

One EMI artist who expressed more than a "slight displeasure" about his being on the same label as the Pistols, and who wasn't afraid to go on record to vent his displeasure, was Cliff Richard, who by this juncture had been with the label some 18 years and was on his way to a knighthood for services rendered.

"I think EMI made a big mistake signing the Sex Pistols for all sorts of reasons," he subsequently said of his fleeting label-mates. "I always thought they couldn't sing and they couldn't play, so what were they doing in our industry? Who were the crazy people who actually gave them some semblance of success? They had absolutely less than zero to offer the industry, just heartache, broken contracts and a few bits of the public who got spat at. I know EMI can't be blamed for what artists do, but I think they kind of knew what this group was gonna do and I think they could have just shoved them to somewhere else, let someone else have that ten-second piece of glory."

Cliff had let his feelings be known to Paul Watts during a wine and dine PR exercise on the eve of his latest UK tour, when, during what Watts would subsequently describe as a "very difficult conversation", the EMI chief used the word "fuck" in Cliff's presence. "The people around the table were shocked when I said, 'OK, they [Sex Pistols] went on TV and said fuck,'" he recalled in *Sex Pistols: 90 Days At EMI*. "I then fought my corner on behalf of EMI and artistic freedom. Cliff wanted to distance himself from it all, and I think he was unhappy about his record company being associated with the Sex Pistols."

Had the "holier than thou" Cliff not been one of EMI's sacred cash cows then Watts might have pointed out that had it not been for Elvis Presley, whose pelvic thrusts had been considered too lewd and suggestive for mid-fifties American TV audiences, then Cliff might well have still been singing for his supper on Old Compton Street.

While there was never any question that Sir John Read would deign to meet with Malcolm or the Sex Pistols in person, as EMI's chairman he knew that it was his responsibility to protect the corporation's image, both home and abroad, as well as pay heed to the interests of its customers and employees. He was also sanguine enough to recognise that while EMI had always sought to behave within contemporary limits of decency and good taste, what passed for "rigid traditional conventions" within one section of society, didn't necessarily mean the same to other more liberal sections.

After all, whilst swearing on national television was unacceptable, and couldn't be tolerated under any circumstances, the opening of the permissive society floodgates a decade or so ago meant that what had been considered indecent or immoral 20 years past didn't necessarily cause offence today. With this in mind, he instructed Bryan Samain to organise a closed-door meeting to explore all avenues. "He [Read] wanted to discuss and understand where a company like EMI drew the line with sensitivity, or with a policy regarding morals, manners and taste," Samain later recalled. "He wanted to invite people associated with or employed by the company who ran businesses or influenced our affairs... and he wanted their wives to be invited."

Amongst those invited to express their views at the meeting – as well as sit through Samain's 25-minute scene-setting video presentation – were non-executive directors former Attorney General Lord Shawcross, Conservative Shadow Cabinet Minister Geoffrey Howe, and Lord Wolfenden, who was also a part-time director of Thames TV. Thames TV was represented by Jeremy Isaacs, Howard Thomas and Verity Lambert. Leslie Hill and Bob Mercer were there to represent EMI Records, while Nat Cohen was there on behalf of EMI Films.

The presentation included various forms of entertainment on general public release such as top-shelf magazines, excerpts from the *Derek & Clive* album, as well as clips from *The Texas Chainsaw Massacre* and *Emmanuelle* – both of which were currently showing in EMI cinemas across the country. "While the Pistols were not specifically on the agenda, it was their behaviour that acted as a catalyst for the meeting," Mercer explained. "I told the meeting that the fact that EMI cinemas were showing films like *Emmanuelle*, without a problem or any censorship from the board, indicated a certain level of hypocrisy in their attitude to the Pistols.

Hill, while recognising this was Read's way of "taking some of the heat out of the situation", had a different take on EMI's hypocritical stance in regard to the Sex Pistols. He found it perplexing that Lord Shawcross, who'd served as Britain's prosecution counsel at the Nuremburg War Crimes Trial, could give a lecture on society's crumbling morality – particularly the all too frequent degradation of women – while EMI cinemas were screening soft porn flicks. As there was little debate on the Pistols per se, Hill considered the evening an inconsequential affair that might have slipped from memory had it not been for Verity Lambert and the attending wives having to sit through Samain's presentation. That nothing conclusive came from the meeting didn't come as much of a surprise to Samain either.

"They didn't so much condemn the sexual conduct and content, but they did all come down on the violence we showed," Samain said. "The other thing was that something should be done to warn mothers, children and old ladies about television and record content. I was so impressed by the force of Lord Shawcross' remarks that I half expected him to resign his directorship of EMI. And had he done so, others would have followed."

Read also had EMI's American interests to consider. In recent years, EMI had invested heavily to expand its brain scanner business, most notably the CAT scanner, and he was anxious that sensationalist headlines in US newspapers about the Sex Pistols might jeopardise potential sales. Bryan Samain, however, while mindful that certain UK executives occupying offices on Manchester Square's sixth floor would point the accusatory finger at the Sex Pistols should EMI's projected sales of its revolutionary scanner fall short of the mark, dismissed the idea of a pop group damaging US sales in EMI's non-musical operations as ludicrous. For though he and Leslie Hill were at loggerheads over the whole Sex Pistols saga, the two at least kept in regular contact which meant the PR guru was aware of the American music market's total disinterest in either punk rock or the Sex Pistols.

Sid Vicious with Vivienne Westwood

For while CBGBs was still packing them in, the US punk – or "new wave" scene as most US pundits were referring to what was going down on the Bowery – had yet to break out of New York, so no one of any import within the American music market was the slightest bit interested in what was occurring over in London. While acknowledging there was a "groundswell of internal interest" about the Pistols within the Capitol Records Building – on account of someone at EMI having sent over a compilation video tape containing footage of the Sex Pistols' appearance on *Today,* and the ensuing media backlash – the American label's head of A&R, Rupert Perry, said in *Sex Pistols: 90 Days At EMI* that as the Sex Pistols weren't in the studio working on an album, ultimately there was no real interest in the group from a "product point of view".

Perry also scoffed at the idea that the Sex Pistols' TV antics could have threatened CAT scanner sales in the US, as the American media apparently seemingly had no interest in the matter whatsoever. Indeed, the Sex Pistols' appearance on *Today* was such a non-news event across the Atlantic that even

Rolling Stone magazine didn't consider it worthy of mention. "The Pistols never really made any impact in America during their time at EMI UK, and neither did punk. It was considered a strange British phenomenon, and the whole spitting and throwing beer around was very non-American behaviour."

What the Sex Pistols' TV antics had affected, of course, was any chance of 'Anarchy In The UK' reaching the upper reaches of the UK singles chart – regardless of how many copies were being sold up and down the country. For while the single would crack the *NME* chart, peaking at number 27, evidence suggests that – just as they did with 'God Save The Queen' five months later – the powers-that-be at the BPI (British Phonographic Institute) put pressure on their opposite numbers at the BRMB (British Market Research Bureau) to nobble the Sex Pistols' debut by dropping all chart-return shops connected with the single, thus causing it to stall at number 38. This of course, meant there was no chance of having to air the record on Radio One, or invite the group to appear on *Top Of The Pops*.

"'Anarchy' got the worst reaction, being banned, and that was banned for no reason," John seethed in *Sex Pistols: The Inside Story*. "It was stopped; it was stopped being made. When it got to 28 [sic], EMI immediately stopped the pressing. That got the worst treatment. The record had no kind of publicity of any kind. If they'd have left it, it would have been a definite number one, easily. At the time there was nothing like it at all. If 'Anarchy' was number one how would someone like Tony Blackburn say, 'And now "Anarchy In The UK".' That's what they were frightened of. It makes them look fucking stupid."

One DJ who was made to look stupid was Aidan Day's Capital Radio colleague Roger Scott, who was made to apologise on air following an irate call from Malcolm for falsely claiming the Sex Pistols had brought in session musicians to record 'Anarchy In The UK'.

As the Caerphilly crowd hadn't raised any objection to a truncated billing, Malcolm saw no need to invite Buzzcocks to fill in for The Damned on their return to Manchester. Another reason for sticking with the tour's amended three-group billing was no doubt due to the Electric Circus management's offering a paltry £240 for the evening's entertainment – less than half of what they were paid 10 days earlier. Buzzcocks' absence on the night meant of course there would be no return to Tommy Duck's, but no one on board the coach appeared overly concerned as the majority of them were suffering hangovers of varying degrees having attended *NME*'s Christmas shindig at Dingwalls the previous evening, the attraction being the free food and drink rather than the musical fare provided by sixties fetishists, Flamin' Groovies.

The last time anyone from the Sex Pistols and The Clash had been at the Camden Lock venue was back in July when The Ramones had played Dingwalls on the second date of their mini UK jaunt. That particular evening had ended in a stand-off with the members of The Stranglers, who'd been one of the support acts on the night. The main protagonists were Paul Simonon and Stranglers' bassist Jean Jacques Burnel, a black belt in karate, who'd squared up to each other in the outside courtyard.

A simmering rivalry already existed between the two camps as many of those within the Pistols inner-circle believed The Stranglers – who'd been treading the boards on London's pub-rock circuit for several years – were guilty of grabbing onto punk's shirttails to further their career, and their securing a support slot with The Ramones served only to exacerbate their grumblings. Though various members of The Damned and Eddie & The Hot Rods were also in attendance at the *NME* party – both bands, of course, having an axe to grind with the Pistols – the evening surprisingly passed without similar incident.

The tour party had probably arrived in Manchester hoping their second visit to the Electric Circus would pass without incident, but of course with it being a Sunday, the city's football hooligans – having already congregated on the terraces the previous afternoon – had had 24 hours notice to spread the word that another night of punk-bashing lay ahead. "That second night was just a riot. There were so many football fans and lunatics throwing bottles from the top of the flats," Peter Hook said in *England's Dreaming*. "It was really heavy, a horrible night. Punk had been completely underground until Grundy: after that it was completely over the top. There were so many punks getting battered."

The Sex Pistols' shows at the Lesser Free Trade Hall had undoubtedly proved an unqualified success, as not only did they lay the foundations for Manchester's burgeoning punk scene, they also acted as the catalyst for the city's much-vaunted "Madchester" late-eighties-to-mid-nineties music scene. This, of course, was before sordid stories about the Pistols began polluting the public's mind to the vile punk rock cult, and while the Electric Circus' management was happy to serve as a port in a storm, its reluctance to match the fee it had paid out first time round was probably due to a suspicion that the kids who'd risked life and limb coming out to Collyhurst 10 days earlier might not fancy the prospect of running the gauntlet again.

"Three dance bands playing the Electric Circus for the second time in 10 days. They're back because the Circus is one of the very few venues in the land that will accommodate them," was how Mancunian madcap Paul Morley chose to open his review of the show for *NME* which appeared in the paper's December 25, 1976, issue. Earlier in the summer, Morley had sensed the impending wind of change after witnessing both of the Sex Pistols' Lesser Free Trade Hall shows, and was one of the hopefuls who'd responded to *NME* editor Nick Logan's request for two "Hip Young Gunslinger" writers to cover the burgeoning UK punk scene. Though Tony Parsons and Julie Burchill had secured the staff jobs, Logan was impressed enough by Morley's efforts to offer him a consolatory freelance role with the paper.

Morley, who has gone on to enjoy a successful career as a journalist and TV presenter, was a true punk aficionado – even going so far as to oversee Manchester punk outfit The Drones' short-lived career whilst writing for the *NME*. Though according to Peter Hook in *I Swear I Was There* he tried inciting the locals to "Get the Cockneys" at the second Lesser Free Trade Hall show, Morley's antipathy towards Londoners didn't extend to the bands themselves. Not only did he praise The Clash for playing vicious, raw, jagged-edged rock'n'roll, he complimented Joe Strummer for playing "crushingly consistent rhythm guitar, and for knowing his "Eddie Cochran rock 'n' roll".

Morley also complimented The Clash on their image and stage style: "The Clash look as aggressive as they sound, all of them moving just right – no perfunctory performances for these boys. From where I'm sitting, they're London's best rock 'n' roll group." And while Joe, Mick, and Paul might have taken exception to Morley's tongue-in-cheek suggestion that their "high energy surges of arrangements are surprisingly only a few steps removed from Showaddywaddy[1]*, in retrospect, he was pretty much on the money with his prescient observations. Given the trio's love of Eddie Cochran, Little Richard, Gene Vincent and other fifties rock'n'roll pioneers, coupled with their fascination for all things Americana, it was perhaps inevitable that the genre would feature heavily in the group's post-punk musical direction – and of course, few would argue that The Clash were England's last great rock 'n' roll group.

"The Clash were the first group to start taking punters away from the Pistols," says Roadent today. "It began at the 100 Club, and became obvious when people started painting their shirts adopting the Clash style, so to speak. The group had made a big impression. They were very accessible."

Morley makes equally appreciative noises about "tourist Johnny Thunders and The Heartbreakers", but whereas The Clash were a group for jiving to, The Heartbreakers – who are "more New York Dolls than the New York Dolls" – were a group to get the audience twisting the night away. Whilst careful not

1   Showaddywaddy were a kitsch rock 'n' roll act known for sporting pastel-shaded Teddy boy drapes and rehashing rock'n'roll hits of yesteryear.

to allude to whatever might have caused Johnny and Co to put in a lacklustre performance on their last visit to the Circus, he acknowledged that they appeared to be "a great deal more together" this time round and they went down a storm. Having cited their music is a "mish-mash of all the New York bands" he brought his critique to a close by praising The Heartbreakers' "regular rock 'n' roll lyrics about love and going steady", which possessed plenty of beat and none of the shit that seemed to afflict many other contemporary American bands. "Buy their singles. And dance."

"The Heartbreakers blew everyone else on the tour away simply because they were more experienced that the Sex Pistols and the other bands," says Leee Black Childers. "They had their roots in rock'n'roll, and rhythm and blues, and were able to draw on all that experience, whereas those other bands didn't have anything to draw on at that point. As I've said before, it didn't matter how anarchic the audience thinks it is, if a group has a bass player that can actually play bass, and the drummer happens to be Jerry Nolan, then they're going to be great."

"I'd always see John Rotten, Steve Jones, and the drummer, Paul Cook, standing offstage studying us," Jerry Nolan said in *Please Kill Me*. "They'd watch the combinations between Thunders and me, how fast we played. Then they'd put the combinations in their act, which they openly admitted."

The Heartbreakers

Perhaps not surprisingly, Morley opened his review of the headliners' performance by saying the Sex Pistols were a group for jumping up and down to – or "pogoing" as the bizarre dance associated with punk rock became known. Yet while opining that the group had become musically self-conscious enough for John to "get snobbish about lacking Damned musical attributes", and for Steve to daub "GUITAR HERO" on the front of his amplifier, while getting "flashy with his fingers during 'Substitute'," he confessed that after three or four songs he was finding the Pistols something of a busted flush, with only "volume and speed disguising basic malfunctions".

Having witnessed the "high standards of musical torment" the Pistols had unleashed on previous visits to the city, Morley could not hide his disappointment at their normality. Though accepting the group were probably lacking "match practice" after having been sidelined for much of the tour, he was unwilling to forgive their sloppiness.

"I remember we played Manchester and a load of people turned up to see the Pistols 'cos they had lots of media attention," Paul Simonon said in *Punk*. "Unfortunately, we did a really good show and the Pistols didn't... but that's the way it goes."

Footage of the Sex Pistols from the second Electric Circus show can be seen in both *The Great Rock 'N' Roll Swindle* and *The Filth & The Fury*. And watching that footage – as disappointingly fleeting as it is – one cannot help but wonder the logic behind Malcolm allowing John and Steve on stage wearing items emblazoned with Nazi insignia when he'd spent the preceding three weeks defending the Pistols against accusations of their supposed right wing proclivities. Morley's ongoing obsession with John, however, remained undiminished and he eulogised about his "demented Pinocchio-type tactics", and of his "10-year-old Hunter/Marriott vocals skidding wickedly".

With the possible exception of 'Substitute', the Pistols' subdued 13-song set went largely unnoticed, but Morley finally found reason to cheer when the group returned to the stage for another run-through of 'Anarchy In the UK'. In these three frustration-channelled minutes the Sex Pistols showed how they could and should have sounded, instead of being the letdown of the evening.

"The difference between the two Clash performances at the Electric Circus was remarkable," Richard Boon said in *England's Dreaming*. "They were glowing. The Pistols had been on the road for most of the year and The Clash hadn't, and really benefited from practical experience."

While the daily press offered little in the way of insightful coverage of the whole Sex Pistols phenomenon, preferring to dwell on the 'outrage' in an almost united negative front, *NME*'s coverage was altogether more intelligent and balanced. "The fact that ninety-nine per cent of their critics have never even seen a live Sex Pistols gig doesn't really matter any more," it pointed out on December 18. "What does matter is that the storm of self-righteous indignation that swept the nation after the episode with Bill Grundy has resulted in Town Hall, local council, University and Rank Leisure officials exercising their virtual monopoly of potential rock venues in this country, and, by doing so, taking away the right of certain young rock bands to play for the people who want to see them.

Joe Strummer and Paul Simonon

"Don't bother with the old Any Publicity Is Good Publicity line; never before has there been a situation where rock bands have been so severely restricted in the right to play their music.

"At the time of going to press, only a handful of gigs had actually been played. This has resulted in huge financial loss all round, especially for the American combo on the tour, The Heartbreakers. It's a long way from CBGBs to the UK when you don't have a recording contract; then when you get here you find you ain't got many gigs either... 'Yeah, we got a few days off,' Johnny Thunders said last Friday.

"The manager of Clash, Bernard Rhodes, wasn't taking it so calmly. 'Kids should have the chance to see the entertainment they want,' he said. 'The Government tells them to work hard for their money and get the nation back on its feet and then they won't give 'em the chance to see the entertainment they want.'

"The Clash have no recording contract and Bernard says the money financing them is coming straight out of his pocket."

The Sex Pistols had ventured as far north as Whitby and Scarborough on their earlier travels, and with The Clash all being English-born they would at least have heard of Cleethorpes – even if they couldn't necessarily pinpoint it on the map. And while Johnny, Jerry, and Leee had made previous visits to England and seen something of its countryside, for Billy and Walter – not forgetting their faithful factotum, Keeth Paul – the bleak mid-December wilds of north-east Lincolnshire gently rolling past the windows as they wended their way to the appropriately named Winter Gardens must have seemed as alluring as the dark side of the moon. Having said that, it's fair to say that no one aboard the tour bus would have been overly thrilled at making the trip to the seaside had it not been for the prospect of actually getting paid. Though they faced a gruelling overnight drive down to Devon immediately following their appearance at the Winter Gardens, with the following night's show in Plymouth definitely going ahead, they would be playing three consecutive dates.

Though the Cleethorpes show was reasonably well attended, Malcolm had already agreed a flat fee of £200 with Winter Gardens' manager James "Jimmy" Jackson. Jackson subsequently claimed to have been unaware of the furore surrounding the Sex Pistols when he'd booked them. Interviewed by the BBC in December 2006 as part of its ongoing 30th anniversary feature on the Anarchy Tour, he stated: "What I didn't realise apparently was that they had to have permission from the mayor in order to perform. I knew it was likely to be a lively do, and by God it was. They whipped the audience up into a sort of frenzy, which was something we had to watch. Yes, we had bits of trouble, one or two scuffles and a window broken outside, that sort of thing. But it was a great relief when it was over."

While playing host to the Sex Pistols has earned Cleethorpes a lasting footnote in the group's chequered history, if truth be told the show at the Winter Gardens (which was demolished in 2007) was a rather nondescript affair for all concerned. Indeed, it seems the only incident worthy of recollection was Glen having to hobble about the stage like "Jake the punk-rocking Peg-leg" as one of the heels had come off the pair of boots he'd purchased from SEX prior to embarking on the tour. Though he'd hardly worn the boots, Malcolm refused to put his hand in his pocket to pay for the necessary repairs.

However, the award for most embarrassing performance on the night went to Paul Simonon who'd spent the afternoon indulging in drinking games with Sex Pistols Steve and Paul as part of his belated 21st birthday celebrations. As a result, he was so out of it when the time came to go on stage that he was unable to decipher the notes he'd stuck onto the neck of his bass guitar to help him remember where to place his fingers.

It was at the Winter Gardens that the inaugural issue of the *Anarchy In The UK* magazine – having arrived at Dryden Chambers from the printers the previous week – first went on sale. At Malcolm's behest, Bromley Contingent stalwarts, and SEX habitués, Debbie "Juvenile" Wilson and Tracie O'Keefe had travelled up by train and set up stall in the Winter Gardens' foyer. The magazine – priced at just 20p, and now a much sought-after collectors item – featured Ray Stevenson's now iconic image of Soo "Catwoman" Lucas in her full feline regalia on the front cover.

Though much had happened to the Sex Pistols since headlining the 100 Club Festival back in September, the majority of the fanzine was given over to the two-day event and contained several pages of Stevenson's photographs of the group in action. Debbie and Tracie had something of a vested interest in the magazine as it featured the photos Stevenson had taken of the Bromley Contingent at play at Linda Ashby's Westminster flat. Paul may have suffered the indignity of having his dirty laundry aired in the *Daily Mail*, but the magazine had devoted a full-page feature to "the luscious Paul Cook".

Not everything was rosy on the literary front, however, for the renowned American music journalist Lisa Robinson had recently rubbished the Sex Pistols in one of her columns. This in itself might not have seemed all that big a deal, but the fact that her column was syndicated in scores of papers across America and Australia meant that her disparaging remarks would reach a significant audience.

CHAPTER THIRTEEN

Plymouth Ho!

> "It's been the most successful tour in musical history to date. We've been banned in virtually every town in the country. They're writing about us all over the world, we make the news at six nearly every night – you can't buy this amount of exposure. So what if we only played a handful of gigs, we become more mysterious and more people will want to see us in the future."
>
> Malcolm McLaren

The issue of *Melody Maker* dated December 25, 1976 – Christmas Day – reported that another date, at Ipswich Manor Theatre on December 23, had been added to the tour, and that the Pistols had lost £10,000 as a result of the cancelled dates. It also claimed the Pistols were furious about the lack of support they'd received from their record company. "We are having regular meetings with Malcolm McLaren and the Sex Pistols and if they are in need of money then I am sure the question has been raised and discussed," an EMI spokesman responded. "We have certainly fulfilled our obligation as far as an advance on their contract is concerned so there is no question on that account. Whether we pay them any more is a matter between EMI and the group."

They'd been treated with similar disdain by the British Establishment, yet unlike the invading Spanish Armada of 1588, the Sex Pistols rode unmolested into Plymouth and – according to despatches received from the front – took the coastal town by storm. As the coach was devoid of bunks, however, the weary tour entourage had been obliged to find what comfort they could during the gruelling overnight slog from north-east Lincolnshire, and after grabbing a few hours' much-needed sleep beneath crisp sheets – as well as a quick freshen up and a bite to eat at the Holiday Inn where they would be based during their short stay in Devon – the three groups made their way over to the venue. Before falling foul of a town planner's wrecking ball in the early eighties to make way for the Drake Circus Shopping Mall, the Woods Centre was situated above a Burtons menswear store, and one cannot help wonder what Montague Burton, the bespoke tailoring chain's founder, would have made of Malcolm and Vivienne's SEX ensembles – particularly John's bondage suit.

While no English punk group had yet visited West Germany, the latest musical happenings in London were obviously attracting interest over there. Germany's leading music magazine, *Bravo*, had dispatched one of its journalists to Plymouth to document the event for its readers. The article, which appeared in the magazine's January 1977 issue, featured close-up photographs of the Sex Pistols and The Heartbreakers on stage, and it is interesting to note that one of the snaps taken whilst The Heartbreakers are strutting their stuff shows several kids sitting cross-legged in front of the stage – one of whom is wearing a parka!

The *Bravo* article also featured several photographs of the more colourful members of the audience – including Steve "Strange" Harrington and his gamine-haired girlfriend – who'd also been in attendance at the Caerphilly show and snapped by Brian Case for his *Observer* piece. In *Steve Strange: The Authorised Biography*, Steve recalls how some unruly elements in the audience were trying to incite a riot, and that: "This huge fight broke out but the punks came off better."

Tracie and Debbie – "Die Punk Mädchen" – who'd accompanied the tour to Plymouth to shift more copies of the *Anarchy In The UK* magazine, were also captured for posterity.

In *My Amazing Adventures With The Sex Pistols*, Dave Goodman says the proceedings at the first Woods Centre show got underway with a short set by EMI's latest punk-related signings, Wire, who, according to Goodman "introduced a level of musical intellectualism to the event". He also mentions how The Clash put in "one hell of a set", and how Joe, Mick, and Paul had refused to vacate the stage until enticed to do so by Johnny Thunders waving a spliff in the air from the side of the stage. The Heartbreakers were – again according to Goodman – also on top form, yet if the soundman is to be believed their being on "top form" meant they "managed to play three numbers in between tuning up, falling over, and swearing at the audience".

For reasons known only to themselves the Sex Pistols chose to keep the 150-strong crowd waiting longer than was perhaps necessary, but the sporadic catcalls and jeering ended the moment the group arrived on stage and launched straight into 'Anarchy In The UK'. Goodman subsequently opined that it was at this point that "all hell broke loose" among the audience, but seeing that Steve Strange is the only one who mentions any violence on the night, the mayhem Goodman is referring to was entirely pro-Sex Pistols. Seeing as he had a microphone at his disposal, Goodman also took it upon himself to act as the Pistols' unofficial cheerleader and encouraged the crowd into applauding them back on stage for not one but two encores. He also says that in his "drug-crazed state they sounded brilliant".

Despite his nine-month involvement with the Pistols, Goodman was still something of a "trippy-hippy" at heart, and had chosen to start his Winter Solstice celebrations early. Nils – in a fit of pique at Goodman's total lack of professionalism – tried retrieving the situation by having Keeth Paul replace Goodman midway through the Pistols' set. The switch failed to bring about much of an improvement to the sound emanating from the stage, however, as the happy-go-lucky American – who if truth be told had little experience at the console, and had simply tagged along for the ride – had also spent the evening dipping into Dr. Goodman's bag of happy pills.

In 1981, looking back on the Anarchy Tour Mick Jones would tell the *New Zealand Listener* that in his opinion the Sex Pistols were far superior to The Clash. "They were just great; the best. Better than us," he enthused. "What they did to an audience never really came through on record, and the papers never wrote about it fairly. But the energy they put into an audience was amazing."

According to Rob Harper's recollections in *The Clash: Return Of The Last Gang In Town*, whilst out on the Anarchy Tour John had confessed to him that he and the other Pistols sometimes "found it difficult to follow The Clash on stage". In *I Was A Teenage Sex Pistol*, Glen Matlock claims that because Harper was not a full-time member of The Clash he was completely ostracised throughout the tour and "became a Herbert in a whole coach-full of people's eyes". Harper, who would subsequently turn down the chance to join a fledgling Dire Straits, says Glen is over-egging the pudding somewhat, for while Joe, Mick, and Paul tended to keep him at arm's length owing to their gang mentality refusal to allow an outsider into the fold, everyone else – notably the two Johnnys – was cordial and made him feel welcome. While no one else has ever heard John say anything positive about The Clash, Harper – who was never anything but a temporary stand-in, and would forever give up The Clash drum stool following the group's New Year's Day Roxy date – would surely have no reason to fabricate such a tale.

It's interesting that Rotten and Thunders went out of their way to be sociable to everyone else on the tour, yet purposely kept each other at arm's length. This could only be down to their respective egos, for while Rotten penned the acerbic lyric to 'New York', Steve, Paul, and Glen played the song most nights, and yet neither Thunders nor Jerry Nolan appeared to hold a similar grudge against them.

"Johnny Thunders and Johnny Rotten didn't like each other at all," Leee Black Childers said in *Please Kill Me*. "That was mutual. I know from talking to each one of them separately that neither one liked the other at all. Thunders thought Rotten was an awful little poseur – phony, social-climbing – you know, just a little twerp.

"I think Johnny Thunders was right. Not to take anything away from Rotten's talent. Rotten had fabulous talent and could hold an audience in the palm of his hand. But he just had no soul. He just didn't get it. He wasn't rock'n'roll at all. He was just an opportunist."

On discovering Thursday's proposed additional show at Ipswich's Manor Ballroom was now definitely off, the local promoter – who'd been so enthused by how things had gone on the night – hurriedly booked a return date at the Woods Centre. While town councils, leisure committees, high-handed university authoritarians and Rank Leisure officials had all played their part in wrecking the Anarchy Tour's original itinerary, the following night's date at Torquay's 400

Ballroom had to be the most bizarre cancellation of all. Devon County Council had initially raised no objections to allowing the Sex Pistols to play the date, but a self-righteous local housewife called Sheila Hardaway – who undoubtedly saw herself as the English Riviera's answer to Mary Whitehouse – had taken it upon herself to protest the council's acquiescence, which had caused them to have a rethink.

Two years earlier, as part of her one-woman "Clean Up Torquay" campaign, the redoubtable Mrs Hardaway had attempted – forlornly, as it turned out – to get a bill passed which would have forced male holidaymakers to keep their shirts fastened whilst out and about the coastal resort's cobbled streets.

Following Malcolm's death in April 2009, Lionel Digby, the local promoter who'd booked the Anarchy Tour date at the 400 Ballroom, told the *Plymouth Evening Herald*: "The authorities rejected the plans to bring them [Sex Pistols] to Torquay because of their anti-social reputation; like head-butting people. They weren't that bad, though. It was just the image that Malcolm had built up for them."

This of course, wasn't Digby's first encounter with Malcolm as he'd booked the Sex Pistols to play three English Riviera dates – the Torquay 400 Ballroom (October 5), Plymouth Woods Centre (6) and Penzance Winter Gardens (7) – all of which were subsequently cancelled. "It was agreed for their fee to be £300, which was a lot of money in the seventies," Digby recalled for the paper. "They weren't good musicians, but Malcolm made them really famous."

Undeterred by Mrs Hardaway's actions, Malcolm had managed to secure an alternative pit-stop at Penelope's Ballroom in nearby Paignton, but since arriving in Plymouth he'd learned the venue's management had undergone a change of heart. In a bid to avoid any further unnecessary expenditure by prolonging their stay at the Holiday Inn, Malcolm instructed the local promoters, Van Dike, to bring the second Woods Centre date forward. However, what had seemed like a sound financial decision was never going to work on a practicable level, as Malcolm hadn't stopped to consider that the eleventh-hour amendment would leave the promoters with little time to advertise the second Woods Centre date.

As a result of Malcolm's non-lateral thinking, the three bands were obliged to play to a near-empty club. He wasn't there to see the error of his ways because he'd gotten wind that the overworked and underpaid road crew were plotting their revenge on Bernard's supposed high-handed management style. Fearing he might suffer similar retribution Malcolm stole off into the night and caught the last train back to London.

Having wrapped everything up at the office a day earlier than anticipated, Sophie – ignoring Malcolm's pleas to the contrary – decided to make the trip to Plymouth to watch the final show of the tour she'd helped organise. Her unexpected arrival brought false festive cheer to Andy the coach driver and the road crew who, having probably feared the worst following Malcolm's powder act, mistakenly assumed she'd brought their end-of-tour wages. Despite Sophie's repeated assurances that everyone would be paid what they were owed on their return to London the following day, the crew – knowing Malcolm's reluctance to open his wallet – were understandably sceptical. It was perhaps fortunate that Sophie was a girl, for the hired hands might well have become physical had Malcolm's lieutenant been a callow youth.

Playing four shows in a row sounds like a flight of fancy after all the cancelled shows, and though Malcolm's unintentional gaff left them playing to a handful of local punks and a small leather-clad clique of local Hells Angels, Glen remembers the second Woods Centre show as the best of the tour: "The last show… at the Woods Centre… was a great show and absolutely packed out. All the bands, The Clash, The Heartbreakers and us – played really well. The promoter loved it so much he decided to put us on again the following night. Hardly anyone turned up. He hadn't had time to advertise it properly and obviously Plymouth is a bit light on word-of-mouth. The entire audience was six Hells Angels and the other bands on the tour. [But] we were all so happy that it was finally over, that we didn't even bother to change into our stage clothes, just played for each other. Each group got up and played and then, as they came off the stage, handed their instruments to the next group."

If Ray Stevenson's photographs from the two Woods Centre shows are anything to go by, then Glen didn't bother changing into his stage clothes the previous night either, whereas John had again worn his bondage suit. The restrictive sateen ensemble perfectly symbolised the constrictive measures the

establishment and its council minions had imposed on the Pistols throughout the tour. While Whitehall's elected officials would continue persecuting the group at every turn for the remainder of their turbulent career, this would be the last occasion John would don the suit.

Though there had been plenty of high-jinks during their cross-country travails, it is something of a time-honoured tradition amongst musicians the world over to celebrate the final night of a tour. In days gone by, it was regarded as rock'n'roll *de rigueur* for rock musicians to trash their rooms, yet while no television sets were hurled out of the windows, according to Sophie's diarised account of the night before it was the lighting crew's room that suffered the brunt of the Colt 45-fuelled carnage. According to Dave Goodman's Purple Hazy recollections, knowing that the evening's frolics were likely to surpass anything that had gone before during the tour, an attempt was made to minimise the chances of disturbing the hotel's other guests and thereby incurring the management's wrath by slapping paper plates of trifle – which came from who knows where – onto the doors of all the designated rooms.

While Glen had been happy for his and Mick's room to serve as "party central" on the tour, he wasn't feeling particularly jovial, and aside from engaging in a bout of play-wrestling with Sophie – the knock-down and submission being captured for posterity by Ray Stevenson – he opted for an early night. "To be honest, I was feeling a bit ostracised by the rest of the Pistols by then, although I could never have expressed it that clearly at the time," he explained in *I Was A Teenage Sex Pistol*. "Maybe hanging out with Mick Jones was a bad move. Maybe the reason I fell out with the rest of them is all down to Mick Jones."

The upmarket Holiday Inn's bar, which was decorated throughout with framed charcoal sketches of the Mayflower leaving for America in 1620, as well as scenes of the English ships of the line sailing out to give battle to the invading Spanish galleons off Eddystone Rocks in 1588, normally catered for tourists with an interest in Plymouth's maritime history, and the occasional business convention. It was therefore woefully unprepared to cope with boisterous end-of-tour naughtiness, which became ever rowdier as the drink flowed.

Having already received numerous complaints from his other guests, the hotel manager decided to end the evening's japes by announcing he was closing the bar. Needless to say, the decision brought a barrage of protest from the revellers who not only questioned his authority, but also his parentage. Not wishing to be seen as a bah-humbug-sucking killjoy so close to Christmas, the put-upon manager relented by granting the revellers a 30-minute stay of execution, which although less than what they'd been hoping for, did at least allow them sufficient time to refill the glasses – as well as stock up on supplies so they might continue the party upstairs.

Sometime during the half-hour respite the lift doors opened to reveal a chair upon which rested a pair of leopard-skin brothel creepers that were readily identified as belonging to Steve. As everyone was pondering the mystery as to what Steve's shoes were doing in the lift, the doors closed and it ascended slowly back whence it came. When the lift returned a couple of minutes or so later, and the doors opened to reveal Steve's neatly folded trousers nestled beside the creepers on the chair, everyone again fell silent in eager anticipation as to which item of Steve's apparel might follow.

The next prop to appear on the scene was Steve's mohair jumper, followed soon afterwards by his cowboy T-shirts. While the others were quizzing Paul as to whether Steve wore underpants the lift's doors opened and the guitarist himself – sporting nothing but a pair of purloined swimming trunks – came charging out with water pistols drawn. Needless to say, the raucous laughter brought the manager at the run, but nothing untoward – with the exception of several of the revellers having wet patches on their clothing – appeared to have occurred owing to Steve having already made his escape in the lift. However, the bar staff were pointing accusatory fingers towards the lift, which at that precise moment began yet another descent.

Thinking the mystery prankster was returning to create more mischief, the manager took up a position in front of the doors. It wasn't Steve who emerged from the lift, however, but rather a visibly shaken Bernard who demanded that he be given another room as someone had defecated in his bed. His indignant outburst brought renewed laughter as everyone was well aware of the road crew's long-standing promise to get even with Bernard for his high-handedness and demeaning attitude towards them throughout the tour. This proved the final straw for the beleaguered manager who closed the bar and ordered everyone to their respective rooms.

"The roadies trashed Bernard's room and shit in his bed. I have a terrible fight with Rotten in the hotel room we're sharing," Nils said in *Vacant: A Diary Of The Punk Years 1976-79*. "After the dust settles he says he really respects me now. What working-class bullshit is this?"

With the lift having been officially declared off limits, the revellers were reluctantly heading for the stairs when either Steve or Dave Goodman noticed that the door leading down to the hotel's basement swimming pool was slightly ajar. The unexpected opportunity to continue the party at poolside was too good to pass up – especially when it became clear that no one was coming to curtail the fun – and the frolics went into sulphate-fuelled overdrive with everyone stripping down to their undies and hurling themselves into the pool.

Spotting Debbie, Tracie, and Jo Faul – who had accompanied Sophie to Plymouth – splashing around in the shallow end, Steve swam across in the hope of getting a little action. The tour was all but over and he had yet to get his "ticket stamped". He knew the doe-eyed Debbie usually had eyes only for John, and what with Jo being Cookie's ex-squeeze, he set his sights on Tracie. Just as has was about to make his move, however, Roadent and Mickey Foote came staggering through the door looking the worse for wear, and before anyone could stop him Roadent dove into the pool's shallow end, splitting his head open on the tiles.

Tracie rushed out to call an ambulance, and while Foote gingerly guided the concussed Roadent up to the reception area to await said ambulance, Steve and the others brought the Anarchy Tour to its chaotic conclusion by hurling tables, chairs, and recliners into the pool before then making their escape up the stairwell. They were met en route by the manager who threatened to call in the police, only to have

Nils Stevenson and Joe Strummer

second thoughts when he realised the bill was as yet unpaid and a late-night eviction could well result in a protracted battle to recover the monies owed.

Having spotted Ray Stevenson pairing off with one of the girls – possibly Jo Faul – Steve followed in pursuit in the hope that his being a Sex Pistol would give him a higher ranking in the shagging stakes than a mere photographer. If that should prove not to be the case seeing as Jo had already bedded a Sex Pistol, then he was perfectly willing to settle for sloppy seconds. Ray, however, having done all the necessary spadework, was naturally reluctant to share his prize and continually ignored Steve's pleas to be allowed into the room. What he hadn't counted on, however, was Steve's perseverance when it came to the opposite sex, as having succeeded in getting his hands on the spare key – either from the mischievous Nils or John – the guitarist had then returned and burst in on the unsuspecting couple.

"There wasn't a lot of free sex on the tour, but I got lucky at Plymouth after the pool incident," Ray Stevenson said in *England's Dreaming*. "The group [Sex Pistols], however, didn't. It must have irritated Steve because he kept hammering on the door and shouting, 'C'mon, Ray, just let me have a look.' Eventually he managed to get my room key off Rotten, and came in and pretended he was searching for something he'd mislaid."

The return journey to London was largely uneventful, but the casual observer would have been unsure as to whether the onboard lethargy was down to a collective hangover, or whether the musicians were each lost in their own private thoughts as to what the coming year was going to bring their respective groups. The Heartbreakers were looking particularly despondent. Although they had elected to remain in London, they didn't have the necessary work permits and acquiring them could prove extremely difficult. Leee Black Childers was somewhat more optimistic than his charges as he believed – as the group's appearance at the Roxy the previous week had indeed proved – that since The Heartbreakers had two former New York Dolls in the line-up it would give them enough kudos on the English punk scene to get them further gigs at the Roxy and various other clubs in and around London.

Another reason for Johnny and Jerry's decision to brave it out in London rather than return to New York was that methadone – a synthetic opiate which was given to heroin addicts to wean them off the supposedly more serious drug – was readily available in the UK on prescription.

The Clash were in an equally sombre mood, for while they didn't need to worry about being extradited to the colonies, they'd been hoping their inclusion on the Anarchy Tour would allow them to finally step out of the Sex Pistols' shadow and stake their claim by making a name for themselves in the provinces. Of course, the Bill Grundy fiasco had pretty much put paid to that idea, and with Rob Harper unwilling to listen to Bernard's overtures to stick with the group, the chance of their landing a recording contract appeared as remote as ever. Indeed, Joe and Paul were so distraught at the prospect of auditioning for yet another drummer they gave serious contemplation to giving Roadent a try-out on drums. While their roadie's brief stint in prison had given him the rough and ready image The Clash were seeking, Mick had dismissed the idea out of hand on the grounds that any prospective drummer should at least possess some musical ability.

Joe's distress was further compounded by his having to abandon the coach which he'd come to regard as a makeshift home: "I was really destroyed because, after a few days, you get used to eating. We were eating hotel rubbish but it was two meals a day," he subsequently bemoaned in *England's Dreaming*. "When I got off the coach I had no money and it was just awful. I felt twice as hungry as I'd ever felt before. I had nowhere to live and I remember walking away from the coach deliberately not putting on my woolly jumper. I walked all the way up Tottenham Court Road and it was really cold but I wanted to get as cold and miserable as I could. I just felt like it was the worst thing in the world that the tour had ended. I wanted it to go on and on. The coach had been like home and I didn't want to get off."

The Anarchy Tour might have been a disaster in financial terms, but the ongoing trials and tribulations had at least – with the obvious exception of The Damned – gone some way to repairing fractious relationships as Nils recorded in his diary: "We've never really got along with The Clash, but this tour has built some bridges. Glen has become particularly friendly with Mick Jones, and if it weren't for Bernard, I would starve – he always makes sure there's some scraps for me when I've sorted out the equipment after the cancelled gigs."

When the coach pulled up on Denmark Street Nils' tour commitments were at an end, but rather than head off to meet up with the Banshees, he and Ray – whose own 10-month association with the Sex Pistols was also set to end – enjoyed a last supper of sorts with the group: "The Pistols had to try and get some cash out of Malcolm because they were all broke, and he gave them each about £15," Ray recalled. "Glen went off alone, but the rest of us walked round to an Italian restaurant on Old Compton Street.

"After we ordered, Steve wandered out and didn't come back for about 20 minutes. When the bill came, Steve didn't have any money, and when we asked him about it he went all bashful. He'd blown it on a woman."

The Sex Pistols may have been front-page news, but they were perhaps in the most perilous position of all. Despite Mike Thorne's oft-repeated assurances that the Christmas break would allow time for the dust to settle at Manchester Square, while he'd been out on the road with the Pistols an increasing sense of foreboding had descended upon EMI's A&R Department. Though Frank Brunger and his team were working towards releasing 'Pretty Vacant' in the coming year, rumours were abounding in the lifts and lower corridors of high-level meetings up on the hallowed sixth floor as to the corporation's position in regard to the Pistols and EMI's contractual obligations to them. Piqued at not being privy to these meetings Malcolm brazenly declared to *NME*: "They [EMI] can't stall any longer. They must state once and for all if they will support the Pistols or drop them."

Though EMI's board remained closed-lipped, evidence that the label would continue its working relationship with the Pistols came with EMI International's second-in-command, Hilary Walker, taking a "business-as-usual" attitude towards the group. 'Anarchy In the UK' might have run its course

in the UK singles chart, but it was about to be released in EMI's overseas territories and Walker was concentrating all her efforts towards persuading the heads of EMI's companies in northern Europe that as the Pistols were still an EMI act they should put together a strategy to market the single in their respective territories.

While the majority of those petitioned vacillated, waiting to see which way the dice might fall in the coming year, EMI Holland set about getting the Sex Pistols a spot on Dutch TV's premier music show, *Disco Circus*. Walker was hesitant to invite the group over to Manchester Square for a meeting to discuss the Dutch promo trip – not least because of unsubstantiated reports that one of the group had been seen urinating in the reception area on an earlier occasion – but she later conceded that all four members had been "as good as gold".

A more immediate show of support came with a courtesy Fortnum & Mason Christmas hamper despatched to Dryden Chambers, the traditional seasonal offering available to all the artists on EMI's roster. Malcolm, something of a gastronome, would have appreciated the grub but he deigned not to attend the meeting with Walker in the belief that the proposed Holland trip was an indication that EMI's resolve was crumbling. If he thought his couched ultimatum in the *NME* would force EMI's hand, however, he was in for a rude awakening. The mere fact that EMI was actually responding to the music papers' questions regarding the Sex Pistols was evidence enough that Sir John Read and the rest of the board were rapidly reaching the end of their tether.

"The outrage started to percolate even further through, to 'them above'. And then up to the chairman's office," said Mike Thorne on the Stereosociety website. "EMI was a pillar of the establishment at that time and the biggest chiefs might reasonably expect an eventual mention in the New Year Honours list and letters to add to the end of their name. But here were these noisy children causing outrage and singing sarcastic songs about our nice queen in the year before her lovely Silver Jubilee.

"Rumours started circulating that top management would unilaterally drop them from the label, over the protests of the A&R and Marketing Departments, all of whom were now unanimously enjoying the show as well as watching records pour out of the stores. Nick Mobbs had an evening meeting with Sir John Read. Nick wore his dark blue suit and a quiet tie, although the hair didn't quite co-operate. Vague questions were asked, and no judgment offered or even hinted at. Going through the motions, we thought."

The Sex Pistols could do nothing other than trust in Thorne's assurances that Leslie Hill and Bob Mercer would prove victorious in their quest to make the EMI board see sense in allowing its Records Division to put its own house in order. There were, of course, rather more pressing internal matters that would need addressing sooner rather than later. Firstly, how could they expect Malcolm to focus on what was happening over at Manchester Square when he appeared more interested in the shop; and secondly, John and Glen no longer appeared to be speaking to each other.

While Steve and Paul would have been loath to admit it, when they'd set off to the Thames studio that fateful Wednesday night – which must have now seemed like a lifetime ago – they'd been equal members of the group, but Fleet Street's ongoing show trial had rendered them little more than sidemen. A telling indication that they – and indeed Glen – were being relegated to supporting roles in the group they had formed, came with the Saturday, December 11, edition of *Record Mirror*. The full-page interview within its pages had been conducted in the days leading up to the group's appearance on *Today*, and yet 95 per cent of the text had been given over to the ranting of Chairman John. The article also featured two of Ray Stevenson's photographs of John posing in the Dryden Chambers doorway in all his manic-eyed glory. Another of Stevenson's photos of John adorned the paper's front cover while Steve, Paul, and Glen had to settle for postage stamp-sized pictures.

The Last Supper

> "A party at Jonh Ingham's Victorian stucco house in Cambridge Gardens. In the kitchen downstairs, members of the Damned, the Clash and the Sex Pistols sit around a large table: the gathering is dominated by Roadent, whose furious scorn turns him into the living embodiment of obnoxiousness. Halfway through the evening, the Heartbreakers arrive, and install themselves in a tight corner near the telephone, which Johnny Thunders uses to make hour-long calls to the United States. Not collect."
>
> Jon Savage's diary entry, December 25, 1976.

Jonh Ingham, who had recently – albeit temporarily – put away his pen to try his hand at music management with Generation X, was actually house-sitting the four-storey property, which makes it all the more remarkable that he and Caroline Coon would think of staging a Christmas banquet for the Sex Pistols, Clash, and Heartbreakers, and expect the day to go well – especially after their having extended a similar invitation to The Damned!

One can only assume that their decision to have everyone gather around the yuletide log was due to *NME*'s festive shindig at Dingwalls having passed without incident. Then again, it's possible that the reason the bands were on their best behaviour at Dingwalls was because the club's management had employed a team of bouncers to ensure nothing untoward occurred. The last time the assorted musicians and their entourages had all been in such close confines was backstage at Leeds Polytechnic some three weeks earlier, and though it was the season of goodwill to all, the ice was showing little sign of thawing.

Caroline would claim that persuading Ingham to declare open house for the day was so that the Anarchy Tour's leg-weary participants could kick back and enjoy a traditional Christmas. Of course, the cynics might argue that her motive was rather more self-seeking, as it ensured she'd spend Christmas Day with her bass-playing beau, Paul Simonon.

"The Heartbreakers and I went to Caroline Coon's house on Christmas Day where she cooked us Christmas dinner," Leee Black Childers recalled. "She was a journalist and she had money whereas The Heartbreakers were a rock'n'roll group so we didn't have anything except some loose change in our pockets. The Sex Pistols, The Clash, and The Damned were also there that day. It was as if she was setting herself up as the queen of punk, but the whole thing was set up so she could seduce Paul Simonon from The Clash. She got laid, and we got fed, so I guess it all turned out OK."

Aside from the four groups, she and Ingham had thought to invite fellow scribes Jon Savage and Steve Walsh. Savage, a Cambridge graduate who 15 years later would write punk's most celebrated tome, *England's Dreaming*, had undergone a seismic conversion to the punk rock cause after seeing The Clash perform at the Fulham Town Hall back in October. He'd returned home that night and wrote in his diary: "Within ten seconds, I'm transfixed, within thirty, changed forever."

He had also recently started-up his own punk fanzine, *London's Outrage*, which in the main consisted of a few select cut-outs from *NME* and his collection of sixties pop annuals interpolated with extracts from Austrian psychologist Wilhelm Reich's 1942 book, *The Function Of The Orgasm*. He'd managed to shift a few copies of the first issue at a recent Damned show at the Hope & Anchor in Islington, which Jake Riviera had organised as a "fuck you" to the Sex Pistols. It featured a lengthy self-penned tirade against Conservative leader Margaret Thatcher, as well as his concerns over the growing rise of Fascism and the violence which accompanied it in mid-seventies Britain's inner cities.

As well as being an occasional guitarist in Sid Vicious' ad hoc group Flowers of Romance, Steve Walsh was also an occasional contributor to punk's pioneering fanzine *Sniffin' Glue*. He'd thought to bring along a copy of the fanzine's three-page Christmas special, which boasted a more than passable caricature of a shades-bedecked Johnny Rotten[1*].

"It was a great big house somewhere in Earl's Court [sic], with four storeys," Walsh recalled in *Punk*. "They [Jonh and Caroline] had invited all these urchins and punks round for Christmas. It was really Dickensian – they had literally invited these urchins off the street. It soon degenerated, with alcohol and drugs."

Nils Stevenson and Steve Jones

1   *NME's* festive edition – which also featured a photo of John on its cover – contained several articles relating to the Sex Pistols, including an "open letter" to the Pistols from the members of The Pat Travers Group, who were offering a direct challenge in that the two groups should play together with all proceeds going to charity.

Savage's rant at Roadent – who readily admits to having been off his face that day – was inspired by his stream of homophobic invective aimed at the hapless journalist. The Clash roadie – who would, of course, decamp to the Sex Pistols the following summer – also earned Ingham's ire after throwing up over his rather expensive suede boots.

The cosy – if somewhat fragile – atmosphere was shattered with the expected arrival of The Heartbreakers, who were accompanied by Leee Black Childers and Keeth Paul. With the exception of Childers, who was feeling homesick for his native Kentucky and therefore grateful for the opportunity to spend Christmas Day amongst friends, the brash Americans showed little respect for either their hosts or their surroundings and were only concerned with cooking up another fix.

Caroline Coon

"It was perfect until the Americans arrived. They were pigs in leather jackets," Caroline Coon said in *Punk*. "They kicked their way into the house. They had no manners, no sense of respect. The family atmosphere was destroyed. Things were stolen, ripped off and they all rang America and ran up a £400 phone bill. Several people were ill; I found out it was because of heroin."

Whilst his charges were making a nuisance of themselves cooking up their own wares, Leee heard the lilting strains of American crooner Jim Reeves drifting out from one of the upstairs rooms and excused himself to investigate. "There was this little guy sitting there crying," he says. "I sat down in the chair opposite and I started crying too."

As they sat listening to Reeves' dulcet tones, the sombre-looking "little guy" – appearing totally oblivious to his surroundings – sat toying with a clockwork doll which Leee was surprised to find had a safety-pin through its nose and a Durex fastened about its neck. "When the record ended, I said to him, 'Wow that was really great. I'm from Kentucky and that was really my kind of Christmas music.' I then introduced myself, and on hearing him say, 'My name's Sid,' I suddenly thought, 'Oh, my God, I'm actually in a room with Sid Vicious.' That was the first time we ever met."

The doll with which Sid was toying had been a Christmas gift from John, who, aside from adding the safety-pin and Durex accoutrements, had also scribbled "Auntie Sue" in blue biro on the doll's forehead in mock reference to Sid having adopted Soo Catwoman as his latest female role model.

Although he'd been a face on the scene for several months, that afternoon was the first time that Steve Walsh encountered Malcolm McLaren. In fact, Walsh found himself sitting next to Malcolm at the table for Christmas dinner, and the aspiring journalist/musician was suitably impressed by what he saw. "Malcolm was intriguing, but also his timing was great," he recalled. "People like Malcolm pick on ideas and just spark things off. I thought, 'This guy knows how to run things.' It was like a scene out of a movie."

Aside from joining in the banter and sharing a few anecdotes from the Anarchy Tour, Malcolm probably gave the gathering an overview of his telephone conversation with Leslie Hill from the previous afternoon. It seemed that while he, Sophie, and Glen had been washing down the corporate Dundee cake with champagne from the courtesy Fortnum & Mason hamper at the Glitterbest office, Hill was ensconced in Sir John Read's office discussing the merits of the word "fuck" with Read and EMI's group director of music, Sir Leonard Wood. Hill apparently told his well-heeled superiors that either of them could wander into John Menzies, or any other leading book store, and purchase up to a hundred books containing the four-letter expletive. He also argued that while the F-word wasn't in common use within the world of corporate boardrooms, it was most definitely now part of the public vernacular.

After the meal was finished everyone moved upstairs into the living room, where Steve set about entertaining the others with his Rod Stewart songs. "By the end of the day the whole house was wrecked," Steve Walsh said in *Punk*. "Steve Jones was doing dodgy Rod Stewart impersonations with a standard lamp that had a live wire coming out of the top. These nice, well-intentioned middle-class journalists had invited all these punks and ruffians round, so they couldn't be surprised when their home was wrecked."

It was while Steve was running through his Faces repertoire – being careful to avoid electrocuting himself on the lamp's loose wiring – that Marc Zermati, the owner of the independent French punk label Skydog, came bursting into the room spewing out vitriolic diatribe in his native tongue, interspersed with the occasional English curse. Before anyone could react, Zermati, who'd turned up uninvited and had been drifting in and out of the house all day, pulled a knife from the waistband of his jeans and began slashing it through the air while demanding the immediate return of his fur coat, evidently a Christmas present from his girlfriend. Back home later that evening Jon Savage recorded in his dairy that Steve Jones had taken it.

Savage also noted how the musicians' "hard-man poses" that had been prevalent most of the day evaporated into the ether the moment the threat of real violence reared its head. The exception to this was Jerry Nolan who leapt up and bundled Zermati out of the front door as though he was taking out the trash. According to Savage, once Zermati had been forcibly ejected the mood inside lifted considerably; not, however, to the point where smouldering resentment could be set aside, and in the coming year the chasms between the three English groups would only widen.

Sid Vicious, Nils Stevenson and Linda Ashby at Linda's flat

WHAT HAPPENED TO...?

Sex Pistols

On Thursday, January 6, 1977, while the Sex Pistols were in Rotterdam as part of the promotional mini-tour of Holland, EMI issued a statement announcing that the company and the Sex Pistols had mutually agreed to terminate the group's recording contract. Malcolm, of course, was unwilling to be quite so diplomatic and later claimed that the Pistols had been sacked from the label. Being dumped by one's record label – especially a major player such as EMI – after one solitary single would have had most bands fearing for their future, but Malcolm was largely unconcerned as the Pistols' notoriety ensured that other record companies would come a-calling sooner or later.

Those anticipating which of the majors would step in where EMI feared to tread were surprised when the group publicly put pen to contractual paper with the rather sedate American label A&M Records at the Victoria Memorial opposite Buckingham Palace on Thursday, March 10, 1977. This, of course, was merely a promotional stunt to promote the group's intended debut A&M single, 'God Save The Queen'/'No Feelings' (AMS7284). The "real" contract – £150,000 over two years – had been signed at the offices of Rondor Music, A&M's UK subsidiary company, the previous afternoon where a celebratory get-together descended into chaos.

A&M's UK director Derek Green, who was largely responsible for acquiring the Sex Pistols, might have been willing to put the catalogue of unsavoury incidents at Rondor's offices down to the group's boisterous over-enthusiasm had this not been followed a couple of days later by an equally unpalatable incident at the legendary Speakeasy club. On the night in question the group and their entourage became embroiled in a drunken fracas with *Old Grey Whistle Test* presenter "Whispering" Bob

The Pistols, with Sid Vicious on the left, sign for A&M Records outside Buckingham Palace

Harris, who just happened to be a close friend of Green's. Despite the Pistols having already recorded 'God Save The Queen', A&M decided that having the outré Sex Pistols on its roster wasn't such a good idea after all and terminated the group's contract[1*].

Another underlying reason behind A&M's decision to terminate the contract and hand over £75,000 in compensation was undoubtedly Malcolm's failure to mention to Green that Glen Matlock – the group's recognised tunesmith – had been replaced on bass by the charismatic but woefully non-musical Sid Vicious, aka Simon John Ritchie. Shortly after joining the group Sid met up with "Nauseating Nancy" Spungen, a 20-year-old American stripper/groupie and heroin addict who in turn introduced him to the drug that would kill him within two years.

Following his departure from the Pistols, Glen formed the Rich Kids with guitarist Steve New, who'd auditioned for the Sex Pistols as a potential second guitarist back in September 1975, and future Ultravox frontman Midge Ure. Somewhat ironically, given that Sid Vicious had replaced him in the Pistols, Glen played bass for what turned out to be Sid's one and only UK solo show at the Electric Circus in Camden on Monday, August 15, 1978. The ad hoc backing group on the night – billed as the Vicious White Cats – also featured Glen's fellow soon-to-be-ex-Rich Kid Steve New on guitar, and had The Damned's one-time tub-thumper Rat Scabies providing the beat.

Of course, Glen's musical dexterity meant his services were always going to be in demand, and when he wasn't touring with the likes of Iggy Pop, or playing with Dead Men Walking, he was busy recording and touring with his bands, The Mavericks and The Philistines. Most recently he achieved what must have been a lifetime ambition by playing bass with the reformed Faces alongside Ronnie Wood, Ian McLagan and Kenney Jones, who had to settle for Mick Hucknall on vocals in place of the uncooperative Rod Stewart.

On Friday, May 13, 1977, the Sex Pistols accepted a reported £15,000 to sign with Richard Branson's Virgin Records for whom they would release three singles while Johnny Rotten was still with the group. 'God Save The Queen'/'Did You No Wrong' (VS181) gave the group their first – albeit unofficial – UK number one single following its release on May 26, 1977, but the resulting furore saw the Pistols caught up in another media maelstrom from which they never really recovered. While 'Pretty Vacant'/'No Fun' (VS184) and 'Holidays In The Sun'/'Satellite' (VS191) gave the group two further UK Top 10 singles in July and October respectively, and the parent album *Never Mind The Bollocks Here's The Sex Pistols* (VS2086) slammed in at number one on the UK album chart with advance orders of 125,000, the now ever-present controversy surrounding the group's every move meant they played but a handful of further shows in the UK.

On Tuesday, January 3, 1978, the group embarked on a seven-date US tour. Like the Anarchy Tour, it had originally been scheduled for 19 dates but it was truncated due to problems over the issuing of visas stemming from the group's criminal records. After the final shambolic show at the Winterland Ballroom in San Francisco on Saturday, January 14, John – who'd decided he'd had enough of being cheated and mismanaged by Malcolm – offered Steve and Paul an ultimatum; they would have to choose between himself and their manager.

Steve and Paul naively chose to follow Malcolm to Rio de Janeiro where they recorded the single 'No One is Innocent' with Great Train Robber Ronnie Biggs, which was released on June 30, 1978. The double A-side with Sid's hilarious rendition of 'My Way' gave the Sex Pistols their fourth consecutive UK Top 10 hit, but to all intents and purposes they were now a group in name only.

With the demise of the Sex Pistols, Johnny Rotten reverted to his real name of John Lydon, and formed Public Image Ltd. (PiL) with his old college friend "Jah Wobble" a.k.a John Wardle, and ex-Clash guitarist Keith Levene. Though the outfit's line-up would undergo many personnel changes over the

---

1   Though A&M supposedly destroyed all 25,000 copies of 'God Save The Queen', a few copies did make it to the light of day and at the time of writing are commanding prices upwards of £12,000.

following decades, they would receive critical acclaim for their avant-garde brand of music and achieve moderate chart success, most notably with their near-eponymous debut single 'Public Image', which gave them a Top 10 UK hit in October 1978, and 'This Is Not A Love Song' which reached number five in 1983.

John has also enjoyed success on his own, working with artists as varied as Afrika Bambaataa and Leftfield, and 1997 saw the release of his first solo album, *Psycho's Path*. A second solo album, the enigmatically entitled *The Best Of British £1 Notes*, which comprised songs from every aspect of John's colourful career, was released in 2005.

In early 2004, John surprised everybody by participating in ITV's tedious jungle extravaganza *I'm A Celebrity Get Me Out Of Here.* Somewhat surprisingly, his plain-speaking, no-nonsense attitude – coupled with his blatant refusal to play ball – endeared him to the viewing public, and resulted in his being given his own TV series, *John Lydon's Mega Bugs*. This led to his being offered two further programmes: *John Lydon Goes Ape*, in which he searched for gorillas in Central Africa, and *John Lydon's Shark Attack* in which he swam with man-eating sharks off South Africa. However, not all of John's TV exploits have been as well received, and in 2008 he was widely mocked for agreeing to appear in a TV advertising campaign for Country Life butter. On the positive side, he evidently used his fee to fund a PiL reunion tour in 2009.

Steve and Paul continued working with Malcolm on *The Great Rock 'N' Roll Swindle* film and its accompanying soundtrack, served as hired hands on Johnny Thunders' 1978 solo album, *So Alone*, and teamed up with Thin Lizzy's Phil Lynott and Scott Gorham for The Greedy Bastards. They also formed The Professionals, who recorded two albums for Virgin and released a clutch of singles, but having failed to achieve mainstream success the duo decided to go their separate ways in 1981.

Steve relocated to Los Angeles where, like Sid, he quickly came to realise that the sum of the Sex Pistols' whole was greater than its individual parts. Aside from being a permanent member of the less-than-successful Chequered Past, he traded on past glories by became something of a "serial ligger", opening for or playing with anyone who would have him. Again, like Sid, the one-time self-proclaimed "guitar hero" developed a heroin habit to take the sting away from his as yet unfulfilled dreams. The habit quickly became an addiction, and one has to wonder what might have become of Steve had it not been for the emergence of glam metal in the mid-to-late-eighties with bands like Mötley Crüe, Hanoi Rocks, and Guns N' Roses all acknowledging the Sex Pistols' worth, and also respectfully paying their dues to Steve.

There's nothing like having one's ego stroked to get the self-esteem pumping and having kicked his habit Steve recorded two solo albums. While neither album troubled the *Billboard* 200, the title track of his 1987 album, *Mercy*, appeared in an episode of *Miami Vice*, and also on the *Miami Vice II* soundtrack album. In 1995, he joined forces with the ex-Guns N' Roses rhythm section of Duff McKagan and Matt Sorum, and Duran Duran's John Taylor, to form the "supergroup" Neurotic Outsiders who released an eponymous album the following year.

In February 2004, after nigh on two decades of making music, Steve became an unlikely DJ when he began hosting his own daily radio programme, *Jonesy's Jukebox*, which started out on LA's Indie 103.1 FM before switching to KROQ six years later.

Paul opted to remain in his native London and after briefly looking after Bananarama – working as producer on the delectable trio's 1982 debut album, *Deep Sea Skiving* – he collaborated with another of Malcolm's former charges, ex-Adam & the Ants and Bow Wow Wow bassist Matthew Ashman, to form Chiefs Of Relief. The group split up after releasing just one album in 1988.

Paul also enjoyed a moderately successful career as a session musician – most notably with ex-Orange Juice frontman Edwin Collins – and he played on Collins' 1994 single 'A Girl Like You' which was a massive hit on both sides of the Atlantic. In 2004, Paul joined forces with Def Leppard guitarist Phil Collen and their mutual friend Simon Laffy to form Man-Raze. The trio's debut single, 'Skin Crawl', was released with little or no fanfare in October 2005, and this was followed two years later with 'Turn It Up' which was released in digital download form. However, owing to Paul and Phil's other group commitments, their debut album, *Surreal*, didn't hit the UK record shops until December 2008.

On completing *The Great Rock 'N' Roll Swindle*, Malcolm returned to music management with Bow Wow Wow, whose 14-year-old Anglo-Burmese singer, Annabella Lwin, was apparently discovered singing in a launderette. Though the group had been predominantly put together to promote Vivienne Westwood's latest fashions, they released three studio albums and enjoyed moderate chart success before calling it a day in 1983. That same year, Malcolm tasted success as an artist with his album *Duck Rock* which spawned two UK Top 10 hit singles, 'Buffalo Gals' and 'Double Dutch'. The following year he scored another hit with his "Techno Poperatic" 'Madame Butterfly' which cleverly set the title song from Puccini's opera to drum machines and atmospheric synthesizers.

In February 1986, Malcolm was reunited with his former charges when John Lydon finally saw his seven-year-long petition to have the Sex Pistols dissolved heard in the high court. The order also ensured that Malcolm would no longer have any legal claim to any aspect of the Sex Pistols' name or back catalogue. Steve and Paul had originally sided with Malcolm against John, but sensibly changed their minds on hearing the catalogue of evidence of their erstwhile manager's mismanagement. The judge sided with the plaintiffs, which ensured that all future moneys earned by the Sex Pistols – or Sex Pistols Residuals – would be evenly distributed between the surviving group members and Sid's mother, Anne Beverley, who was the executor of her son's estate. The fact that Anne Beverley earned far more from the Pistols that Glen Matlock did not sit well with the only member of the band with any real musical chops.

Whereas John had painstakingly built up his case, Malcolm had done nothing to counter the claims, and had entered the courtroom that day knowing full well what the outcome would be. Having surreptitiously filled his pockets with cash from the Glitterbest account, he boarded the night train to Paris where – owing to his association with both the Sex Pistols and Vivienne Westwood, whose sartorial star was steadily rising – he became something of a cause célèbre in the fashion world.

On Tuesday, March 18, 1996, the seemingly impossible came to pass when John, Steve, Paul and Glen staged a press conference at their old stamping ground, the 100 Club on Oxford Street to unveil plans for their 78-date "Filthy Lucre" reunion world tour, which commenced three months later on June 21, at the Messila Festival in Hollola, Finland. This, the four aging original Sex Pistols had us believe, was so that they could sign off in style – something which had been denied to them back in January 1978 – as well as perform for those fans too young to catch their act back in the day.

2000 saw the cinematic release of *The Filth & The Fury* film in which – with Julien Temple once again at the directorial helm – John, Steve, Paul, and Glen gave their version of the Sex Pistols' colourful history which, needless to say, varied greatly from Malcolm's account. That should have been it, but having enjoyed being in the limelight again the reconstituted Sex Pistols had no intention of going quietly and reunited again in 2002 in order to commemorate Queen Elizabeth II's Golden Jubilee celebrations with a one-off show at the Crystal Palace National Sports Centre. This was followed the following year with a three-week "Piss Off Tour" of US cities.

In November 2007, to commemorate the 30th anniversary of the release of *Never Mind The Bollocks*, the group booked two dates at the 5,000-capacity Brixton Academy. Owing to the demand for tickets, this was extended to five nights with other shows subsequently added in Manchester and Glasgow. The following summer saw the group embark on their "Combine Harvester" tour of European festivals before returning to London for a sell-out show at the Hammersmith Odeon on September 2, 2008.

At the time of writing, the Hammersmith Odeon show is the last Sex Pistols UK outing, but with 2012 being Queen Elizabeth II's Diamond Jubilee year, the boys might well be tempted to stick a rusting safety-pin through the royal nose.

Though Malcolm flitted between his homes in Paris and New York, now that punk rock had been assimilated into the system, he was frequently invited back to the UK to talk about the Sex Pistols and the musical revolution in which he had played such a pivotal role. Indeed, such was his standing in the British capital that he contemplated throwing his hat into the ring for the 2000 mayoral contest.

Malcolm's "Midas" touch may have proved transitory at times, but the ideas continued to flow freely. Having penned a song for Quentin Tarantino's 2004 film *Kill Bill Vol 2*, he secured a Hollywood deal as an ideas man for Steven Spielberg. He also became an outspoken critic of the burger industry by co-producing the 2006 film *Fast Food Nation*. And in November 2007, it seemed as though Malcolm would be following John's footsteps through the jungle by participating in the latest series of *I'm A Celebrity... Get Me Out Of Here*, only to pull out at the eleventh hour. He did, however, take part in *Big Brother Celebrity Hijack* which was broadcast on E4 the following year.

In October 2009, whilst working on a film project, Malcolm was diagnosed with peritoneal mesothelioma, a rare cancer that attacks the lining of the abdomen. Though he sought treatment at various hospitals, he succumbed to the disease less than six months later on Thursday, April 8, 2010, in a clinic in Switzerland. Following a funeral service at One Marylebone Church in central London where Glen and Paul were among the congregation, Malcolm was laid to rest in Highgate Cemetery on April 22. Despite his lasting enmity, on hearing of Malcolm's passing John paid the following tribute: "For me Malc was always entertaining, and I hope you remember that. Above all else he was an entertainer and I will miss him, and so should you."

The Clash

On Thursday, January 27, 1977, The Clash signed a five-album record deal with the American label CBS. They, like the Sex Pistols before them, had expected to sign with Polydor – having been courted for several weeks by Polydor's punk-loving head, Chris Parry. Like Malcolm, however, Bernard had his eye on the bigger prize, for if all record companies were indeed "whores", then it made sense to go to the one with the biggest assets. Polydor was only able to table an offer of a £25,000 advance plus all recording costs, whereas CBS was offering an advance of £100,000, which was astonishing given the fact that The Clash had been together for just seven months and had played fewer than 30 gigs.

While only Bill Grundy chose to publicly pass judgment on the Sex Pistols' hypocritical greed in signing to EMI, The Clash came in for plenty of criticism when the news of their six-figure signing to CBS was made public, most notably from Mark Perry at *Sniffin' Glue*, who openly accused the group of having "sold out". In context, however, £100,000 wasn't the fantastic sum of money it seemed. Not only did Bernard – as was his right as per his managerial contract with the group – take a hefty 25 per cent (net), but all recording costs and tour support would have to be paid out of the advance. Also, hidden away in the contractual small print was CBS's right to take up an option to extend the deal to 10 albums.

CBS was naturally keen to see an immediate return on its investment and, although The Clash were still on the lookout for a permanent drummer, the label booked the group into Whitfield Street Studios to begin work on their debut album. To solve the drumming problem,

Bernard approached Rob Harper – who'd rejoined the fold for The Clash's New Year's Day show at the Roxy. When Rob surprisingly refused, Bernard had little option but to coerce Terry Chimes into helping out in the studio.

The Clash's debut single, 'White Riot'/'1977' (CBS 5058), was released on March 18, 1977. Despite a total lack of daytime radio play, it managed to break into the UK Top 40 peaking at number 38. The eponymous album (CBS 32232) followed one month later to mixed reviews, and narrowly missed a Top 10 slot, peaking at a very respectable 12.

In May of that year, The Clash, with newly installed drummer Nicky "Topper" Headon, embarked on their own punk-package nationwide UK tour with The Jam, Buzzcocks, and The Slits in support. It played to packed houses every night – including a sell-out show at the 9,000-capacity Rainbow Theatre in Finsbury Park – but "White Riot Tour" accrued losses estimated at £28,000.

The protracted disagreements between The Clash and their corporate paymasters hove into view when CBS released 'Remote Control'/'London's Burning' (CBS 5293) – both of which, of course, appeared on the album – as the follow-up single without consulting the group while they were midway through the tour. Mick had penned 'Remote Control' in response to the "bores and their laws" they'd encountered on the Anarchy Tour, and now here they were being subjugated by their own record label. In response to this, the group vented their anger in a new song 'Complete Control' which was released as the third single, that September.

In 1978 The Clash did two nationwide UK tours and enjoyed moderate chart success with the singles 'Clash City Rockers'/'Jail Guitar Doors' (CBS 5834), the superb reggae-influenced '(White Man) In Hammersmith Palais'/'The Prisoner' (CBS 6383), and 'Tommy Gun'/'1-2 Crush On You' (CBS 6788), which served as the introductory single from the group's – arguably overproduced – second album *Give 'Em Enough Rope* (CBS 32444), which was released on November 10, 1978, and reached number two on the UK album chart. Despite respectable sales of *Give 'Em Enough Rope* on both sides of the Atlantic, by year's end The Clash were reportedly £250,000 in debt to CBS. They'd also parted company with Bernard Rhodes which cost them a further £25,000 in severance pay.

Prior to the release of their seventh single, 'English Civil War'/'Pressure Drop' (CBS 7082), in February 1979, The Clash embarked on their first US tour. However, the nine-date "Pearl Harbour '79 Tour" as it was called, was plagued by problems with CBS's sister company, Epic, which was constantly griping about the tour budget, the group's choice of support acts, and perhaps most important of all – poor album sales. The latter consideration led to Epic going behind the group's back by promoting the tour under the same name as the album, and relations were soured even further when Joe and the boys refused to pose for the obligatory corporate photograph with Epic's besuited high-flyers. On a more positive note, however, The Clash's raunchy brand of rock'n'roll went down well with the audiences – with most of the shows selling out in advance.

Back in London, the group moved into Vanilla Studios in Pimlico – little more than a nondescript backroom above a garage – where they set about penning the songs that would make up their third album, *London Calling*. As Bernard had had the group's assets to date frozen, in order to bring in some much-needed cash the group released *The Cost Of Living*, a four-track EP which included a blistering cover of the Sonny Curtis classic 'I Fought The Law', and a re-recording of 'Capital Radio' – originally given away as a promotional freebie via *NME* – as a means of thwarting the black marketeers who were selling the original *Capital Radio* EP for extortionate prices.

In July 1979, Epic finally bowed to pressure from the group's growing number of American fans by releasing a modified version of *The Clash*, which up until that time had only been available in the US as an expensive import. In September, the group embarked on their second US tour: "Clash Take the Fifth Tour" (as in the Fifth Amendment of the US Constitution, which gives every American citizen the right to remain silent in the face of incrimination), but once again strained relations between the group and Epic marred the tour.

On December 7, 1979, The Clash released 'London Calling'/'Armagideon Time' (CBS 8087) as the lead single from the forthcoming *London Calling* (CBS CLASH 3), which, despite being the group's finest album in terms of musical diversity, received mixed reviews on its release in the UK the following week. Though The Clash had expanded musically, and had long-since shed their natty punk threads, they doggedly held onto their punk ethos in ensuring their fans got value for money by insisted that the double album retailed at £4.99, the same price as that of a single album. As *London Calling* wasn't released in the US until January 1980, *Rolling Stone* magazine subsequently voted it the best album of the eighties.

In January 1980, The Clash embarked on a nationwide UK tour to promote *London Calling*. Buoyed by the success of the 'London Calling' single, which reached number 11 on the UK chart, they announced a non-stop UK singles campaign. The first single was intended to be 'Bankrobber'/'Rockers Galore... UK Tour' (CBS 8323), but once again the group met with record company obstinacy and the single didn't actually come out until later that summer by which time Joe, Mick and Topper were in New York recording songs for the next intended studio album. Paul was in Canada appearing in the film *Ladies And Gentlemen: The Fabulous Stains* with Steve Jones and Paul Cook, and *Scum* actor Ray "Johnny Strummer" Winstone.

The Clash's creativity was so prolific during this period that they recorded enough material for a triple album – the eclectic *Sandinista* (CBS FSLN1). Once again, however, the group insisted on giving their fans value for money by retailing it at £5.99 which meant that they had to forgo royalties on the first 200,000 copies sold. This was a bold move given the fact that its predecessor *London Calling* had sold only 180,000 copies all told. Playing latter-day Robin Hoods was all well and good, but by the end of the year The Clash was in hock to CBS to the tune of £500,000, and so Joe, fearing that the group was facing financial meltdown, instigated Bernard's return[2]. 1980 also saw the release of the Dave Mingay/Jack Hazen film *Rude Boy,* in which The Clash can be seen recording *Give 'Em Enough Rope* as well as out on tour.

The following year did not augur well for The Clash, as none of the three singles culled from *Sandinista* – 'The Call Up'/'Stop The World' (CBS 9339), 'Hitsville UK'/'Police On My Back' (CBS 9480), and 'The Magnificent Seven'/'The Magnificent Dance' (CBS A1133) managed to trouble the UK charts. Plans for a full-scale UK tour were downsized to a few selective dates, before being shelved altogether.

Believing that their popularity in the UK was on the wane, The Clash began putting together a massive 60-date US tour in a bid to break through into mainstream America, which made perfect sense given that over half of the sales for *Sandinista* had been in the US. While this tour ultimately fell through, Bernard did at least manage to salvage something from the ashes by proposing a series of seven-night residencies starting in New York at Bonds Casino on Times Square. Though the first night at Bonds went ahead as scheduled, unfortunately for both the group and their American fans – who would take their protest out on to the street and cause a mini-riot – the city's fire chiefs made an unannounced visit to the venue and declared that the supposed 4,000-capacity represented a fire risk and restricted the rest of the shows to a capacity of 1,750.

The Clash, however, were unwilling to allow either adversity or petty political bureaucracy to stand in their way, and they not only agreed to extend the residency to 16 nights – including additional matinee shows, but also to absorb the extra costs. Having warmed to the residency concept, the group staged similar events at Paris' Mogador and again at London's Lyceum Ballroom, which formed part of their long-delayed UK tour. However, the year would end on something of a low note with the single 'This Is Radio Clash'/'Radio Clash' (CBS 1797) barely breaking into the UK Top 50, and Topper being arrested at Heathrow airport for attempting to smuggle heroin into the country

By the beginning of 1982, The Clash had neared completion on their fifth album, *Combat Rock*

---

2   During his enforced exile, Bernard had looked after the interests of Subway Sect, Specials AKA, and the soul-rebel era Dexy's Midnight Runners.

(CBS FMLN2), which it had been hoped would be ready for release in time for the group's tours of Australia, New Zealand and South-east Asia. Topper's spiralling heroin problem, coupled with Mick's high-handedness over the new album's production, meant that CBS didn't actually take possession of the master tape until April, which delayed the official release until May 14, 1982. Prior to the album's release CBS tested the water by releasing 'Know Your Rights'/'First Night Back In London' (CBS A2309), but as with the group's recent efforts the single faired poorly on the UK chart.

By the time of the album's release, The Clash were supposed to be in the midst of a 19-date UK tour, but the first of these dates had to be cancelled as Joe had seemingly gone AWOL. It later transpired that Bernard had been behind Joe to fake his disappearance in order to drum up publicity for the forthcoming tour as ticket sales were poor. The idea had been for Joe to visit his namesake, the American Tex-Mex troubadour Joe Ely, but Joe outfoxed Bernard by catching the boat train to Paris without telling anybody his true destination. So while Bernard was playing up Joe's "mysterious" disappearance, his singer had gone into hiding for real. Joe was eventually located and brought back into the fold, but within weeks of his return Topper was sacked. Topper's drug problems would get so bad that at one point – having sold all his Clash memorabilia to feed his habit – he was forced to drive a cab to make ends meet until the group's long-standing CBS contract was renegotiated to allow their back catalogue to be reissued on CD.

Despite the poor showing of 'Know Your Rights', *Combat Rock* soared to number two in the UK album chart in its second week of release – equalling *Give 'Em Enough Rope*'s feat of four years earlier. Unlike its predecessor, however, *Combat Rock* would stay in the charts for 23 weeks, making it the group's most successful album to date. The problem facing The Clash now, however, was that they were about to embark on a US tour to promote the album without a drummer. With no time to waste on recruiting and breaking in someone new they once again called on the services of their old pal Terry Chimes, and although the tour was beset with problems, the group sold out five consecutive nights at the 3,800-capacity Hollywood Palladium.

A short UK tour followed, but the group didn't have time to collect its collective breath before embarking on another month-long US tour, which stretched into October as a result of the group accepting an offer to support The Who on the American leg of their supposed "retirement tour" – including two consecutive nights at New York's Shea Stadium. The American audiences probably viewed the shows as a symbolic handing over of the baton between the outgoing kings of British counter-culture to the one group best suited to take their mantle, but the vast majority of The Clash's British fans viewed this as a double betrayal of the group's ideals: not only were they publicly kowtowing to one of the reviled sixties "dinosaur groups" which punk had supposedly railed against, but they would be doing so in vast stadiums. To their minds, The Clash couldn't be the same group that had once championed a world with "No Elvis, Beatles, or Rolling Stones".

In late October 1982, Mick Jones' remixed version of 'Rock The Casbah' (CBS A2479) was released in the US, which thanks to a combination of exposure from their guest appearances on The Who's farewell tour and the accompanying video's heavy rotation on the new cultural phenomenon known as MTV served to propel the single to number eight on the US charts. This in turn helped *Combat Rock* to climb to number seven on the *Billboard* 200, and sell over a million and a half copies which at long last put The Clash in the unique position of actually turning a profit.

1982 proved something of a gruelling year for The Clash, and the three long-standing members had already decided to take a few months' holiday in order to recuperate and recharge their batteries for as yet unspecified objectives in the coming year. Terry, however, although thoroughly enjoying his second stint with The Clash, didn't have the luxury of CBS royalties to pay the bills and was also less than convinced that the group would actually get back together as relations between Mick and Joe had degenerated almost to breaking point. Knowing that he couldn't afford to waste six months hanging around waiting to see if there would still be a group to rejoin, he accepted Johnny Thunders' offer to replace Jerry Nolan in The Heartbreakers, before subsequently teaming up with Billy Idol.

Terry is now a fully qualified chiropractor and travels the world giving seminars.

The friction growing like a cancer at the heart of The Clash stemmed from Mick – or "Wack Attack" as he was known to Joe and Paul – having fallen in love with hip-hop while growing tired of conventional guitar-based rock music. He wanted the group to experiment with their sound by adding drum machines, synthesizers and samples. Joe and Paul, however, were equally determined to ensure that the group didn't drift away from its punk roots. By February 1983, rumours of a split were beginning to appear in the music press, and although little was happening on the public front, behind the scenes Joe, Mick, and Paul had returned to their old Camden Town stomping ground Rehearsal Rehearsals where they tried to rebuild bridges by writing new material together. They were also actively seeking a new drummer, and from the 300 or so would-be Toppers that responded to the *Melody Maker* ad, the trio finally settled on 23-year-old Pete Howard from the Bath-based group Cold Fish, who also happened to be signed to CBS.

In May, The Clash flew out to America to play a series of low-key dates that were intended to break in their new drummer before headlining the New Music Day of the second annual US Festival, which saw them earn an unbelievable $500,000. Though The Clash's three long-standing members returned to the UK with bulging wallets, the on-going rift between Mick and Joe was clearly getting worse, and arguments over how best to use the cash windfall only served to exacerbate the problem.

Nothing was heard from the group for the next four months or so, and then on Thursday, September 1, 1983, a "Clash Communiqué" announced that Mick had been sacked for having apparently "drifted away from the original idea of The Clash".

It wasn't until January of the following year that The Clash resurfaced with a five-piece line-up, and it was surely a telling sign of Joe's and Paul's appreciation of Mick's talents that they felt the need to bring in two guitarists. First to join was 23-year-old Nick Sheppard, formerly of Bristol punks The Cortinas, and in December the line-up was augmented further still by Vince White who also just happened to be 23[3*].

The "rejuvenated" Clash then embarked on a short US tour before returning to the UK for a month-long tour with the group taking to the stage each night backed by a wall of television screens each showing separate images of current cultural and political events. At the end of March, they embarked on a second, more extensive, US tour that ran through until the end of May. Although The Clash were once again active on the live circuit, they had no new product with which to promote the tour which led to some venues falling to sell out. This obvious shortcoming saw the group head into the studio to begin work on a new album.

Cut The Crap (CBS 26601) was released to harsh critisism in November 1985, and apart from the single 'This Is England' (CBS A6122) – generally regarded as the last great Clash song – which climbed to a respectable 24 in the UK chart the previous month, the album contains 11 sub-standard offerings that many critics believed to be unworthy of bearing The Clash logo. The anticipation of a new Clash release amongst the group's fanbase, however, allowed the album to reach number 16 in the UK chart before sliding away into obscurity. It faired little better in the US, stalling at a dismal 88 on the *Billboard* 200.

In May 1985, The Clash embarked on what could perhaps be described as their craziest venture to date – hitch-hiking up and down the UK playing a string of busking dates at various towns and cities including Leeds, Nottingham, Gateshead, York and Edinburgh. This spate of back-to-basic impromptu performances gave the group's die-hard fans renewed hope, but it was to prove a false dawn and The Clash's swansong came on Tuesday, August 27, 1985, when they headlined the Greek Music Festival at the Olympic Stadium in Athens.

By this time, of course, Mick Jones was already enjoying chart success with his new group Big Audio

---

3   *NME* took great delight in revealing that White was a Physics and Astronomy student at University College, London, whose real name was actually Greg.

Dynamite[4*] (BAD), and although Joe would go on to achieve recognition for his solo projects, as well as with The Mescaleros, rumours would often surface of a possible reunion between one of the greatest songwriting duos in the history of contemporary music, for which The Clash received an Ivor Novello Award in 2001.

Although a reconciliation of sorts did come to pass in the mid-Eighties, the pair fell out again over Mick's decision to use a BAD song ('Rush') to accompany 'Should I Stay Or Should I Go' (CBS A2646), when The Clash song – originally released in June 1982 – was selected for a Levi's TV commercial; this resulted in the group achieving its first-ever UK number one some six years after they'd disbanded. Joe and Paul patched up their differences with Mick, and although the rumours of a Clash reunion continued – with several serious cash offers being tabled – the reunion was sadly not to be.

On Friday, November 15, 2002, 19 years since they had last done so, Joe and Mick shared the same stage – typically during a benefit gig for striking miners – at the Acton Town Hall in London, and those lucky enough to be in the audience that night were treated to an encore of 'Bankrobber', 'White Riot' and 'London's Burning'.

Mick's decision to get up on stage that night was purely spontaneous, but both he and Joe were in favour of a one-off classic line-up reunion to celebrate The Clash's long-overdue induction into the Rock 'n' Roll Hall of Fame scheduled for March 2003. Topper was also up for the one-off appearance, but Paul – though he enjoyed his time playing with Havana 3AM – was rather less enthused about the idea as he had made a name for himself outside of music and therefore had little desire to set aside his oils and watercolours in favour of picking up a bass guitar again. Although determined to get Paul to change his mind, Joe had placed Mani from Primal Scream on standby.

Whether Paul would have had a change of heart and agreed to join his old muckers on stage one last time became a moot point when Joe died suddenly at his Somerset home shortly after returning from walking his two dogs on Sunday, December 22, 2002. He was 50 years old. The subsequent autopsy revealed that he died from a congenital heart defect and not a heart attack as was originally suspected. Unbeknownst to anyone – including himself – Joe had been born with the defect where a main artery went through his heart instead of around it and could have claimed him at any point during his life.

The Damned

On Friday, February 18, 1977, The Damned released their second single 'Neat Neat Neat'/'Stab Your Back' (BUY 10), the same day they released their debut album, *Damned Damned Damned* (SEEZ1). They then set yet another precedent by becoming the first punk group to tour the United States. Having released two singles and an album in less than six months, to the casual observer it must have appeared as though The Damned were leaving their punk peers behind. A third "limited edition" single

4   When first putting BAD together Mick offered the drum stool to Topper, but the drummer's ongoing drug problems soon led to his departure.

'Stretcher Case Baby'/'Sick Of Being Sick' (DAMNED 1) – initially given away at the group's one-year anniversary shows at the Marquee – followed in July, but doing everything at a sulphate-fuelled frenetic pace inevitably came at a price.

By the time they went into London's Britannia Row Studios to record their second album tensions were mounting because Brian James – upon whom the group relied for the majority of their songs – was insisting they recruit a second guitarist so that he could adopt a more virtuoso role. Despite grumblings from the other three members, James won the day and Robert "Lu" Edmonds joined the line-up shortly before the group went into the studio.

To herald the impending release of *Music For Pleasure* (SFF75), Stiff released 'Problem Child'/'You Take My Money' (BUY 18) as the Damned's third official single. Though the single cracked the Top 30 on the *NME* chart, it failed to trouble even the Top 75 on the official UK chart. The parent album – which was considered a disappointment by both critics and fans alike – faired even worse and didn't shift enough copies to reach the Top 100 on the UK chart. One of the reasons for the failure was undoubtedly the group's choice of producer. Instead of calling on Nick Lowe who'd produced *Damned Damned Damned*, they had initially tried to lure former Pink Floyd frontman, Syd Barrett, out of his self-imposed seclusion, but when the enigmatic Syd refused The Damned – rather unwisely as it turned out – agreed to allow another Floyd stalwart, Nick Mason, to take the controls.

The Pink Floyd drummer may have been attuned to the needs of his own outfit, but he had little or no understanding of what The Damned were about. Owing to the disappointing response to the album and to the subsequent single 'Don't Cry Wolf'/'One Way Love' (BUY 24) – which again failed to make any impression on the UK chart – Rat Scabies announced his departure. Although the group managed to limp on for several months with other drummers – including Jon Moss, who would also temporarily occupy The Clash drum stool before achieving worldwide fame with Boy George's Culture Club – Brian had also lost heart and made the unilateral decision to dissolve The Damned in February 1978.

Brian wasted little time in grieving over The Damned and formed Tanz Der Youth, before then going on form the relatively more successful Lords Of The New Church. Singer Dave Vanian joined the Doctors Of Madness, while Captain Sensible teamed up with The Softies to record a cover version of the New York Dolls' classic 'Jet Boy', before then going on to form his own short-lived group King[5*]. By this time Rat had put together his own group, The White Cats, and he also teamed up with Glen Matlock and Steve New for the aforementioned "Sid Sods Off" show at Camden's Electric Circus in August 1978.

Being the drummer in Sid Vicious' ad hoc backing group, however, was as good as it was going to get for Rat in regard to attracting any interest in The White Cats so he approached his old mate Captain Sensible with the view to putting another group together. Sensible was more than up for the idea as his post-Damned career was also in perpetual freefall. Having reverted to lead guitar, his instrument of choice, the Captain recruited Softies bassist, Henry Badowski, and with Dave Vanian back in the fold, the four-piece christened themselves The Doomed, and embarked on a European tour.

The tour, however, was beset with problems both on and off stage, with Rat almost being incarcerated in a French prison for having set fire to his hotel room. Shortly after their return to the UK, Badowski announced his departure and was replaced by ex-Saints bassist, Algy Ward. By the end of 1978, having first secured Brian's blessing, the group reverted back to The Damned and in the spring of 1979 the group, now signed to Chiswick Records, enjoyed chart success with the single 'Love Song/'Noise Noise Noise' (CHIS 115), which reached number 20 in the UK chart and earned them an appearance on *Top Of The Pops*.

Later that year The Damned went back into the studio to begin recording their third album, *Machine Gun Etiquette* (CWK 3011), for Chiswick. Prior to the album's release, Chiswick released 'Smash It Up'/'Burglar' (CHIS 115), which – though regarded as a "punk classic" – stalled at number 35 on the

---

5   Not to be confused with the group of the same name once fronted by Paul King, the MTV VJ.

UK chart owing to Radio One's refusal to give the single any daytime airplay over its perceived anarchistic theme. Despite 'I Just Can't Be Happy Today'/'Ballroom Blitz' (CHIS 120) – the third single culled from the album – failing to make much impact on the singles chart, the parent album was well received both in critical and commercial terms. However, the in-house squabbling, notably between Rat and Algy Ward, which was ever-present in the Damned camp resulted in Ward's departure shortly before the end of the year. Algy's replacement was Paul Gray, formerly of Eddie & the Hot Rods, who joined in time for a short European tour before accompanying the group in the studio during the recording of their fourth album.

The resulting *Black Album* (CWK 3015), which was released as a double album in the UK, yet only as a single disc in the US, was a commercial failure despite being praised by the critics for containing some ground-breaking material. This failure saw The Damned part company with Chiswick after four years, but they managed to find another – albeit temporary – home with Bronze Records, for whom they recorded their fifth album, *Strawberries* (BRON 542), in 1981. *Strawberries* became The Damned's first Top 20 success, probably due to the group's decision to experiment with their sound by augmenting the line-up with keyboardist Roman Jugg.

1982 brought more – perhaps totally unexpected – problems for The Damned when Captain Sensible scored a surprise UK number one with his version of the *South Pacific* song 'Happy Talk'. The media exposure from Sensible's success may have resulted in increased sales for The Damned's new album, but it did little to endear him to the rest of the group. In order to promote the new album they embarked on another European tour before heading out to the US, where financial mismanagement turned the tour into a complete fiasco and at one point saw the near-penniless group holed up in a seedy motel sharing a solitary hamburger.

If the latter half of 1982 was an unhappy time, 1983 was a particularly grim year for The Damned as the group again succumbed to the "curse of the bass players". In-house squabbling between Rat and Paul Gray resulted in Gray's departure in February. Gray's replacement was Bryn Merrick, a friend of Jugg's, who took up bass duties in time for their guest appearance on the anarchic BBC2 show *The Young Ones* starring Rik Mayall and Ade Edmondson on which they performed 'Nasty'. However, this line-up was destined to be short-lived as Sensible quit the group to pursue a solo career, a move that saw Jugg switch from keyboards to guitar.

After 18 months of relative obscurity The Damned resurfaced and headed back into the studio in a "make or break" bid to secure a new record deal. The quality of the songs on the resulting demo tape was enough to secure a deal with MCA, whose initial scepticism was swept away on the tide of success following the group's first single, 'Grimly Fiendish' (GRIM 1), which reached number 21 in the UK chart in 1985, their highest chart placing since 1979.

On the strength of this success, MCA released the group's sixth album, the pop-orientated *Phantasmagoria* (MCFW 3275), which was closely followed by further singles 'The Shadow Of Love' (GRIM 2), which reached number 25 on the UK chart, and 'Is It A Dream' (GRIM 3), which peaked at number 34. MCA was probably already pleased with having three Top 40 hits from the album, but the fourth single – a cover version of the Paul & Barry Ryan song 'Eloise' (GRIM 4) – surprised everybody by climbing to number three.

This, however, would prove to be zenith of The Damned's career-to-date as their follow-up album *Anything*, released during the summer of 1986, was a commercial failure despite their version of Love's 'Alone Again Or' receiving extensive airplay in the US. It would be 15 long years before the world saw another Damned album, *Grave Disorder*, released on Nitro Records in 2001. And although Sensible had rejoined the group for a string of successful reunion shows, which culminated in a triumphant 10-date US tour, hopes of a permanent reunion of three members of the group's original 1976 line-up were shattered when Rat departed in acrimonious circumstances.

2008 saw the release of The Damned's tenth album, *So, Who's Paranoid?*, which featured the single 'Little Miss Disaster' which was released back in 2005 via the group's own Lively Arts label. Although The

Damned's hedonistic days are well and truly behind them now, the group is still active on the live circuit and can rely on a loyal fanbase to ensure that the current line-up, which still features original stalwarts Dave Vanian and Captain Sensible, will be playing to packed houses for some time to come.

The Heartbreakers

In April 1977, The Heartbreakers signed a six-album, three-year deal with Track Records – the very same label that had been poised to sign the New York Dolls the night Billy Murcia died five years earlier. The following month saw the group embark on a short European tour, taking in Holland, France and Belgium, before then returning to the UK to continue work on the debut album – tentatively titled *Like A Motherfucker* – which they'd first set about recording back in February prior to signing with Track. With Track having released 'Chinese Rocks'/'Born To Lose' as the group's debut single, things did finally appear to be on course, but of course anything might happen when Johnny and Jerry were out on the road, and after a show in Leeds during a mini UK tour, the group found themselves being held at gunpoint by police. (The fingerprints taken by the police that night were subsequently used as part of the artwork for the front cover of *Like A Motherfucker*.)

That August, Johnny took time out to marry his long-term American girlfriend, Julie, who'd joined him in London earlier in the year. The marriage, however, was destined to be short-lived.

In October 1977, The Heartbreakers embarked on a lengthy UK tour to promote their long-awaited and highly anticipated album. However, the production was so bad on the finished product that the album was received with universal disappointment, which led to Jerry Nolan quitting the group. Jerry was temporarily replaced by Paul Cook, and although he rejoined midway through the tour, Thunders and the rest of the group issued a terse statement announcing that Jerry had rejoined as a "hired musician", and not as a full-time member of The Heartbreakers.

Finding himself a hired hand in the group he'd helped form was never going to sit easily with a firebrand like Jerry, and within a month he'd quit again to be replaced by Terry Chimes. That same month Track Records released 'It's Not Enough' as the group's second single. However, the financial implications over poor sales of the *L.A.M.F.* album had already sounded the label's death knell, and it folded shortly thereafter. The Heartbreakers brought their tour to a climax with two sell-out shows at The Vortex, but the loss of record label support – as well as the end of the Johnny/Jerry nucleus – saw The Heartbreakers quickly disintegrate. Walter and Billy flew back to New York, supposedly for the Christmas holidays, only to then decide that they wouldn't be returning to London in the New Year. When a possible new deal with CBS fell through at the last minute Leee Black Childers announced his departure and followed Walter and Billy to New York.

The opening months of 1978 saw Johnny put together an in-house Speakeasy supergroup from the pool of musicians frequenting London's famous watering hole at that particular time. The group, which usually performed under the name The Living Dead, included Paul Cook and Steve Jones, Peter Perrett from The Only Ones, and Paul Gray and Steve Nicol from the Hot Rods. This series of impromptu gigs helped Johnny secure a solo deal with the newly established Real Records, a WEA subsidiary, and the majority of these musicians – as well as Walter Lure and Billy Rath who flew over from New York – would appear as guests on the resulting album, *So Alone*, released the following October.

Johnny's solo career finally seemed to be on the up, but he was brought back down to earth again when the official receivers brought in to handle the liquidation of Track Records' assets discovered that The Heartbreakers had inadvertently spent £29,283, over and above the contractual £50,000 and were threatening to initiate court proceedings unless they received payment within 14 days.

In August, Johnny – again accompanied by Walter and Billy – returned to New York to play a one-off Heartbreakers reunion gig of sorts at Max's Kansas City, but with Ty Styx on drums instead of Jerry Nolan. In October Johnny returned to London where he performed a solo show at the Lyceum to promote his solo album with a backing group again consisting of his old Speakeasy buddies. After the show he informed the music press that he was planning to go to New Orleans where he intended to hand-pick musicians for a new group. This plan, however, came to nothing for by June 1979 Johnny was in Ann Arbor, Michigan, recording demos with former MC5 guitarist Wayne Kramer for an early version of the group Gang War, which would subsequently go on to play gigs in various US states but failed to secure a record deal.

Having agreed to help Johnny secure a new deal, in November 1981 Leee Black Childers took the Track demos to France which appeared to be the only country still interested in what Johnny had to offer. Although Leee returned to the US empty-handed, he did at least manage to secure a deal with Fresh Records. Unfortunately for Johnny, however, the label folded less than six months later.

By March 1982, Johnny was back in the studio recording demos with Rolling Stones producer Jimmy Miller at the controls, and with a host of musicians – including Jerry Nolan. On a personal level, however, Johnny's life appeared to be in freefall as he was living in a squalid New York basement apartment and had sold off his guitars to feed his heroin habit. At the end of that month he flew out to Sweden to perform a song on TV, but he hit the headlines for all the wrong reasons when his drug proclivities brought him to the attention of the Swedish police.

In April, he returned to the UK to undertake a tour of London performing at venues such as the Hope & Anchor, the Venue, as well as the Rock Garden in Covent Garden. Once again, however, the performances were marred by his prodigious drug intake. At The Venue on April 22, Johnny was joined on stage by Sylvain Sylvain who was astounded that his buddy couldn't remember the chords to 'Chinese Rocks'. Johnny was also forgetting to stash his rocks securely for on arrival at Heathrow following a short trip to Sweden, he was arrested and charged with possession of heroin and spent the night in Pentonville prison.

On July 15, 1982, Johnny celebrated his thirtieth birthday with a show at New York City's Irving Plaza. He also formalised a management agreement with Christopher Giercke, who would be instrumental in landing Johnny a deal with Jungle Records – which had risen phoenix-like from the dying embers of

Fresh Records. Giercke also arranged for Johnny to see a Harley Street doctor who was also a psychiatric specialist. The good doctor placed Johnny on a methadone programme on which he would remain for the rest of his life.

Johnny was also briefly reunited with Leee Black Childers, who had finally got hold of the paperwork which proved that the rights to *L.A.M.F.* legally reverted back to his own management company when Track folded. Childers then set to work on remixing the album for a Heartbreakers reunion tour.

In December, Johnny returned to Sweden for the Christmas holidays where – just as Jerry had done several months earlier – he met and fell in love with a local girl. Her name was Susanne Blomqvist, and Johnny remained in Sweden with his new flame until the end of January when he returned to London to oversee the remixing of *L.A.M.F.* Once the album had received its makeover, Johnny then took the reconstituted Heartbreakers out on a promotional UK tour. After only a few dates, however, Walter decided that there was more to life than rock'n'roll and returned to New York where he resumed his prior career as a Wall Street commodity broker.

In August 1984, the three-piece Heartbreakers became the first and only group to play five consecutive nights at London's hallowed Marquee Club, and the following month they embarked on a tour of Scandinavia. There must have been something in the Swedish water as Billy Rath also found himself a Swedish partner and subsequently remained in Stockholm once the tour had ended. With his rhythm section firmly ensconced in Sweden, Johnny brought in new musicians including Terry Chimes. He also joined Hanoi Rocks for the metal group's up-and-coming tour; the proviso being that his own group was booked as support.

The early part of 1985 saw The Heartbreakers tour extensively – including a 10-date tour of Japan. But once again Johnny was focusing all his energy on chasing the dragon rather than putting fire into his music. Although he voluntarily placed himself on a six-week detoxification programme, he quit the programme after just three weeks.

Having parted company with both Blomqvist and Giercke, Johnny returned to New York in April to play three nights at the Irving Plaza. But the plaza triumvirate was not the triumphant homecoming that Johnny or his fans had been hoping for. By October, Johnny and Susanne were back in each other's arms, and such was Johnny's renewed ardour that when the time came for him to return to the US to go on tour he purposely crushed his hand in a car door so that the tour would have to be postponed.

The rescheduled US tour finally got underway four months later, but after the final show in New York, the road crew – suspecting that Johnny was holding back their wages – barged into his room at the Chelsea Hotel and threw all his belongings out of the window. Johnny was so freaked out by the incident that he fled back to Stockholm, only to return to London the following month for a show at Dingwalls where he unveiled his latest group, which included a rhythm section consisting of Glen Matlock and Jerry Nolan. Johnny and Jerry had recently formed a 50/50 partnership, with Jerry's new wife, Charlotte, acting as the pair's manager. The summer was taken up with tours of Japan and Bangkok, which was followed in September by a two-week tour of Australia. En route to one of the Australian shows Jerry suffered a broken collar bone when the tour bus came off the road, but the drummer somehow managed to see out the remainder of the tour.

In January 1987, by which time Arthur "Killer" Kane had replaced Glen Matlock, The Heartbreakers embarked on a tour of the US that was a New York Dolls reunion of sorts. But although the tour was a success, Johnny and Jerry fell out again over money. In May, Johnny flew to London to begin work on his new album *Copy Cats*, again for Jungle Records. But he was back in Sweden with Susanne before the week was out having been dissatisfied with the recordings, leaving red-faced Jungle executives wondering whether the album would ever be finished.

He returned to London two months later to renew work on the album, only to then lose his voice and he still wasn't happy with his vocal efforts when the time came to return to Stockholm. That August Nina Antonia's long-awaited book *Johnny Thunders: In Cold Blood* finally went to press.

Things went quiet for a while, but in August 1988 Johnny unveiled a new six-piece group which – barring having to replace the bass player the following year – would remain with him until his death. The next 12 months were taken up with extensive touring, including a tour of the UK, but poor attendances resulted in neither Johnny nor his backing group being paid.

In September, Jerry Nolan flew into London to collect his methadone prescription, but was subsequently arrested at Gatwick Airport whilst en route to New York for being in possession of 540 5mg. tablets. After spending six days in Lewes Prison he appeared before magistrates at nearby Horsham, but was released without charge. He was so delighted at being acquitted that he vowed to cut down on his daily methadone dosage.

In February 1990, Johnny flew out to Paris, principally for a few dates at the city's Gibus Club, but ended up moving in with his old friend, and former Dead Boy, Stiv Bators, in order to work on the latter's new album alongside Dee Dee Ramone. Johnny's input on the project would prove short-lived, however, as the ex-Ramone accused him of having stolen his money. In a fit of rage, Dee Dee smashed Johnny's guitar and poured bleach over his clothes.

Although Johnny decided to remain in Paris and moved into a hotel, he was down to his last dollar and was forced to rely on hand-outs from Jungle Records. In April, he returned to the UK for an acoustic tour, but was detained by Immigration which resulted in his missing the opening date in Dublin; the rest of the tour went ahead as scheduled. Two months later, Johnny – flush with cash from the acoustic tour – was finally able to put down some roots by acquiring an apartment in New York. In September, he booked himself into a health farm from which he emerged six weeks later totally detoxed for the first time in almost 16 years.

In January 1991, Johnny – the eternal nomad – was back living in Paris, but the New Year saw him slide back into old habits. Now he was also taking tranquilisers as well as heroin. In early April, following a quick stop-off in London where he re-established contact with his Harley Street doctor, Johnny embarked on another tour of Japan before flying on to Thailand for a short vacation. He returned home to New York for a brief visit, and then flew out to Germany where he recorded a song with Die Toten Hosen.

On Monday, April 22, 1991, Johnny finally made good on his promise of 13 years earlier by flying to New Orleans where he booked into the St. Peter House Hotel. He never got the chance to fulfil his dream of hand-picking a backing group from the city's black street musicians, however, as he was found dead in his room the following morning. The coroner's report stated that Johnny's death may have been drug-related as empty methadone packages and a syringe were found in the en-suite toilet, but many of his fans believe he was murdered. He was just 38 years old.

Within eight months of Johnny's demise, Jerry Nolan was also dead. The 45-year-old drummer lapsed into a fatal coma while in hospital undergoing treatment for bacterial meningitis and pneumonia. Jerry's dying wish was that he be buried next to Johnny in Mount Saint Mary Cemetery in Queens.

Buzzcocks

While supporting the Sex Pistols at the Electric Circus on the Anarchy Tour brought about a suitably climatic finale to 1976 for Buzzcocks, the first quarter of 1977 was to bring contrasting fortunes for the Mancunian outfit. In February of that year – with financial assistance from friends and family – they released their seminal four-track EP *Spiral Scratch* (ORG 1) on the independent New Hormones label. The ground-breaking disc received excellent reviews which helped to shift the initial pressing of 1,000 copies. But this success proved to be something of a double-edged sword for Buzzcocks, as Howard Devoto believed his having released a single now fulfilled all his pop star ambitions and he announced that he was quitting the group. The self-enforced exile didn't last long, however, for he resurfaced later in the year fronting a new group, Magazine.

Despite the loss of their lead singer and main songwriter, Buzzcocks were determined to carry on. Pete Shelley took over Devoto's mantle whilst continuing sawing away on his Woolworths guitar, and Steve Diggle switched to guitar – the role he'd secretly been coveting since joining the group – and an old school friend of Shelley's, Garth Smith, was brought in on bass. The new line-up soon became something of a regular attraction at the Roxy, and such was Buzzcocks' growing prestige amongst London's punk cognoscenti that they were invited to participate in The Clash's now-legendary White Riot Tour.

Buzzcocks, left to right: John Maher, Steve Diggle, Pete Shelley & Garth Smith

On Tuesday, August 16, 1977, the same day that Elvis Presley died, Buzzcocks signed to United Artists, with the official contract signing taking place at the Electric Circus. Their first single for the label – released in November of that year, was the highly controversial Devoto/Shelley composition 'Orgasm Addict'/'What Ever Happened To…?' (UP 36316) which centred on the delights of masturbation. It was a true measure of the potential that United Artists saw in its latest acquisition that the label was willing to allow the group to choose a song which had little or no hope of receiving radio airplay.

The follow-up single, 'What Do I Get?'/'Oh Shit' (UP 36348), released the following February, scraped into the UK Top 40. But this success coincided with another temporary setback when Garth Smith was dismissed over the bassist's excessive drunkenness. Smith's replacement was another Mancunian, Steve Garvey, whose introduction brought about what many fans believe to be Buzzcocks' all-time classic line-up.

March 1978 saw the release of Buzzcocks' debut long-player, *Another Music In A Different Kitchen* (UAG 30159), which received glowing reviews, and to promote the album United Artists released 'I Don't Mind'/'Autonomy' (UP 36386) – both of which appeared on the album – as a double A-side single. A fourth single, 'Love You More'/'Noise Annoys' (UP 36433) followed later in the summer. Buzzcocks' seemingly-effortless ability to create perfect three-minute highly infectious guitar-driven pop vignettes about teenage love and heart-rending angst was cemented in stone with the release of their second album, *Love Bites*, just six months later.

Although both albums enjoyed success in the UK album charts, neither would receive an official US release until many years later. Despite the lack of interest from our American cousins, 1978 was still a fantastic year as Buzzcocks shed their punk skin and entered the pop mainstream, notching up five Top 20 singles in the process. Their most successful single to date: 'Ever Fallen In Love (With Someone You Shouldn't've?), released in November 1978, would prove a massive US hit in 2004 following its inclusion on the soundtrack for the film *Shrek 2*.

During the first quarter of 1979, Buzzcocks embarked on a full European tour with fellow Mancunians Joy Division in support. This was followed in May with an invitation to record a session for John Peel's late-night radio show. A promotional tour of America followed the release of the group's long-awaited third album, *A Different Kind Of Tension* UAG 30260), and the tour was considered enough of a success for IRS to release the singles collection album: *Singles – Going Steady*, Stateside, which was subsequently released in the UK.

1980 saw Buzzcocks announce a reduction in their live schedule in order to concentrate on recording and their next project for United Artists was an innovative idea which saw them record three singles – none of which possessed either 'A' or 'B' sides and were entitled Parts 1, 2, & 3 respectively. That same year United Artists was bought out by EMI, which resulted in Buzzcocks' new paymasters calling a halt to the recording of a planned fourth album in favour of the group going out on tour to promote the UK release of *Singles – Going Steady*. Their steadfast refusal to comply led to EMI holding back the advance money needed to cover the ongoing new album's studio recording costs. By 1981, however, having spent the best part of five years living in and out of each other's pockets, relationships within Buzzcocks were falling apart and shortly after the release of the third of the new singles they called it a day.

Pete Shelley immediately embarked on a solo career, and had a hit in several European countries with the quirky techno-orientated 'Homosapien' – culled from the album of the same name, which was widely believed to have been intended as one of the songs for Buzzcocks' 'Part 4'. Steve Diggle also recorded a solo record before going on to form Flag Of Convenience, which, despite boasting two ex-Buzzcocks (John Maher was on drums) in the line-up, was destined to remain in the musical wilderness releasing just four singles in five years.

Throughout the eighties, rumours abounded of a possible Buzzcocks reunion – no doubt fuelled by the fact that many of the then-current leading indie bands such as The Soup Dragons, Primal Scream and Jesus & Mary Chain were citing them as a major influence. In 1989, rumour finally became reality when the group's classic line-up reformed and embarked on a world tour. However, the much-vaunted and long-awaited reunion lasted less than 12 months as Maher – although happy to play a few dates here and there with his old mates – was far more interested in pursuing a career in dragster racing than being a full-time Buzzcock. His replacement was ex-Smiths drummer Mike Joyce, and this new line-up remained together for the next three years until Joyce left in order to pursue other interests. This was the cue for Steve Garvey to also announce that he was calling time on the group in favour of relocating to New York with his family.

On Sunday, June 23, 1996, Buzzcocks again found themselves supporting the Sex Pistols when the latter group performed at Finsbury Park as part of their 'Filthy Lucre' world tour. In September 2002, at the KROQ/Levi's Island Invasion 2, Buzzcocks once again lined up to play alongside the Sex Pistols, and also – somewhat ironically – The Damned.

Pete Shelley and Steve Diggle – who to all intent and purposes have always been the general public's perception of Buzzcocks – wasted little time in recruiting a new rhythm section in the form of ex-Lack of Knowledge duo Tony Barber on bass and Phil Barker on drums. This line-up would remain together for the next 11 years, until Barker announced his departure in 2008 to be replaced by Chris Remmington who was already familiar with many a Buzzcocks tune owing to his being the long-standing bassist in Steve Diggle's solo group, and Phil Barker was replaced by Danny Farrant.

Since the 1989 reformation, Buzzcocks have recorded five studio albums: the critically-acclaimed *Trade Test Transmissions* (1993), *All Set* (1996), *Modern* (1999), *Buzzcocks* (2003), and *Flat-Pack Philosophy* (2006), which all served to reaffirm that Buzzcocks could appeal to a new global audience while still remaining true to their original ideals. Another Buzzcocks reunion of sorts occurred on Saturday, September 2, 2000 at London's ICA when, after a gap of 23 years, Pete Shelley and Howard Devoto shared a stage as "Buzzkunst" (Kunst being the German word for art). And their collaboration – not to mention the original 21st century material – was so well received that an album followed in 2002.

May 2012 will see Howard performing the four tracks which make up *Spiral Scratch* with the Buzzcocks 1976 line-up that had also supported the Sex Pistols on the Anarchy Tour. These two commemorative shows in Manchester and London will also see the classic Shelley, Diggle, Garvey, Maher line-up performing together for the first time in 20 years.